School Food and Nutrition Service Management

For the 21st Century

School Food and Nutrition Service Management

For the 21st Century

Sixth Edition

DOROTHY PANNELL-MARTIN, MA
JULIE A. BOETTGER, PHD, RD

SFS21, LLC
Aiken, South Carolina
Crown Point, Indiana

Library of Congress Cataloging-in-Publications Data
Library of Congress Control Number 2013919805
School Food & Nutrition Service Management for the 21st Century, 6th ed
Co-Authors: Pannell-Martin, Dorothy, and Boettger, Julie A.
Published by SFS21, LLC, PO Box 6383, Aiken, SC29803, www.SFS21.com.
Printed in the United States of America.

ISBN (printed) 978-0-9666121-2-7
ISBN (ePub) 978-0-9666121-3-4
ISBN (ePDF) 978-0-9666121-4-1

1. School—food, 2. School—nutrition, 3. Food services management, 4. School cafeterias, 5. School lunch, 6. School foodservices

Books are available through www.SFS21.com.

Printing and Binding: BookMasters

Cover Photo Credits: ThinkStock by Getty Images (clockwise) Valueline/iStock, Wavebreak Media, Valueline/Monkey Business, Purestock, and Comstock Images, Shutterstock/Elnur's (background tray), Shutterstock/kanate (yellow memo note).

CONTENTS

About the Co-Authors

Dorothy "Dot" Pannell Martin, BS, MA, is president of SFS21, LLC and a consultant. She is a former director of Food and Nutrition Services for Fairfax County (VA) Public Schools, and prior to that assistant director of Food Services for Prince George's County (MD) Schools. Dot and Gertrude Applebaum founded inTEAM Associates, Inc., and Dot was the company's first president.

Dot is a native of Tennessee and Mississippi, earned a bachelor's degree at Mississippi College and a master's degree at University of Mississippi. Her first job in foodservices was as assistant director for Morrison's Management Company at Mississippi College Dining Services. Following her master's degree she became director of foodservice for Chapel Hill Carrboro (NC) City Schools. She taught at the University of Maryland, Prince George's County (MD) Community College, and Northern Virginia Community College.

She has authored and co-authored numerous publications including: *Controlling Cost in the Foodservice Industry* (1998); *School Foodservice Facility Guide*, California Department of Education (1993); *Cost Control Manual for School Foodservices, 3rd Ed.* (2004); *Cost Control Manual for School Foodservices, 2nd Ed.*, Massachusetts Department of Education (1998); *Cost Control Manual for School Foodservices,* Kentucky Department of Education (1992, 2004); *Cost Control Manual for School Foodservices,* New York State Department of Education (1998); *Cost Control Manual for School Foodservices,* Virginia Department of Education (1996); *Cost Control Skills for Foodservice Administrators and Managers,* Mississippi Department of Education (1999); *Management Skills for School Foodservice Managers,* Mississippi Department of Education (1987); *Menu Planning Guide for School Foodservice* (editor), U.S. Department of Agriculture (1980); *inTEAM Food System Manual for Administrators* and *inTEAM Food System Manual for Managers* (co-authored), inTEAM Associates, Inc. (2005); and *Assisted Nu-Menu Manual* (1996).

Dot has received IFMA's Silver Plate in Elementary and Secondary Schools, Most Distinguished Pacesetter Award presented by the National Roundtable for Women, named Food Service Executive of the Year by the Restaurant Association of Metropolitan Washington, and was recognized by ASBO International with the Eagle Service Award for Outstanding Contribution to Schools. Her professional memberships include the South Carolina School Food Service Association and the School Nutrition Association. She is married, has two grown children and six grandchildren, and lives in Aiken, South Carolina.

Julie Ann Boettger, PhD, RD is the director of Food and Nutrition Services for School City of Hammond (IN) and vice president of SFS21, LLC. Prior to working in Hammond, she was a consultant for inTEAM Associates, Inc., where she worked with clients such as Orange County Public Schools (FL) on the use of technology for their financial turnaround, New Mexico Department of Education on a USDA Administrative Review and Training (ART) Grant project, Pittsburgh Public Schools (PA) to integrate technology and operations, and the School Nutrition Foundation for Prime Purchasing Practices online learning course and the national Breakfast in the Classroom project.

She began her school foodservice career as a district supervisor for Chicago Public Schools, establishing an award-winning training program for the district's 550 foodservice managers. After seven years as a school foodservice director in a Chicago suburb, she joined SNAP Systems, Inc. (later known as School-Link Technologies). She has spoken at state and national conferences for the School Nutrition Association, ASBO International, Academy of Nutrition and Dietetics, North American Food Equipment Manufacturers

(NAFEM), as well as companies such as Tyson, Performance Food Group (now part of Key Impact), and Schwan Foods. She has written articles including "Rx for a Healthy School Nutrition Program" published in *School Business Affairs* and the *Inventory Tracking and Reference Guide* and accompanying trainer's guide published by the National Food Service Management Institute.

Julie earned a bachelor's degree in the Purdue University's dietetic program and a master's degree in Instructional and Training Technology from Governor's State University. She received her PhD in Foodservice and Lodging Management through the Child Nutrition Leadership Academy at Iowa State University. Her dissertation title was "Effects of Organizational Attributes on Adoption of Technology for Supply Chain Management in Large School Nutrition Programs."

She has been actively involved in the state and national School Nutrition Associations, serving as Illinois state president. Currently she is co-chair of the Professional Development Committee for the Indiana School Nutrition Association. She is a member of the Academy of Nutrition and Dietetics and is currently serving on the nominations committee for the School Nutrition Services Dietetic Practice Group. She is a member of the Indiana Association of School Business Officials, the Institute of Food Technologists, and the Illinois Chapter of the International Society for Performance Improvement. Julie is married, has two grown children, five grandchildren, and lives in Crown Point, Indiana.

PREFACE

The first edition, *School Foodservice,* was published by AVI Publishing Company in 1974. Nearly 40 years later, the sixth edition addresses the current requirements of the programs that drive foodservice at school.

This edition has a co-author. The title change to *School Food and Nutrition Service Management for the 21st Century* is because nutrition has become such a vital part of school foodservice. This revision embraces the many changes that have occurred over the past 10–12 years. The economy, nutrition issues, and social media are forces at the root of the changes. This user-friendly edition is a reference for administrators, new and experienced directors of small to large school districts, and managers of school foodservices. The trainer and college professor will find the book a good introduction to school foodservice management. The advantages of the co-authorship are years of experience and the current day realities.

School nutrition has become the standard description for school meal programs. However, the local cafeterias, where management, preparation, and serving of food take place, make it happen. This book focuses on the management of foodservice and execution of the menus. Schools do not have good nutrition without appealing food and good customer service. As nutrition becomes the centerpiece of the program, it is important to not lose sight of all the aspects of managing, including the execution. For the program to be a successful business, it must ultimately have the acceptance of the customers and customers' parents.

Local administrators may find overwhelming the federal, state, and local regulations, the accountability requirements, and community interest in nutrition, and being in charge of "what is for lunch" at school. This book includes up-to-date federal regulations (as of publication date) and the impact of the regulations. Because numerous books on the market cover personnel management, purchasing, and the design and equipping of kitchens, these subjects are not detailed here.

"Food at school" programs will see equal or greater changes in the next decade. It is important to apply the classic principles of school foodservice management but with a renewed focus on nutrition and wellness. Several new topics and features are in this edition, including:

- New regulations brought forth by the Healthy, Hunger-Free Kids Act of 2010
- Changes in menu requirements and competitive foods
- The emergence of social media in marketing to young customers
- The role of the school nutrition supply chain in procurement and food safety
- The new approach to food safety using Hazard Analysis and Critical Control Points
- A whole chapter devoted to solving financial problems
- A story to open each chapter and illustrate the challenges experienced
- Study questions to help readers identify key concepts and multiple choice questions to check for retention
- Online resources to provide additional information about the topic

This edition emphasizes financial management and problem solving. As the federal reimbursements provide a greater share of the revenue, the management of expenses will become more difficult for many school districts. Whereas, school districts in states/school districts with low labor cost may have no problem breaking even, others may find it impossible.

We are interested in your feedback on our latest edition. To join one of the latest trends in marketing, *School Food and Nutrition Service Management for the 21st Century* has its own website, SFS21.com, where we will blog about how the book is used to address some of today's challenges and where you can post your comments and questions. Enjoy!

ACKNOWLEDGMENTS

Where did it start? It was 1974 when I wrote the first edition of *School Foodservice*. I was an unknown, a mom of two school-age children, and assistant director of foodservices in Prince George's County (MD). I had written a master's thesis on the school lunch commodities, and I knew the need for a basic textbook. Thanks to the director of the newly opened Food and Nutrition Information Center of the National Agricultural Library in Beltsville (MD) for sharing the treasury of knowledge during the writing of the first edition, I spent months exploring the books, journals, and state developed materials. My thanks go to USDA for the opportunity to learn from the Food and Nutrition Service staff, while developing guidance materials for major changes in menus and regulations of the late 1970s.

This is 40 years later and the 6th edition. So much has happen since the 1970s. My thanks go to Julie Boettger for agreeing to co-author this edition. She brings a fresh point of view and expertise that is very valuable. As leaders of training seminar in over 40 states, Julie, Gertrude, and I learned the challenges of others trying to carry out federal and state regulations with limited money. We recognize today the renewed dedication of people in school food and nutrition services across the country.

We extend appreciation to the many colleagues and friends, who we have worked with in both small and large school districts, on state staffs, in colleges, and in the industry. We thank the many outstanding school staffs and directors that have shared and inspired this edition and Susan Dillard for creating the book cover concept. Also, we cannot thank Kathy Duncan, Gertrude Applebaum, and Jerry Cater enough. They spent many hours reading each chapter and giving us feedback to help with accuracy, updates, and trying to make a complicated subject more understandable. We are grateful for their dedication to this book.

Special acknowledgment is to the "story" writers—twelve carefully selected people, who have shared their experiences and advice in their stories that introduce each chapter:

Gertrude Applebaum, BS
Julia Bauscher, BS, SNS
Jerry Cater, PhD
Brent Craig, MS, RD, SNS
Angela Haney, BS, SNS
Lora Gilbert, MS, RD
Jana Landrum, BS, SNS
Claudie Phillips, MA
Jean Ronnei, BS, SNS
Barry Sackin, BA, SNS
Cyndie Story, PhD, RD, CC
Mary Swift, BS, RD, SNS

Lastly, we thank our families for their understanding and endurance of the endless hours of work we put into this revision. We offer our deepest thanks to Clyde and Bryan for their contribution to this edition and encouragement.

Dot Martin
Julie Boettger

Chapter 1

Introduction

STUDY QUESTIONS

1. Why do schools serve meals?
2. What meals are available in schools?
3. What funding is available to help support school meals?
4. What changes to meals help students with "special needs"?
5. What process ensures regulations are followed?
6. What criteria qualify students for free or reduced-price meal benefits?
7. Why has participation in the breakfast program grown recently?
8. What organizations provide education and training to school food and nutrition professionals?
9. What organizations offer grants to schools wanting to expand meal service or improve meal quality?
10. How will school meal programs be different in the future?

Chapter 1

"FROM THE BEGINNING" by Gertrude Applebaum, BS

Consultant, Former Food Services Director and Assistant Superintendent for Corpus Christi (TX), and Former Vice President of inTEAM Associates, Inc.

In 1946, I was hired as a foodservice director in Corpus Christi Schools at a salary of $2,400/year, and began my career in school foodservices. This was the year President Truman signed the National School Act into law, providing 5¢ for each student's lunch and regulations to govern the program.

I remember the 1940s when a keyboard was a place to hang the keys and a hard drive was driving home in a rainstorm. The job was simple in Corpus Christi. Managers bought food at the local grocery stores and planned their own menus. Cooking was from "scratch" and the employees worked 8-hour days at 25¢/hour.

The 1950s was an era of breathtaking change and learning. The population in Corpus Christi exploded, new cafeterias were built, and old ones remodeled. Suddenly I found I had to be an expert on equipment and layouts. Food changed, as convenience foods hit the market. The first one I used was potato flakes, and the potato peelers became white elephants.

The 1960s was a decade of turmoil, rebellion, and more change. We became a mobile society, and regional food differences were blurred. We piloted the breakfast program, but it was not a hit. A study in the late 1960s revealed malnutrition and hungry children in the United States. President Nixon responded by requesting special consultant, Dr. Jean Mayer, to conduct a White House Conference of Food, Nutrition, and Health in Washington, D.C. On December 2–6, 1969, a group of us met. I remember mothers from Watts crying that their children were hungry. The biggest changes were free lunches funded and reduced-price lunch established.

The 1970s brought an increase in participation and more funds. In the late 1970s school foodservice was under attack for what schools were serving students and the amount of plate waste. This gave rise to menu changes, offering choices, instituting offer versus serve.

The 1980s was marked by the Reagan budget cuts. I was School Nutrition Association president and traveled the country promoting optimism and that we would survive. We made the cost cuts necessary, and the programs did survive.

In the 1990s I retired from Corpus Christi and began my second career as vice president of inTEAM Associates, Inc. We traveled across the country teaching a system of management, cost control, and financial management. The twenty-first century is continuing with changes, which I embrace. I still appreciate the opportunity to serve, and try to make a difference, as a private consultant.

Schools in the United States have been feeding students for more than 150 years. Food and nutrition managers play a critical role in supporting the educational process by making nutritious school meals available to students. Research has proven that students are more attentive and learn better when they are not hungry. In the early 1900s, children were happy to receive hot soup and a glass of milk, however students and their parents today are more selective about student menu offerings. The challenge is to find the right balance of foods with student appeal, with good nutrition, and at a price within the food and nutrition program's tight budget. This chapter introduces different nutrition programs available to schools, program regulations, and future trends in the school food and nutrition market.

INTRODUCTION TO SCHOOL FOOD AND NUTRITION

Today, public and nonprofit private schools may participate in a variety of nutrition programs authorized and funded by the federal government. Since President Truman signed the National School Lunch Act of 1946 into law, school nutrition programs have continued to expand and reach more students.

What began as a single meal with limited menu choices served during the school day is now a complex foodservice operation serving meals throughout the day, week, and year. Not only are school nutrition operators offering high-quality nutritious meals in the cafeteria, they are also taking nutrition messages into the classroom and influencing food offerings all over campus. The timeline in Exhibit 1-1 illustrates the evolution of the school nutrition programs.

> *Volunteers served the first school meals in 1853 from the Children's Aid Society in New York City. Today more than 31.7 million lunches and 11.67 million breakfasts as well as after-school snacks and dinners are served daily to schoolchildren.*

For someone just starting a career in student nutrition or a school district administrator responsible for student nutrition programs, it is important to understand the regulations, policies, and

Exhibit 1-1 Evolution of School Nutrition Programs

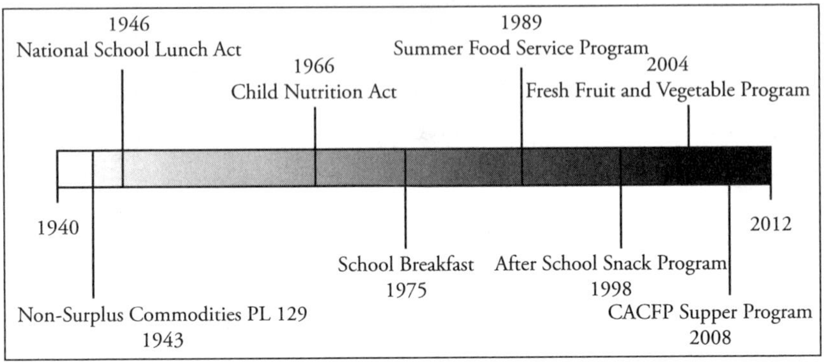

guidelines for the various programs available to schools. This chapter will discuss food programs administered by the U.S. Department of Agriculture (USDA) and state agencies. Ultimately, the local school district is responsible for the school nutrition program and following regulations. This task can be especially challenging and overwhelming to those new to school food and nutrition programs. This section includes a brief history and the major provisions of each program.

National School Lunch Act

President Harry S. Truman (Exhibit 1-2) signed the National School Lunch Act into law in 1946. It became a law primarily because:

1. During physical examinations for military service, many young men were malnourished.
2. An outlet was needed for agricultural commodities produced by flourishing farms after World War II.

> *The purpose of the law is in the introduction—*
>
> *"... as a measure of national security, to safeguard the health and well-being of the Nation's children and to encourage the domestic consumption of nutritious agricultural commodities and other food...."*
>
> Source: *National School Lunch Act*. 79 Pub. L. 396, 60 Stat. 230.

3. Lunch at school promoted a better situation for learning to take place.

Exhibit 1-2 The National School Lunch Act Signed Into Law on June 4, 1946, by President Harry S. Truman (seated)

Witnesses were (left to right): Clinton P. Anderson, Secretary of Agriculture; Rep. Malcolm C. Tarver (Georgia); Sen. Richard B. Russell (Georgia); Sen. Allen Ellender (Louisiana); Rep. Clifford R. Hope (Kansas); Sen. George D. Aiken (Vermont); Rep. John W. Flannagan (Virginia). Photo provided by Department of Agriculture, Courtesy of Harry S. Truman Library.

By the end of 1946, the National School Lunch Program (NSLP) had surpassed the size it had been prior to World War II. Schools were serving nutritious lunches that met established meal requirements. However, the uncertainty of the program and the limited funds caused school administrators to be cautious in starting the program.

From the beginning, each state's education agency administered the NSLP. Participating schools had to agree to do the following:

- Serve lunches that meet minimum nutritional requirements prescribed by the U. S. Secretary of Agriculture.
- Serve meals without cost or at a reduced cost to children who were determined by local school authorities to be unable to pay the full cost of the lunch.
- Make no discrimination against any child because of his/her inability to pay the full price of the lunch.
- Operate on a nonprofit basis.
- Utilize foods declared by USDA as being in abundance.
- Utilize free commodities made available by USDA.
- Maintain records of receipts and expenditures and submit a report to the state agency as required.

The USDA defined three types of lunches according to how they met minimum nutritional requirements: Type A, Type B, and Type C. Originally the Type A lunch contained (Gunderson, 1971):

- ½ pint of fluid whole milk
- 2 oz. protein-rich food (e.g., meat, poultry, cheese, egg, beans, or peanut butter)
- ¾ cup serving of two or more vegetables or fruits, or both
- 1 portion or serving of bread, cornbread, biscuits, rolls, muffins, etc., made of whole grain or enriched meal or flour
- 2 teaspoons of butter or fortified margarine

The Type A meal pattern was the requirement, with only minor changes, for more than 30 years (1946–1977). The Type B lunches contained smaller quantities of the components in the Type A lunch and were served primarily in those schools with inadequate cooking facilities. Type C lunches consisted only of ½ pint of fluid whole milk served as a beverage.

In the 1950s and 1960s, many school foodservice programs were providing free lunches out of funds from the paying students. Imagine how difficult it was to pay the cost of preparing two lunches (one being free) out of the money intended for one lunch. Making students work for their lunches, scrutinizing free-lunch applications, and serving a different lunch to the free-lunch student sound harsh, but the lack of funds forced adoption of such practices in some parts of the country. It was a matter of pure survival for the school lunch programs.

Child Nutrition Act of 1966

During the mid-1960s, Congress took a greater interest in nutrition and poverty in various parts of the country. As a result, the Child Nutrition Act of 1966 became law. It provided the first substantial funding for needy children's meals, guidelines for identifying the needy, and a pilot breakfast program. The Act provided state administrative funds as well as funds to purchase school foodservice equipment in low-income areas.

In 1968, several groups brought national attention to some of the consequences of poverty. The publication of *Their Daily Bread* (Fairfax, 1968) identified poverty as one of the main reasons for unrest in America. That same year, the Citizens Board of Inquiry into Hunger and Malnutrition in the United States focused on poverty in their book, *Hunger, USA* (1968).

In 1969, with the Child Nutrition Act of 1966 in place and with adequate funding, needy children began to receive meals free and at reduced prices. Since the addition of the free meal program to the regulations, the number of free meals has risen steadily and in the mid-1990s exceeded the number of paid meals (Exhibit 1-3).

Exhibit 1-3 National School Lunch Program Average Daily Participation (millions of meals)[1]

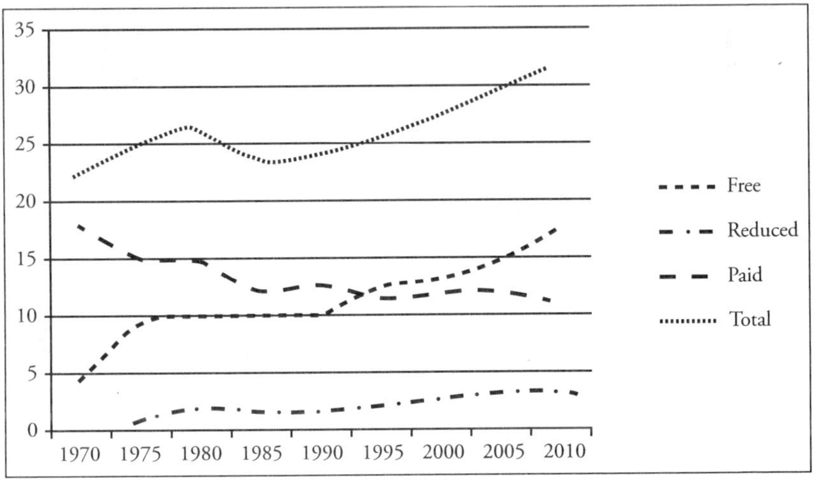

[1]Free and reduced-price meals reported together until 1971.

Free and Reduced-Price Meals

Prior to the Child Nutrition Act of 1966, each school district disqualified students for free meals using local criteria. The Child Nutrition Act created a standard set of criteria for all states to ensure that students qualified for meals on a fair basis. The poverty rate established by the Department of Health and Human Services is the basis for income guidelines. Household income less than 130 percent of federal income poverty guidelines qualifies students for free meals. At less than 185 percent of poverty guidelines, students qualify for reduced-price meals. Two methods are currently used to qualify students for free lunches, and a third will be available beginning July 2014.

1. Direct certification
2. Annual household meal application
3. Community eligibility

Direct Certification

Direct certification of students is required at least three times per year. It is based on data from the Supplemental Nutrition Assistance Program (formerly known as Food Stamps) (SNAP), Temporary Assistance for Needy Families (TANF), and other programs. This method is efficient and effective in reducing fraud. As a result, it has gained in popularity and is now a required method for determining eligibility.

Annual Household Meal Applications

Families whose qualification for meal benefits cannot be directly certified may apply for meal benefits each year by filling out an application. Applications are evaluated based on income and family size or the family's participation in another program (e.g., SNAP and TANF). These programs have the same, or more restrictive, income criteria as the school nutrition programs. Applications are available online or scanned into software greatly reducing errors and making the approval process faster.

In order to control fraudulent applications, verification of income or categorical information is required for 3 percent of applications by November 15 of each year. Although verification is done based on random selection, applications considered "error-prone" or within $100 of the monthly income guideline are first selected.

In 1994, Congress authorized Provisions 1, 2, and 3 to reduce the amount of paperwork involved with processing applications. Schools with a high percentage of low-income students may reduce the frequency of collecting applications. These provisions also allow all students within a school to eat at no charge.

The most popular of these provisions, Provision 2, allows application collection during a base year (year 1), which is then compared with meals served and counted based on student eligibility. A monthly percentage establishes meals claimed as free, reduced-price, or paid; this percentage is then used for monthly meal claims in years 2 through 4.

Community Eligibility

The newest method of certifying students for meal benefits is the community eligibility provision. This provision is an alternative to household applications in high-poverty districts and schools. To be eligible:

- Forty percent of students in a school, a group of schools, or a school district must be "identified" (Identified Students) as directly certified for free meals as of April 1 of the preceding year.
- Breakfast and lunch must be available at no cost to all students.
- Non-federal funds must be used to pay the additional cost of meals over the federal reimbursement.

The community eligibility provision is for four years. If the district or school continues to meet the criteria for Identified Students, they are eligible to continue for another four years.

Example of Community Eligibility Reimbursement

10,000 students enrolled

6,000 directly certified

6,000/10,000 = 60% of students are directly certified

60% x 1.6 = 96% of meals reimbursed at free rate

Reimbursement is determined based on the percentage of Identified Students as of April 1 in the year preceding the first year of the program. Through 2014, the percentage of students is multiplied by 1.6 to establish the percentage of meals reimbursed at the federal free reimbursement rate. After 2014, USDA is permitted to change the multiplier. The remaining meals are reimbursed at the paid rate.

Pilots of this option began in July 2011. Districts and schools in all states will be eligible beginning July 1, 2014.

FEDERALLY SUBSIDIZED SCHOOL NUTRITION PROGRAMS

Most programs offered in schools have finances from participation or the number of reimbursable student meals served. In order to receive the maximum amount of money, the program must reach as many students as possible. The NSLP, School Breakfast Program (SBP), Afterschool Snacks in the NSLP, Child and Adult Care Food Program (CACFP), and Summer Food Service Program are all reimbursable meal programs. Each year, USDA sets per meal reimbursement rates for free, reduced-price, and paid meals. The 48 continental states all receive the same reimbursement rate (Exhibit 1-4). Hawaii and Alaska receive higher rates due to the high cost of living. In this book, referenced rates refer to the rates paid to the continental states.

Exhibit 1-4 Example of Reimbursement Rates for School Meal Programs[1]

Program	Paid	Reduced-Price	Free
Breakfast	$0.28	$1.28	$1.58
Lunch	0.34	2.59	2.99
Snack	0.07	0.40	0.80

[1]Base reimbursement rates for SY2014, including performance-based $.06 for each lunch in continental United States.

National School Lunch Program

The NSLP is the largest student nutrition program in the United States and the first student nutrition program established by Congress. The lunches were originally to provide half of the recommended dietary allowance (RDA) and meet recommendations of the *Dietary Guidelines for Americans* (7 CFR 210, 2012). RDAs are no longer a primary value for planning food of groups and individuals. In 2000, the Institute of Medicine issued the Dietary Reference Intakes, which provides guidance for planning dietary intakes for individuals and groups.

Menus use a food-based system, discussed in Chapter 3, "Nutrition and Menu Planning." The lunch requirements have changed several times since 1946. In SY2014, a lunch consists of the following:

- 2 oz. of meat or a meat alternate
- 1 serving of fruit
- 2 servings of vegetables
- 1–2 servings of bread or grain product
- 1 serving of fat-free or low-fat milk

Lunches are available to students free, at reduced price, and at a locally set full price. The basis for free, reduced price, and full price is household income. The price for a reduced-price lunch cannot exceed $0.40.

The student price for a paid lunch must be similar to the free reimbursement rate minus the paid reimbursement, according to the Paid Lunch Equity Provision. Requirements mandate school districts raise the student meal price annually by at least $0.10 per year until achieving price equity. This requirement has meant many school districts have had to increase the prices charged to paid students.

> *For example, If federal free lunch reimbursement is $2.99 and federal reimbursement for paid is $0.34, the student price for a paid lunch will be a minimum of $2.65. If currently the student meal price is $2.00, the price must be increased at least $0.10 annually until price equity is achieved.*

Some states provide additional funds for lunches. Programs serving a high percentage of free and reduced-price meals may qualify for an additional federal reimbursement per lunch (2 cents in SY2014).

School Breakfast Program

Although smaller than the NSLP, the SBP served more than 11 million students in 2012. There is a push to expand breakfast programs because research shows that eating breakfast has a positive effect on tardiness, attentiveness, and test scores (Levin, 2010).

In SY2014, a typical breakfast consisted of:

- 1 serving of fruit
- 2 servings of whole grain-rich bread
- 1 serving of fat-free or low-fat milk

Programs serving a high percentage of free and reduced-price meals, referred to as severe need, may qualify for a higher reimbursement ($0.31 in SY2014). Just as with lunch, the price charged to students for breakfast must be similar to the reimbursement for free breakfast. The price of a reduced-price breakfast cannot exceed $0.30.

Since the inception of the breakfast program, the number of free breakfasts has risen sharply. It is still only a fraction of the number of lunches served (Exhibit 1-5).

Exhibit 1-5 School Breakfast Program Average Daily Participation (millions of meals)

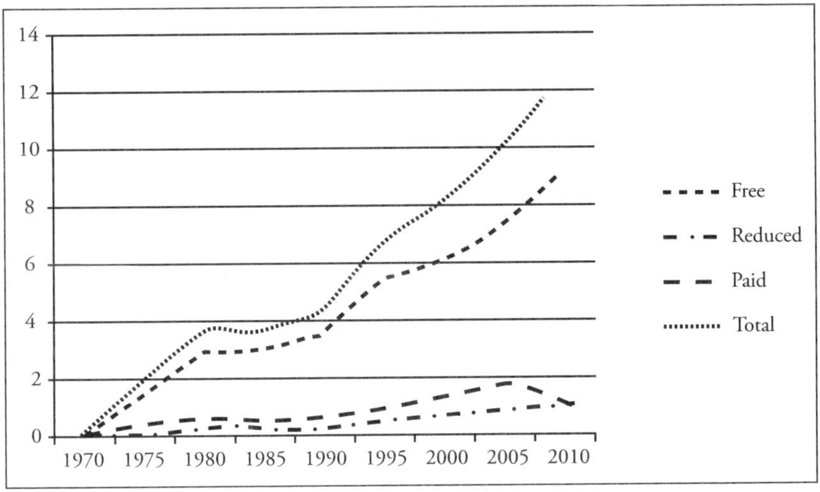

Other School-Based Federal Meal Programs

The number and types of meals served in schools expanded in recent years. Afterschool Snacks in the NSLP, Summer Food Service Program, and CACFP are a way to reach more students who come from food-insecure households. These programs extend meal accessibility throughout the day, week, and year.

Afterschool Snacks

Afterschool Snacks are for students who participate in After-school Care Programs. Qualifying for participation in this program includes an educational component. More than half of all school districts now offer snacks in at least one after-school care program site (SNA, 2011).

Schools serving free and reduced-priced meals to more than 50 percent of students qualify as "area eligible" and may serve all snacks at no charge. In more affluent areas, students may still receive snacks; however, the students who do not qualify for free meals must pay a portion of the cost.

Summer Food Service Program

Hunger does not stop when school ends for the summer. For this reason in 1975, the Summer Food Service Program was established to provide meals to low-income students. Breakfast and lunch are available at no cost in schools, parks, community centers, or other areas where children are located. By 2012, approximately 43 percent of school districts participated in this program (SNA, 2011).

The tracking and reporting of summer meals increased administrative costs. Therefore, meals are at a reimbursement rate higher than NSLP lunches. Because the extra paperwork presented a barrier to school district participation in the program, the Seamless Summer Option was extended to all school districts in 2007. This program does not require the collection of cost information, and it reimburses school districts at the same rate as NSLP meals.

Child and Adult Care Food Programs

According to the School Nutrition Association (SNA) study, 10.8 percent of the school districts in 2012 offered meal programs under CACFP. Unlike meals served under the NSLP and SBP, these meals and snacks are available after school, on weekends, and during school vacation periods.

USDA administers CACFP at the federal level. In most states, it is under the same agency that manages the school lunch and breakfast programs.

CACFP "At Risk" Afterschool Snack and Meal Program students may participate in the NSLP and SBP and CACFP afterschool meal or snack. The students cannot receive the same meal from both programs (e.g., NSLP snack and CACFP snack).

Meals and snacks may be served at sites located in eligible areas or an attendance area of a public school where at least 50 percent of the students are eligible for free or reduced-price meals. "Area eligible" meals and snacks are offered at no charge to the student. Meal reimbursement is the same as for the NSLP free meals and snacks.

FOOD DISTRIBUTION PROGRAM

The Food Distribution Program provides food for schools to use in the meal programs. "USDA Foods" previously were referred to as donated commodities. Compared to the reimbursement for free and reduced-price meals, the commodity rate for USDA Foods has risen very little (Exhibit 1-6).

Exhibit 1-6 National School Lunch Meal and Commodity Rates for USDA Foods (dollars per lunch)

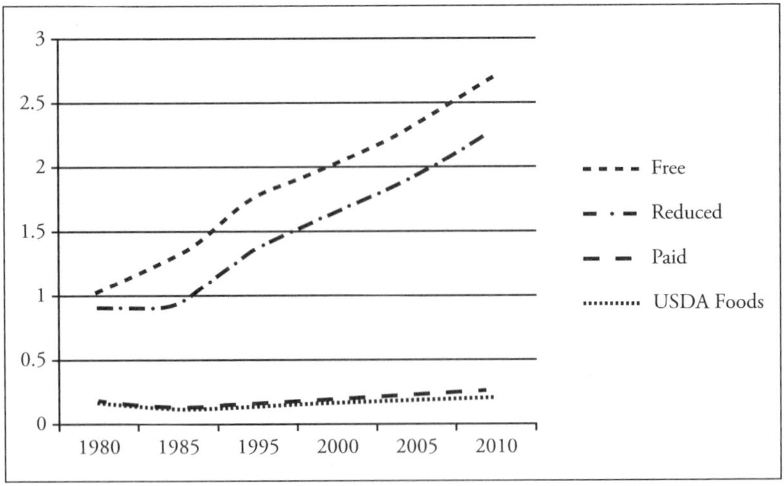

The USDA Foods allocations are based on the number of lunches served the prior year multiplied by a reimbursement rate ($0.2325 in SY2014). These are "entitlement" USDA Foods. In addition to entitlements, bonus USDA Foods are occasionally available when excess product floods the marketplace; for example a record harvest of cherries would perhaps make cherries available to school programs.

Some alternatives to the commodity program were tested in the 1990s, such as Commodity Letter of Credit (CLOC) and Cash in Lieu of Commodities (CASH). A study by Kansas State University showed that both pilot programs were effective in providing greater value to schools; however, the pilots were not expanded. The programs were so well received by the pilot districts that they were allowed to continue.

CACFP earns USDA Foods for lunches served but may elect to receive "Cash in Lieu" of food products. USDA Food allocations also are available in Summer Food Service Programs; however, the rate is lower than the NSLP and CACFP.

The availability of products varies by state. USDA Foods may be diverted to a food manufacturer for processing into a more acceptable form (e.g., raw chicken into roasted chicken pieces). In some states, the Department of Defense makes available fresh produce to schools and takes the value from the USDA Foods allotment.

STUDENTS WITH SPECIAL NEEDS

The intention of school food and nutrition programs is to reach all students, including those with special needs. The NSLP and SBP regulations require that students with disabilities have appropriate menu substitutions. The regulations also stipulate that students not be discriminated against because of disabilities. Serving these students may require accommodations in the serving line and dining area or changes in the menu. In order for a student to receive menu substitutions, some conditions apply:

- The condition qualifies as a disability (see side panel).
- A licensed physician certifies disability.
- Student is unable to eat school meals planned for the regular school population.

> To qualify for special needs, the parent must provide a physician's statement with the following information:
>
> - Student's disability
> - Why the disability affects the student's diet
> - Major life activity affected by the disability
> - Food or foods to be omitted from the student's diet and the appropriate substitutions

Most allergies are not disabilities under this law; however, students with severe or anaphylactic reaction to a particular food are covered. Schools may choose to accommodate other food intolerances or milder allergies but are not obligated to do so. Accommodations are not required for dietary restrictions based on religion; however, if the school serves a large number of students from a given religious group, it is good customer service to consider their needs.

FEDERAL REGULATION COMPLIANCE

When a school district first offers one or more school nutrition programs, they agree to follow all provisions of the school meal regulations. The meal programs, reviewed periodically by the state agency, ensure that all provisions are met. Beginning in 2013, the reviews consolidated under one system are an Administrative Review. The Administrative Review includes the NSLP, SBP, Afterschool Snacks, Special Milk, the Seamless Summer Food Service Program, and the Fresh Fruit and Vegetable Program (FFVP). School Food Authorities (SFA) and agencies offering other programs, such as CACFP, may have additional reviews.

Administrative Review

The Administrative Review developed a unified accountability system that was put in place to ensure consistency and improve efficiency of the auditing process. An Administrative Review is required at least once during every three-year cycle. This review consists of three distinct areas:

1. Performance Standard 1
2. Performance Standard 2
3. General

Noncompliance with Performance Standard 1 (PS1) and Performance Standard 2 (PS2) areas may result in fiscal action. A follow-up review depends on the extent of the infraction. If corrective action is needed after a follow-up review, or if new problems are discovered, the state can withhold reimbursement payments.

PS1 certifies that all free, reduced, and paid meals are available to students eligible for those benefits. An SFA's system for counting and claiming meals is inadequate if 10 percent or more of the meals are claimed incorrectly. Specific tasks contained under PS1 include:

- Meal benefit issuance
- Meal counting by category at the point of sale
- Meal reporting and claiming

PS2 requires that all meals claimed for reimbursement contain the required components, including vegetable subgroups, and meet dietary specifications and nutritional goals. An SFA's system for accounting for meals is inadequate if 10 percent or more of the meals are missing one or more of the required components or items.

Administrative Review "General" refers to areas of major program requirements considered during the review process. The General areas include:

- Food safety plan and other food safety requirements
- Civil rights training, accommodation of students with special needs, and reporting requirements
- Onsite monitoring
- Reporting and recordkeeping
- Availability of water
- Competitive foods or items sold at the same time meals are served
- Wellness policy
- Resource management

PROFESSIONAL ORGANIZATIONS AND RESOURCES

Several organizations offer technical resources and training for those interested in federal nutrition programs. SNA, National Food Service Management Institute (NFSMI), and the Food and Nutrition Information Center (FNIC) Healthy Meals Resource System provide excellent resources.

The SNA offers membership to personnel working in nutrition programs and industries serving the student nutrition market. Members may participate in a certification program or may test to earn School Nutrition Specialist credentials. The SNA Foundation offers scholarships to members who would like to complete higher education goals.

USDA funds support NFSMI for development of training, research, and other technical resources related to school meal programs. The NFSMI offers a document library, training seminars, and online training in subjects from financial management to culinary arts.

FNIC offers a lending library and online resource center. The resource database includes the Healthy Meals Resource System (HMRS) and the Food Safety Education and Training Materials databases. The HMRS includes school meal materials developed by state agencies.

TRENDS

Two shifts in the past decade directly affect the management of school nutrition programs. First, media and community interest play a significant factor in changing the quality of school nutrition programs and initiation of new regulations. Second, the economy and public pressure to reduce government expenditures take a toll on education budgets, forcing both government agencies and local school districts to find ways to operate more efficiently while maintaining or increasing the quality of programs. The changes in school nutrition result from these trends and more detail is found in the chapters to follow.

Disease Prevention

The expectation is that meals served in schools will help prevent diseases and serve as positive examples for healthy eating.

- Menu planning patterns and nutritional goals are changing the types and quantities of food offered during and outside of meals. (Chapter 3, "Nutrition and Menu Planning," offers examples.)
- Wellness policies set the expectations for the nutrition environment for the entire school campus and throughout the day.

- Professional standards are being set for education and skills of school nutrition personnel at all program levels, including the state agency. (Chapter 5, "Personnel and Staffing," discusses this further.)

Program Independence from Federal Support

Most school food and nutrition programs in the United States operate under the NSLP; however, the increase in unfunded mandates for this program is causing districts to reconsider offering the program. School districts in affluent areas may find that the small subsidies from meal reimbursement and value of USDA Foods do not provide enough financial support to implement all federal requirements, especially those that curtail the types of foods sold. Some districts, such as Chesterfield County, Virginia, participate in the NSLP at the elementary and middle school levels but not at the high school level. In several states (e.g., Alabama, Montana, Nevada, Pennsylvania, Utah, Wisconsin), school meals are not required (SNA, 2013). Other states mandate schools serving low income populations to offer one or more meal programs. Each school district must evaluate the needs of the population they serve to determine the best way balance nutritional needs of students with realistic financial models.

Grant Programs

In addition to the reimbursable meal programs, some programs operate on a grant basis. Schools must apply for these competitive grants that are generally awarded on the basis of the demographics of the school. In addition to the government-funded grants described here, many other private grants are available to schools from organizations such as the SNA Foundation, the Robert Woods Foundation, and food and equipment manufacturers.

The design of the FFVP grant is increasing the exposure and consumption of fresh fruits and vegetable. Eligibility is limited to elementary schools with more than 50 percent of students qualifying for free or reduced-price meals. Because funding is limited, schools typically must have more than 70 percent low-income students for a grant.

Team Nutrition offers grants annually to state agencies. Some states utilize the funds to create training and resource materials for local programs, and other states use their funding to provide local grants for nutrition education projects.

The HealthierUS Challenge is a Team Nutrition awards program recognizing school-based programs that meet certain nutrition and physical activity targets. Schools may earn bronze, silver, and gold level recognition by meeting and documenting program targets.

Chefs Move to Schools is another Team Nutrition program that facilitates the involvement of certified chefs in developing new menu items that are both nutritious and appealing to students. A database matching volunteer chefs to school districts wanting to involve chefs in their program is located on the Team Nutrition website.

SUMMARY

Improving the nutritional health of students, preparing students for learning, and expanding domestic consumption of agricultural commodities are the goals of federal school nutrition programs.

Nearly all public schools participate in NSLP, and most offer breakfast. Many low-income districts offer supper and meals throughout the summer. More than half of school districts offer after-school snacks in at least one site.

Schools receive cash reimbursement for all meals served under NSLP and SBP. The schools qualify for USDA Foods. In recent years, grant money has become a source of revenue for special programs and local nutrition initiatives.

"Special needs" students with documented disabilities qualify for meal modifications as specified by a physician. Students with diet restrictions not classified as disabilities are accommodated at the discretion of the school district.

Only eligible students receive free, reduced-price, and paid lunches. Meals are to be accurately counted and reported by category (e.g., free, reduced-price, and paid). Meals must contain the required components and meet nutritional goals.

School meal programs will be different in the future. The meal programs may:

- Play a more prominent role in the educational process.
- Extend wellness policies outside the cafeteria and throughout the school day.
- Focus on disease prevention through menu planning.
- Require management personnel to be certified or trained in key areas such as menu planning and financial management.
- Place more emphasis on grant funding for significant efforts to improve nutritional quality of meals and increase availability of nutrition education.
- Decrease the number of schools participating in federal meal program because of the requirements.

QUESTIONS AND ANSWERS

1. The National School Lunch Act was signed into law in:
   a. 1853
   b. 1935
   c. 1946
   d. 1966
2. The Child Nutrition Act of 1966 established:
   a. Criteria for free and reduced-price meals
   b. Nutrition education
   c. Meal patterns used today
   d. USDA Foods
3. Today, more students are served federal breakfast than lunch.
   a. True
   b. False
4. Food substitutions may be provided to children with special needs.
   a. True
   b. False
5. Criteria to receive free and reduced-price meals are based on:
   a. State-by-state cost of living
   b. Household size and income
   c. Food and labor costs at the school
   d. Unemployment rate in the school district

ANSWERS: 1.c., 2.a., 3.b., 4.a., 5.b.

REFERENCES

Child Nutrition Act of 1966, Pub.L. 111-80. Retrieved from *http://www.fns.usda.gov/cnd/lunch/AboutLunch/ProgramHistory_6.htm.*

Citizen's Board of Inquiry into Malnutrition and Hunger in the United States. 1968. *Hunger U.S.A.*, Boston: Beacon Press.

Fairfax, J. 1968. *Their daily bread.* Atlanta, GA: McNelley-Rudd Printing Service.

Gunderson, G. 1971. *The National School Lunch Program: Background and development.* U.S. Government Printing Office, 1971 0-429-783, Washington, DC: USDA.

Levin, M. 2010. *Breakfast for learning: Scientific research performance.* Washington DC: Food Research and Action Center.

Martin, J., & Oakley, C. (Eds.). 2008. *Managing child nutrition programs: Leadership for excellence,* 2nd ed. Sudbury, MA: Jones and Bartlett.

Miller, C. 1999. *The case for commodity letter of credit.* Presentation at the California School Food Service Association Annual Meeting. Palm Springs, CA.

National Food Service Management Institute. 2006. *Handbook for children with special food and nutrition needs.* University, MS: Author.

Richard B. Russell National School Lunch Act, 79 Pub. L. 396, 60 Stat. 230. Retrieved from *http://www.schoolnutrition.org/uploadedFiles_old/ASFSA/childnutrition/govtaffairs/nsla.pdf.*

School Nutrition Association. 2011. *The little big fact book: Essential guide to school nutrition.* National Harbor, MD: Author.

School Nutrition Association. 2013.

School Meal Mandates and Reimbursements Across the U.S.

School Year 2013-2014. Retrieved from http://www.schoolnutrition.org/uploadedFiles/School_Nutrition/16_LegislativeAction/2013-2014 State%20School%20Meal%20Mandates%20and%20Reimbursements.pdf?n=1039

7 CFR Part 210. 2012. National School Lunch Program. Retrieved from *http://www.fns.usda.gov/cnd/Governance/regulations/7cfr210_12.pdf.*

7 CFR Part 220. 2012. School Breakfast Program. Retrieved from *http://cfr.regstoday.com/7cfr220.aspx.*

7 CFR Part 225. 2012. Free and Reduced-Price Eligibility. Retrieved from *http://cfr.regstoday.com/7CFR225.aspx.*

U.S. Department of Agriculture, Food and Nutrition Service, Child Nutrition Division. 2011. *Coordinated review effort procedures manual.* Retrieved from *http://www.fns.usda.gov/cnd/Guidance/CREmanual.pdf.*

U.S. Department of Agriculture, Food and Nutrition Service. 2012. National School Lunch Program: Participation and lunches served. Retrieved from *http://www.fns.usda.gov/pd/slsummar.htm.*

ONLINE RESOURCES

Chefs Move to Schools
http://healthymeals.nal.usda.gov/resource-library/chefs-move-schools

Child & Adult Care Food Program
http://www.fns.usda.gov/cnd/care/

Food Allergy Research & Education
http://www.foodallergy.org/managing-food-allergies/at-school

Food Research and Action Center
http://frac.org/

Fresh Fruit and Vegetable Program
http://www.fns.usda.gov/cnd/ffvp/

Healthier US Challenge
http://www.fns.usda.gov/tn/healthierus/

Healthy Meals Resource System
http://healthymeals.nal.usda.gov

National Food Service Management Institute
http://NFSMI.org

Robert Wood Johnson Foundation
http://www.rwjf.org/

Schools/Child Nutrition USDA Food Programs
http://www.fns.usda.gov/fdd/programs/schcnp/

School Nutrition Association
http://www.schoolnutrition.org/

Summer Food Service Program
http://www.fns.usda.gov/sfsp/summer-food-service-program-sfsp

Team Nutrition
http://www.fns.usda.gov/team-nutrition

USDA Child Nutrition Programs
http://www.fns.usda.gov/child-nutrition-programs

USDA Guidance for Accommodating Children with Special Dietary Needs
http://www.fns.usda.gov/cnd/Guidance/special_dietary_needs.pdf

Chapter 2

Financial Management

STUDY QUESTIONS

1. Why is financial management important?
2. How much revenue is available for breakfast? Lunch?
3. What does it cost to produce and serve a lunch?
4. Is the food and nutrition service program to be self-supporting?
5. What are three important financial reports?
6. What is the difference in cash accounting system and accrual accounting system?
7. Why should the director understand the statement of revenue and expense?
8. What are the benefits of a budget?
9. What is the difference between a budgetary fund and an enterprise fund?
10. What is the break-even point?

Chapter 2

"Beating the Financial Odds" by Jerry B. Cater, PhD

Consultant, and former Research Scientist for the Applied Research Division, National Food Service Management Institute

In the mid-1970s, after several years of classroom teaching, I decided to make the move to school nutrition. First, I had to find a position in the area, so I began networking. It paid off! I was offered a job in a nearby school district, and so began my long journey into the world of school nutrition.

During the first days of my employment, the superintendent began training me on the responsibilities of a district administrator. Part of my orientation included studying the nutrition program's financial records from the previous year and to hear the financial history of the program. It seems that a long-time director had retired a couple of years before, and the school board decided to try a management company. After two years, both the school administration and the management company decided the arrangement was not feasible for a small district that fed 2,400 students, so the contract was not renewed. However, the June 30 balance sheet showed enough undesignated, unreserved funds to cover 1.5 months of operation for the new school year I felt great about my new job.

When I met with the superintendent, he indicated he had several financial goals for the school nutrition program and I began working toward those goals. I was heavily engrossed in the things new school nutrition directors do, meeting with vendors, getting to know the school nutrition employees, studying school board policy, and well you get the picture. July passed and school started in August. I ordered food to start the year and developed purchase orders for supplies. The superintendent requested new dining tables for an elementary school, so I started the bid process. I had a wonderful bookkeeper who was supportive of her new boss in every way. Everything was great!! Then the bombshell!

My bookkeeper was opening and sorting mail, when she suddenly startled me with a loud, "I don't believe this! It cannot be correct!" What? It seems we had just received a "final" bill from the management company for the last month's operation of the previous school year, and that bill wiped out most of the funds necessary for the operating expenses to begin the new school year. After doing the math, I realized I had $1,500 left in the account after payment to the management company. I called the superintendent; he was dumbfounded. Long story short, it was called "creative bookkeeping" and yes, the school district owed the company the full amount of the invoice. Less than two months into my job, I had the challenge of my life; to turn this program around overnight, literally. We had bills and payroll to pay and $1,500, even in the mid-1970s, was not going to cover much of anything.

I did not want to ask for a bailout, so decided to try it without school board money. I gathered the employees together, gave them the full picture and said, "We can do this. We are going to succeed, but I need your help." The superintendent was in our corner. It was a year of counting pennies daily, using every cost-cutting procedure known to mankind, working with vendors to give us more time to pay (probably couldn't do that today), and marketing the program. On July 30, at the end of my first year, we finally paid the milk company in full and ended the year with a 1.5-months' operating expense. This time it was real.

Management of finances is important to a successful, sound school food and nutrition service program. Managers/directors should operate the program with the revenues generated, which is usually the goal of superintendents, school boards, and upper management. School districts are often on tight budgets and may not be prepared to subsidize the school food and nutrition service program. Managers and directors need to know what the school superintendent and school board expect of them. Is the program to be self-supporting? The site manager's first question may be simply, "How much money do I have to spend?" This is a question management needs to answer.

> *A good accounting system provides accurate data on a timely basis and in a form that management can understand and can use to make decisions.*
>
> *Without accurate, timely financial information, no one should be held responsible for financial management.*
>
> *A month's financial report should be available within 20 days after the end of the month.*

IMPORTANCE OF FINANCIAL MANAGEMENT

The school food and nutrition service fund is one of the most challenging school district accounts to manage because of the many variables. A good accounting system is essential. It should follow generally accepted governmental accounting principles. The school food and nutrition service fund is an enterprise fund. An "enterprise fund" generates its own income and is different from a "budgetary fund." The program fund parallels an enterprise account in that it produces goods, provides services, and charges for those goods and services.

A valuable source of financial guidance is the U.S. Department of Education's Financial Accounting for Local and State School Systems publication (available through "Online Resources" at end of this chapter). The business office or finance office may take care of accounting for the food and nutrition service program, but

Definitions:

BUDGETARY FUND—Revenue generally received from taxes (e.g., a school district's education budget is referred to as the "general fund"); the funds do not generate revenue as with a business and are generally in preset amounts.

ENTERPRISE FUND—Revenue generated by producing goods and services that are sold (e.g., school foodservice and bookstore); sometimes referred to as proprietary or revolving fund.

that does not relieve the person in charge from the responsibility. Finance is the second chapter in this book because it is so important to the success and survival of the program.

DETERMINE THE REVENUE AVAILABLE

The revenue, or income, for food and nutrition service program usually comes from five sources:

1. Cash payments from customers
2. Federal subsidy (cash reimbursements and USDA Foods value)
3. State subsidy
4. Possibly local subsidies
5. Interest earned

In fiscal year 2011, the federal subsidized breakfast program served nearly 85 percent of the breakfasts at free and reduced prices. Slightly less than 35 percent of the students participating in the National School Lunch Program (NSLP) paid full prices for their meals (they did not qualify for free or reduced-price meals). More than 50 percent of the revenues in many school districts come from federal subsidy, and the amount is growing. Numerous sources of revenue for schools are shown in Exhibit 2-1. Chapter 1, "Introduction," provides descriptions of most of the different programs and federal requirements.

Exhibit 2-1 Example of Revenue Sources for a School District's Food and Nutrition Service Program

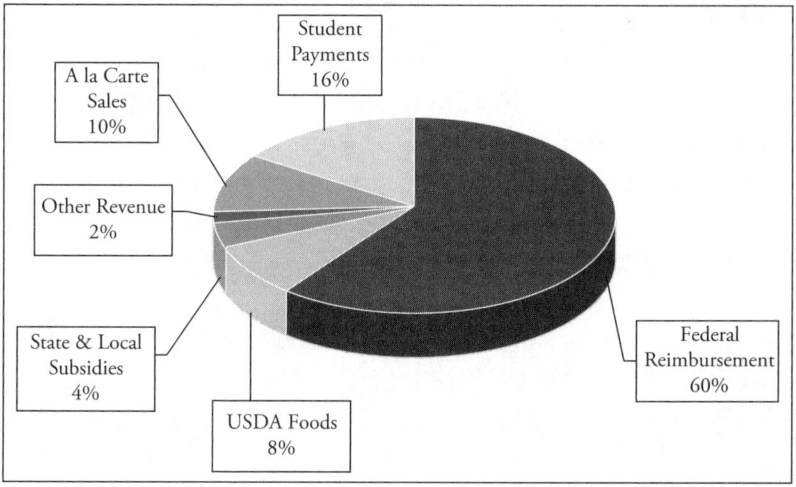

An additional source of revenue for some districts, particularly at middle and high schools, comes from a la carte sales.

Other services, such as daycare meals, senior citizen meals, vending, and special functions/catering, may provide revenue. However, none of the services mentioned should operate at the expense of the federally subsidized school nutrition programs. Any revenue gained (profits) from these sources can be used to subsidize the school breakfast and/or lunch programs or assist with the purchase of equipment.

The state subsidy and the value of USDA Foods can make a real difference in the revenue. In states such as Utah and Louisiana, where state subsidy is high, the revenue received per meal ranks among the highest in the country. At least three states have no state cash subsidy. Good utilization of USDA Foods will also help increase the revenue. For example, because of the effective use of USDA Foods, school districts in Georgia average more commodity value per lunch than most states, which in turn lowers the purchased food costs.

Breakfast Revenue

All breakfasts served in compliance with federal and state regulations under the Child Nutrition Act of 1966 qualify for federal reimbursements. Exhibit 2-2 shows historically how the federal reimbursements have increased over selected years. No USDA Foods are available for breakfast, but USDA Foods may be used in preparation of breakfast.

Exhibit 2-2 Historical Example of National School Breakfast Program Minimum Federal Reimbursements

		FREE BREAKFAST		REDUCED-PRICE BREAKFAST	
Periods	Paid Breakfast	Regular	Severe Need	Regular	Severe Need
7/88–6/89	$0.1400	$0.7925	$0.9475	$0.4925	$0.6475
7/89–6/90	0.1750	0.8600	1.0200	0.5600	0.7200
7/97–6/98	0.2000	1.0450	1.2450	0.7450	0.9450
7/99–6/00	0.2100	1.0900	1.3000	0.7900	1.0000
7/12–6/13	0.2700	1.5500	1.8500	1.2500	1.5500
7/13–6/14	0.2800	1.5800	1.8900	1.2800	1.5900

Source: USDA, 2013.

Directors need to know how to arrive at income or revenue for breakfast. The total revenue includes income from student payments and reimbursements from federal, state, and local funds.

Exhibit 2-3 is an example of revenue based on the SY2014 reimbursement rates.

A school may be eligible for higher rates of federal reimbursement for breakfasts served to students who qualify for free and reduced-price meals. USDA's criteria for "severe need" are on a **school** basis, not by school district. The percent of lunches served free and at reduced price two years prior determines the severe need.

Lunches Served Free/Reduced-Price 2nd Preceding Year = 40% or Higher → **"Severe Need" Breakfast School**

Exhibit 2-3 Example of Revenue for Federally Subsidized Breakfast

Source	Elementary Paying Student	Secondary Paying Student	FREE		REDUCED-PRICE		Adult
			Regular	Severe Need	Regular	Severe Need	
Cash Sales	$1.60	$1.75	N/A	N/A	$0.30	$0.30	$2.25
Federal Reimbursement[1]	0.28	0.28	$1.58	$1.89	1.28	1.59	N/A
Local Funds	N/A	N/A	N/A	N/A	N/A	N/A	N/A
State Subsidy[2]	0.02	0.02	0.02	0.02	0.02	0.02	N/A
TOTALS	$1.90	$2.05	$1.60	$1.91	$1.60	$1.89	$2.25

[1] Based on FY2014 reimbursement rates.

[2] The amount varies from state to state, and some states provide no cash subsidy.

Lunch Revenue

Schools participating in the NSLP program receive federal reimbursement and USDA Foods. Exhibit 2-4 shows historically how the federal reimbursements and USDA Foods have increased.

In the past 10 years, the main source of revenue has been the federal government. Over 60 percent of the students participating in the NSLP received the lunch meal free or at a reduced price.

Sources of Revenue:

- Federal reimbursement
- Value of USDA Foods
- State subsidy
- Student payment
- Interest earned
- Other services provided

If a school district serves more than 60 percent of lunches free or at reduced prices, the **school district** qualifies for additional funds and all student meals are reimbursed at a higher rate (e.g., as of SY2014, 2¢ per lunch).

Lunches Served Free/Reduced-Price 2nd Preceding Year = 60 Percent or Higher → **Over 60% School District**

Exhibit 2-4 Historical Examples of Minimum NSLP Reimbursement and Entitlement USDA Foods (for Continental United States)

Source	Paid Lunch	Free Lunch	Reduced-Price Lunch	Entitlement USDA Foods Per Lunch
7/88–6/89[1]	$0.1400	$1.4625	$1.0625	$0.1225
7/94–6/95[1]	0.1700	1.7575	1.3575	0.1450
7/99–6/00[1]	0.1900	1.9800	1.5800	0.1475
7/02–6/03[1]	0.2000	2.1400	1.7400	0.1500
7/11–6/12[1]	0.2600	2.7700	2.3700	0.2225
7/12–6/13[1,2]	0.2700	2.8600	2.4600	0.2275
7-13–6/14[1,2]	0.2800	2.9300	2.5300	0.2325

Source: USDA, 2013.

[1]Additional 2¢ available if served 60% or more of lunches free and reduced-price.

[2]Additional 6¢ available if met new meal requirements.

The Healthy, Hunger-Free Kids Act of 2010 allows school districts to apply for and receive an additional $0.06 per student reimbursable lunch. The school districts must certify compliance with the new meal pattern requirements to receive the additional funding. Chapter 3, "Nutrition and Menu Planning," provides the new meal pattern requirements.

Directors particularly need to know how to arrive at income or revenue for a lunch. A school district can miss receiving federal funds if the district fails to apply for the funds. Exhibit 2-5 is an example of revenue for a lunch based on the minimum SY2014 reimbursement rates plus USDA Foods value. The differences in minimum and maximum federal reimbursement rates in the continental United States in SY2014 were considerable.

Exhibit 2-5 Example of Revenue for Federally Subsidized Lunch

Source	Elementary Paying Lunch	Secondary Paying Lunch	Free Lunch	Reduced-Price Lunch	Adult Lunch
Cash Sales	$2.7500	$3.0000	N/A	$0.4000	$3.7500
Federal Reimbursement[1]	0.2800	0.2800	$2.9300	2.5300	N/A
USDA Food Value[2]	0.2325	0.2325	0.2325	0.2325	N/A
State Matching Funds[3]	N/A	N/A	N/A	N/A	N/A
Local Funds	N/A	N/A	N/A	N/A	N/A
TOTALS	$3.2625	$3.5125	$3.1625	$3.1625	$3.7500

[1]The minimum federal reimbursement rates for SY2014.
[2]USDA Foods entitlement value for SY2014.
[3]Some states provide cash subsidies.

USDA FOODS, formerly referred to as "commodities" or "donated foods," are revenue value when received and expense when used.

USDA and state agencies refer to school districts as School Food Authority.

The following reimbursement is based on SY2014 plus USDA Foods value, the "severe need" supplement, and the supplement for meeting meal requirements:

<u>Student Paid Lunch</u>: \$0.28 minimum + \$0.2325 USDA Foods value + \$0.02 severe need supplement + \$0.06 supplement for meal requirements = \$0.5975

<u>Free Lunch</u>: \$2.93 + \$0.2325 + \$0.02 + \$0.06 = \$ 3.2425

<u>Reduced-Price Lunch</u>: \$2.53 + \$0.2325 + \$0.02 + \$0.06 = \$2.8425

The value of USDA Foods for SY2014 was \$0.2325 per lunch based on the number lunches served the previous year. The value is more or less, depending on the usage. In addition, "bonus" foods are unpredictable extras. USDA's website has current rates and other federal revenues available.

A la Carte and Other Food Sales

A la carte sales include any items sold in addition to the unit-priced breakfast and lunch. In some states, a la carte sales are discouraged and limited to the sale of milk and items on the menu. The sales of individual items are "extra food sales," or nonprogram food sales.

A la carte may be a service needed by the students who cannot afford or do not want entire meals, particularly in high schools. If priced appropriately, school districts find a la carte sales help subsidize lunches.

The Healthy, Hunger-Free Kids Act of 2010 requires that the revenue from sales of nonprogram foods, such as a la carte, cover the cost. Subjective pricing of products and services can be dangerous. It is easy to believe a food item or service is costing far less than it does and even be selling the product or service to an outside group below cost. Chapter 11, "Resolving Financial Problems," discusses other factors to consider.

IDENTIFY THE EXPENDITURES

Expenses usually fall in direct and indirect categories. Direct expenses come from costs of items, such as food, paper supplies, and the labor involved in preparation and service. Often, the school administration charges indirect expenses for services they provide, such as maintenance of equipment, costs of running the central foodservice office, printing, utilities, and other items. The state department of education sets the yearly indirect cost rate that each school district may use.

<u>Cost of meals and individual food items include:</u>

- Direct labor
- Ingredients used (food and supplies)
- Proportionate share of indirect costs
- Proportionate share of all other costs to operate the program

Definitions:

DIRECT COSTS—Identified items of cost (e.g., food and paper supplies and labor).

INDIRECT COSTS—Costs that cannot be directly identified because the amount is prorated across several programs (e.g., utilities).

For a food and nutrition service director and manager to know the costs of each food item and each service (e.g., breakfast, after school snack) may be difficult. However, management does need to know the costs of the various services. This information is important for making decisions about whether to add a new food product to the menu or how much to charge for a service provided.

Other classifications of expenses include "fixed costs" and "variable costs." When costs are too high, a manager has more control over the variable than fixed costs. Whereas, a director or upper administration has more control over the fixed costs. More detail on costs is provided later in this chapter.

Definitions:

FIXED COSTS—Costs that remain relatively constant or the same during a given period of time regardless of the number served.

VARIABLE COSTS—Costs that vary in direct proportion with volume of sales or number of customers served (e.g., food and disposable products).

The fixed costs ("overhead") are the preset expenditures such as administrative costs, management salaries, and miscellaneous operating costs of the program. In order to charge the operating costs, or overhead costs, against each product and service, it is useful to determine the operating costs per dollar of revenue. This rate is used to arrive at the pro rata share for each service. In this way the operating costs are charged proportionately (e.g., if breakfast provides 25 percent of the revenue, it would be charged 25 percent of the overhead).

Examples of variable costs are direct labor that is adjustable, and food and supplies used or wasted. Managers can influence these costs that will vary in direct relationship to number meals served.

Management needs actual product costs in order to make wise decisions regarding:

- Prices to be charged
- Justification of prices charged

It is not easy to arrive at the "real cost," or the actual postcost, because so many variables are involved. It is important to know the precost of preparing and serving a lunch and the actual cost of preparing and serving a lunch. One without the other misses the full value of the exercise. If the precost and postcost are very different—more than 2 percent—management needs to find out why and reduce the difference.

The cost of producing and serving a breakfast and a lunch varies from one school district to another. A study by the National Food Service Management Institute (NFSMI, 2010) showed the average cost of a lunch at $2.56.

When total revenue is used to pro-rate overhead, all revenue should be included: value of USDA Foods, federal and state subsidies, all cash sales, and so on.

For example, a school district's revenue for the year was $1,450,000. Each program/school was to be charged a percentage of the overhead cost. The percentage of overhead costs a high school in that school district (with revenue for the year of $250,000) would be charged is:

$$\$250{,}000 \div \$1{,}450{,}000 = .17 \text{ or } 17\%$$

In 2010, the average cost of a lunch was $2.56 and breakfast was $1.58.

The NFSMI study shows two-thirds of schools spent more producing and serving breakfast than they received in revenue.

Food Costs

In recent years, food costs have increased. In some schools, food costs are higher than labor costs. The food costs from school to school, where food is prepared on site, are more difficult to control than are labor costs. According to the School Nutrition Operations Report of 2011, management's top two issues are:

1. Implementation of new nutrition standards and meal patterns
2. Cost of food

The value of entitlement USDA Foods realized by a school depends on the usage. State agencies select what foods will be received and whether the foods will be processed or in the raw form. States may or may not receive input from school districts. Frequently, USDA makes bonus foods available to the school district. Effective use of USDA Foods can reduce purchased foods costs.

An accurate inventory at the end of the month is necessary to determine food cost. Computerization accomplishes this task of determining food costs if an accurate perpetual inventory is kept. Chapter 9, "Technology," offers suggested uses of technology in food production.

The most common way to determine food costs starts with a beginning inventory. All purchased and USDA Foods received during the month are added to value of beginning inventory. The ending inventory is subtracted to determine the food used. USDA

Example of food cost for a month:

Beginning of month purchased and USDA Foods inventory	$ 7,984
Plus (+) Food purchased during month + USDA Foods value received	14,424
Minus (-) End of month purchased and USDA Foods inventory	6,376
Equals (=) Cost of purchased and USDA Foods used for month	$16,032

does not require a separate inventory for purchased foods and USDA Foods; however, states may require they be separated.

To determine the percentage of revenue used for food, divide the cost of food (purchased and USDA Foods) used by the total revenue earned, as follows:

$$\frac{\text{Food Cost}}{\text{Revenue}} = \text{Food Cost \%}$$

Management should use these percentages when comparing schools and costs from month to month and year to year.

Labor Costs

The goal should be to keep labor costs (including benefits) to no more than 40 percent of the revenue. Maintaining this ratio is becoming more of a challenge because of the increased emphasis on the use of fresh fruits and vegetables and cooking with raw ingredients. This trend requires more skilled labor hours.

Using percentages helps make the financial reports more meaningful. Percentages make it possible to compare one school with another and one month's data with another month.

To determine the percentage of labor costs, divide the month's payroll plus benefits by the total revenue for the month. If no revenue is realized during the summer but labor costs do accrue, it is important to prorate the costs over the months with revenue.

$$\frac{\text{Labor Cost}}{\text{Revenue}} = \text{Labor Cost \%}$$

In order to analyze labor cost, it is important to include all costs. The manager's salary and benefits are a 9½-month expense even if the manager's salary is paid over a 12-month period.

Productivity in the foodservice industry has not increased in the past five years. Among the different ways to measure productivity rates, the most common way in school foodservice is "meals per labor hour." Productivity rate is the output (number of meal equivalents produced) divided by the number of labor hours. Chapter 5, "Personnel and Staffing," offers more detail on this subject.

Other Costs

The other costs include overhead, such as utilities, maintenance, some supplies, technology, transportation or travel expense, and administrative costs. Because food and labor usually consumes 80 to 85 percent of the revenue, little room is left for "other costs." Therefore, each cost categorized as "other" needs to be identified and questioned. The question that needs to be asked is "Can the cost be reduced?" Chapter 11, "Resolving Financial Problems," addresses this question in greater detail.

USE FINANCIAL REPORTS

It is important for management to know the type of accounting system used for the school foodservice account. Is it an accrual-based or a cash-based system? An accrual-based system provides the most meaningful information.

In the past, many school district accountants used cash-based accounting for foodservices because the other departments in the

Definitions:

ACCRUAL-BASED ACCOUNTING—A system of accounting that records revenues when received and records expenses in the period they occur.

CASH-BASED ACCOUNTING—A system of accounting that records revenues when received and records expenses in the period they are paid.

school district (for general funds) used cash-based accounting. If a cash-based system is used, the school food and nutrition service program management will not know exactly how they are doing financially until the end of the financial year.

Accrual-based accounting shows revenue earned and measurable for the same period of time as expenses are incurred. Accounts receivables (e.g., federal reimbursement due for current month) and accounts payable (e.g., payroll through end of current month) post for the month. The chance is that a food and nutrition service director and manager will become overconfident if all the expenses are not included in the financial report.

The three main financial statements needed by an enterprise account, such as a school foodservice account, are:

1. Balance sheet
2. Statement of revenue and expenses, or revenue gain (profit) and loss
3. Budget

Definitions of Terms Used in Financial Reports:

ACCOUNTS PAYABLE—The money owed creditors for goods and services (e.g., food and supplies and unpaid payroll). "Prepaid" student tickets may be considered accounts payable.

ACCOUNTS RECEIVABLE—The money that is owed the foodservice program for food and services rendered (e.g., federal reimbursement and contract meals).

EXPENDITURES (LIABILITIES)—The costs that are incurred for food, supplies, services, etc.

(*Continued*)

REVENUE (ASSETS)—Money that is received for food and services and accounts receivable.

LOSS (DEFICIT)—The expenditures exceed the revenue, resulting in a loss or decrease in the fund balance.

PROFIT (GAIN)—The revenue is in excess of the expenditures, resulting in an increase in the fund balance.

FUND BALANCE—The amount of revenue available after liabilities have been paid. The fund is restricted by USDA and must be kept separate from general funds. The fund balance will show a "gain" when the revenue for a year is greater than the expenses.

Balance Sheet

A balance sheet or statement of net assets is a basic financial statement that provides a "snapshot" of the financial condition of a fund at any given point and compares current balances with balances at the end of the prior year.

Assets or Revenue *(cash, accounts receivable, and inventories)*

(–) Liabilities or Expenditures

(=) Fund Balance or Fund Net Asset

The balance sheet shows cash on hand (including the value of food and supply inventory). A school district usually does not include the value of equipment as an asset.

Available Fund Balance

The difference between revenue and expenses is either a gain (profit) or a deficit (loss). The gains accumulate and become the fund balance. It is advisable to maintain a two- to three-month operating balance. Federal and state restrictions are important to follow.

Statement of Revenue and Expense

A statement of revenue and expense (in the business world it's referred to as a profit and loss statement or operating statement) shows the financial results at the end of an accounting period—usually the end of the month. Because the philosophy is that school food and nutrition programs are not profit making, most school districts refer to it as a statement of revenue and expense. It provides:

- Summary of the income or revenue
- Cost of goods and services
- Bottom line or net income (Exhibit 2-6)

The bottom line reflects either a gain in fund balance (profit) or a deficit (loss)—the balance once the expenditures are subtracted from the revenues.

Comparing percentages of revenue spent is more meaningful than comparing dollars spent. Exhibit 2-6 illustrates this point. It is important to know what percentage of revenue/income is spent for food and labor and keep this within 80 to 85 percent.

A manager needs an accurate monthly statement of revenue and expenses. The school district director

Fund balance is limited by federal regulations to three months of operating cost. Exceptions are allowed with state agency approval when major expenditures are planned (e.g., large equipment purchases).

Compare Statement of Revenue and Expense:

- Current and previous months and prior year
- Other school districts
- Industry standards

Other Comparisons:

- Previous year's monthly meal counts with revenue
- School by school in district; elementary schools separate from middle and high

Note:

- Highest participation may be during January and February; therefore, the revenue will usually be higher.
- Cost of labor may be highest in September, December, and June because of the days when employees are paid with no revenue coming in (holidays, in-service training days, days paid for "setup" and "closing" time prior to opening and closing).

needs the individual schools' monthly statement of revenue and expenses and the overall district's report. Note that the food and supplies costs in Exhibit 2-6 total 42 percent of the revenue, and the labor cost is 46 percent (year-to-date). In recent years, food costs have increased more than labor for some schools because of increased emphasis on use of fresh fruits and vegetables.

In Exhibit 2-7, Sample High School is operating at a deficit. It is caused by a combination of high food cost (which includes purchased food used and USDA Foods value used) and high labor costs. When the administrative salaries are added to the labor cost, it is over 52 percent. Chapter 11, "Resolving Financial Problems," includes ways of reducing costs. Food and labor costs that are more than 80 percent of total revenue by only 1–2 percent can make the difference in a gain to the fund balance and a loss.

> In Exhibits 2-6 and 2-7, the values of USDA Foods are considered as both revenues and expenditures.
>
> The value of USDA Foods used and cost of purchased food used make up the total food cost. The percentages are of revenue.

Many stories tell of school food and nutrition service directors who have turned the financial losses into gains in the fund balances. For example, in 2002, the Orange County (FL) School District reported a loss of $2.5 million, nearly exhausting the fund balance. The district named a new director who made many changes to turn the financial situation around. Within two years, the deficit had been wiped away by centralizing the program, increasing productivity, planning district-wide menus, and implementing competitive bidding practices. The "Story" introducing Chapter 11, "Resolving Financial Problems," provides the details.

According to federal regulations, the school district food and nutrition service program cannot show a deficit. It must show sufficient revenue so the program has at least a zero balance at the year's end. The school district will be required to subsidize the program.

Exhibit 2-6 Example of School District Statement of Revenue and Expenses

	Nov. 2011	% of Rev.	Dec. 2011	% of Rev.	Ytd $	% of Rev.
REVENUE	$	%	$	%	$	%
Breakfast:						
Students Paid	6,364	1.0	6,660	1.4	22,680	.9
Students Reduced-Price	506	.1	512	.1	1,943	.1
Federal Reimbursement	10,435	1.7	10,979	2.2	39,674	1.6
Lunch:						
Students Paid	148,653	24.3	119,644	24.6	572,590	23.8
Students Reduced-Price	4,020	.7	3,927	.8	18,137	.8
Federal Reimbursement	244,884	40.0	193,509	39.7	1,033,85	43.0
State Reimbursement	14,300	2.3	14,300	2.9	57,200	2.4
Adults	32,206	5.3	19,400	3.9	96,559	4.0
A la Carte Sales	96,201	15.7	86,204	17.6	387,391	16.1
Special Functions	6,329	1.0	4,263	.9	17,350	.7
USDA Foods	22,979	3.7	10,572	2.2	61,691	2.6
Contracts	25,690	4.2	18,021	3.7	96,191	4.0
TOTAL REVENUE	612,567	100	487,991	100	2,405,256	100
EXPENDITURES	$	%	$	%	$	%
Labor Cost:						
Wages—School Based	172,131	28.1	161,037	33.0	684,725	28.5
Benefits	37,869	6.2	34,428	7.1	151,290	6.3
Salaries—Central Office	53,293	8.7	52,460	10.7	218,775	9.1
Benefits	13,323	2.2	12,005	2.5	53,203	2.2
TOTAL LABOR	276,616	45.2	259,930	53.3	1,107,993	46.1
Food Used:						
Purchased	180,094	29.4	139,077	28.5	696,351	29.0
USDA Foods	49,618	8.1	37,555	8.2	186,824	7.8
Paper & Supplies	34,308	5.6	24,887	5.1	128,000	5.2
TOTAL FOOD/SUP.	264,020	43.1	201,519	41.8	1,011,175	42.0
Equipment	17,800	2.9	- 0 -		53,064	2.2
Overhead	26,400	4.3	25,400	5.2	97,367	4.0
Indirect Cost	25,040	4.1	22,040	4.5	100,696	4.2
TOTAL EXPENDITURES	609,876	99.6	508,889	104.3	2,370,295	98.5
NET INCOME (OR LOSS)	$2,691	.4%	($20,898)	(4.3%)	$34,961	1.5%

Note: December often has high labor costs because of the number of paid holidays. This school district has a profit year-to-date, even though both food and labor costs are higher than recommended. The overhead and indirect costs are low.

Exhibit 2-7 Statement of Revenues and Expenses with Accruals

School: Sample High		Month: January 2012		
Source	**For Month**	**% of Revenue**	**Year to Date**	**% of Revenue**
REVENUE				
Student Payment	$17,382.50	53.1	$77,574.90	53.9
Adults	525.00	1.6	2,275.00	1.6
Federal Reimbursement	6,048.00	18.5	26,208.10	18.3
State Subsidy	837.00	2.6	3,627.46	2.5
A la Carte Sales	6,375.00	19.5	27,625.00	19.2
Value of USDA Foods	697.50	2.1	3,022.50	2.0
Other Income	893.75	2.6	3,539.10	2.5
TOTAL REVENUE	$32,758.75	100%	$143,872.06	100%
EXPENDITURES				
Food Costs:				
Beginning Inventory	$3,921.40		$5,570.20	
Food Purchased	13,878.00		62,204.46	
USDA Food Received	697.50		6,201.20	
(Ending Inventory)	(4,230.00)		(7,645.50)	
TOTAL FOOD COSTS	$14,266.90	43.6%	$66,330.36	46.1%
Labor Costs:				
Payroll	$9,995.91		$47,048.94	
Benefits	2,798.77		12,320.67	
TOTAL LABOR COSTS	$12,794.68	39.1%	$59,369.61	41.3%

(Continued)

Source	For Month	% of Revenue	Year to Date	% of Revenue
Operating Expenses:				
Paper Supplies	$1,230.35	3.7	$5,431.52	3.9
Cleaning Supplies	768.96	2.3	3,383.42	2.4
Maintenance	320.00	1.0	1,500.00	0.9
Administrative Costs:				
Admin. Salaries	3,350.90	10.2	15,754.50	11.0
Office Supplies	28.00	.1	201.00	.1
Delivery Charges	27.00	.1	320.60	.2
Travel	12.00		49.00	
Data Processing	25.00	.1	125.40	.1
Utilities and Trash Removal	695.00	2.1	3,475.00	2.4
Large Equipment	2,230.00	6.8	5,350.00	3.8
TOTAL OPERATING COSTS	$8,687.21	26.6%	$35,590.44	24.7%
TOTAL EXPENDITURES	$35,748.79	109.1%	$161,290.05	112.1%
GAIN (LOSS)	$(2,990.04)	(9.1)%	$(17,417.99)	(12.1)%

In Exhibits 2-6 and 2-7, the percentages are based on total revenue. For example, in Exhibit 2-7 the total revenue in January was $32,758.75. The cost of purchased food and USDA Foods used was $14,266.90 or 43.6% of revenue. The purchased food and USDA Foods inventories are combined.

Budget

A budget is a financial management plan. It helps a manager/director forecast revenue and expenses based on the prior year's data and planned changes. By comparing the projected revenue and expenses during the budget year with actuals on a monthly basis, a manager or director can determine whether budget goals are going to be met.

A school district's general fund budget is the authority to spend money. The food and nutrition services program, being an enterprise fund, may exceed budget or come in under budget. The food cost, for example, may exceed budget if the number of meals served increases. This increase in costs needs an increase in revenue.

Plan a budget by forecasting:

1. Participation and sales
2. Federal reimbursement and state subsidy
3. All other income
4. Increase (or decrease) in food cost
5. Increase (or decrease) in labor cost based on raises and staffing
6. Equipment needs and other cost

Many centralized school districts have district-wide budgets without individual schools being involved in the budget process (which is the "top-down" approach). When a budget is developed at the top and "passed down" for implementation, top management is ultimately responsible for meeting the budget.

A school district made up of more than one school may start with the individual school's budget—the "bottom up" approach.

Definitions:

BOTTOM-UP APPROACH—A decentralized approach to budget planning, whereby each cost center (school) plans a budget and the school district's budget is made up by combining all the budgets together.

TOP-DOWN APPROACH—An approach whereby a centralized budget is planned for a combination of cost centers.

> *BASELINE BUDGET—A budget based on the assumption that all the previous year's expenditures were necessary and will be duplicated.*
>
> *ZERO-BASED BUDGET—A budget planned as if for the first time by determining revenue for number served and sources of revenue and determining expenditures by costing out all line items.*

The latter approach provides a separate budget for each individual school site, and the totals of all school site budgets become the district's budget.

Zero-based budget planning is safer and more accurate, particularly for the revenue portion of the budget. Baseline budgeting is frequently used with the general fund budget and may be helpful in determining expected expenditures. It is important to adjust up or down for anticipated increases or decreases in participation.

Budgets are usually prepared a year in advance and may involve several processes before final approval. Exhibit 2-8 gives an example of a school district's budget with details as to the projected revenues and expenditures. Unlike the general fund (education) budget, the school food and nutrition service budget is based on estimated revenue/participation, and the figures are projections made as much as a year in advance.

In recent years, food costs increased at a greater percentage than in previous years. Labor costs also increase annually in most school districts as a result of raises and increases in costs of benefits.

Exhibit 2-8 Example of Zero-Based School District Budget with the Sources of Revenue Calculated in Detail

REVENUE SOURCE	TOTAL $	PERCENT %
BREAKFAST (number × rate reimbursement/ price):		
18,000 Paying Elementary × $1.50 Price Charged	$27,000	
15,300 Paying Secondary × $1.60 Price Charged	24,480	
13,500 Reduced Price × $0.30 Price Charged	4,050	
7,000 Paying Adult × $2 00 Price Charged	14,000	
33,300 Student Paid × $0.27 Federal Reimbursement[1]	8,991	
13,500 Reduced Price × $1.21 Federal Reimbursement[1]	16,335	
108,000 Free × $1.51 Federal Reimbursement*	163,080	
TOTAL REVENUE FROM BREAKFAST	$257,936	7.3%
LUNCH (number x rate reimbursement/price):		
432,000 Paying Elementary × $2.50 Price Charged	$1,080,000	
243,000 Paying Secondary × $2.75 Price Charged	668,250	
27,100 Reduced Price × $0.40 Price Charged	10,840	
19,800 Paying Adult × $3.25 Price Charged	64,350	
675,000 Student Paid × $0.26 Federal Reimbursement	175,500	
27,100 Reduced Price × $2.37 Federal Reimbursement	64,227	
288,000 Free x $2.77 Federal Reimbursement	797,760	
990,100 Reimbursable × $0.05984 State Subsidy[2]	59,248	
TOTAL REVENUE FROM LUNCH	$2,920,175	82.5%
OTHER REVENUE:		
A La Carte Sales	$142,200	
Special Functions/Catering	28,000	
Interest	4,200	
USDA Foods	103,000	
USDA Foods Rebates	2,020	
Other Income/Grants	83,302	
TOTAL REVENUE FROM OTHER SOURCES	$362,722	10.2%
TOTAL REVENUE	$3,540,833	100.0%

(Continued)

REVENUE SOURCE	TOTAL $	PERCENT %
EXPENDITURES		
FOOD COSTS (Including value of USDA Foods used)	$1,483,473	41.9%
LABOR COSTS: School Staff Wages and Salaries Fringe Benefits, Employer's Share Central Office Staff Salaries	 1,100,907 144,108 197,112	
TOTAL LABOR COSTS	$1,442,127	40.7%
SUPPLIES, DETERGENTS, AND DISPOSABLES	$180,136	5.1%
SMALL EQUIPMENT AND OFFICE SUPPLIES	$35,320	1.0%
LARGE EQUIPMENT	$134,219	3.8%
OTHER OPERATING EXPENSES	$234,000	6.6%
TOTAL EXPENDITURES	$3,509,275	99.1%

[1]Based on SY2012 reimbursement rates.
[2]State subsidy differs from state to state.

Data-Driven Financial Management

With increased computerization has come more and more data. The questions may be "Are the data being used?" and "Are the data timely and accurate?" Good financial data help drive good decision making. Many comparisons can be made, and the information helps managers and directors determine where corrective action is needed. Point-of-sale data provide information for management on, not only how many the school served, but other data (e.g., number of customers per cashier, number of customers per meal period, and what percentage of revenue comes from free, reduced-price, and paid meals).

The use of financial data is further discussed in Chapter 9, "Technology," and Chapter 11, "Resolving Financial Problems."

Determine the Break-Even Point

When cost accounting is used, the break-even point (BEP) is an excellent tool to use. It is simple, but it requires a lot of information. It is one of the least-used tools. The BEP can be established for each service provided (e.g., breakfast, lunch, after-school snack). It can be used to set goals. It can be determined and compared daily if the total revenue and expenses are being determined daily.

The BEP is that time when total revenues and total expenses are equal. It is that amount of sales (revenue/income) needed to cover the fixed cost (FC) and variable cost (VC). Any sales beyond that point will provide some gains in fund balance (profits). When revenues do not reach the BEP or surpass it, the operation will have a loss (deficit).

BEP FORMULA

$$\frac{\text{Fixed Cost (FC\$)}}{100\% - \text{Variable Cost (VC\%)} = \text{Contribution Margin (CM\%)}} = \text{Break-Even Point}$$

Break-even point occurs when total revenues and total expenses are equal.

Fixed costs (FC) are the costs that do not vary with the day-to-day or week-to-week volumes of sales or numbers of customers served (e.g., manager's salary, maintenance cost). The most common FC items are:

- Central office cost
- Manager's salary
- Basic telephone charges

- Core staff (not including substitute cost)
- Trash removal (unless by weight)

Fixed costs stay relatively constant. For example, the school food and nutrition services may serve 600 lunches Monday and 625 the next day, but the fixed costs are the same for both days. If the school district or school determines the amount of gain it wants to add to the fund balance, the amount of gain can be added to the fixed cost in the formula.

Variable costs (VC) are the costs that vary in direct proportion with volumes of sales or numbers of customers served. For example, food, supplies, and some labor are VC. These are costs that increase and decrease in direct ratio to the sales. The most common VC items are:

- Food
- Supplies, paper goods
- Some labor (temporary and part-time)

The **contribution margin (CM)** is the percent of the revenue that can be used to pay the FC. In other words, if the CM is 49 percent, then 49 cents of every dollar in revenue goes to pay the FC (manager's salary, indirect costs, etc.) as shown in the formula that follows.

$$\frac{\text{FC (\$)}}{\text{CM (\%)}} = \text{BEP (\$)}$$

If daily FC are $400 and VC are 51 percent, the CM is 49 percent, or .49 (the percentage is converted to a decimal point .49), and the FC figure of $400 is divided by .49 to arrive at the BEP of $817. The 100% represents the total revenue or all the revenue.

$$\frac{\$\,400\ \text{FC}\ (\$)}{100\$ - 51\%\ (.51)\ \text{VC} = 49\%\ (.49)\ \text{CM}} = \$817\ \text{BEP}$$

When establishing a BEP for the individual schools and other services, the overhead costs need to be determined. The foodservice central office labor costs are charged against the schools—as overhead costs.

A decision is whether this cost will be "fixed" or "variable." It is easier to compile when considering overhead as a fixed cost. Annually the central office can allocate the cost to each school based on meal equivalents served or revenue in dollars. If the a la carte and other nonprogram sales contribute considerably to the revenue, the percentage is based on dollars.

The BEP can help management determine where financial problems are and how much change is necessary to resolve a financial problem. Exhibit 2-9 provides an example of using the BEP for a high school. The following information is available, as an example:

- Average revenue per day is $2,200 (example was based on serving 350 lunches, 200 breakfasts, and $400 in extra sales).
- Fixed costs are broken out as shown in dollars.
- Variable costs have been determined by dividing costs for the prior month by the revenue for the prior month.

In Exhibit 2-9, the high school has a loss (deficit) and over a year, it will add up to a large loss (deficit). Other schools in the district will have to cover that loss. The problem can be resolved by (1) reducing fixed costs, (2) reducing variable costs, (3) increasing revenues, or (4) a combination of the previous three approaches.

Exhibit 2-9 Example of Determining the Break-Even Point (BEP) for a Day

Item	Fixed Cost ($)	Variable Cost (%)
Revenue for Day $2,200 (includes value of USDA Foods received)		
Food Cost: Purchased Value of USDA Foods		39%
Labor Cost: Management Core Staff Benefits Total Fixed Labor	 $175 501 175 851	
Overhead	374	
Substitute Labor Costs		2%
Telephone/Internet	3	
Trash Removal	5	
Paper/Supplies		4%
Total Costs	$1,233	45%
$\frac{\$1{,}233\ (FC)}{100\% - 45\%\ (VC) = 55\%\ (CM)}$ = $2,242 BEP (rounded up) *CM is converted to decimal point of .55, which is divided into FC.*		

The following description indicates how little the change has to be to break even.

- Reduce FC (e.g., reduce labor cost by $32)

  OR

- Reduce VC (e.g., reduce food costs 2%)

  OR

- Increase revenue (e.g., increase number of lunches served by 13–14)

When the revenue is greater than the BEP, the difference is a fund balance gain (profit). If the revenue is not as much as the BEP, the difference is a decrease in fund balance (deficit). When the goal is to make a specific profit add the dollar amount to the FC in the formula. Chapter 11, "Resolving Financial Problems," discusses ways of reducing costs and increasing revenues.

If the BEP for the district food and nutrition service program is higher than revenue, the district has the options of subsidizing the program or taking some other action.

> *Is it possible to break even? Not always.*
>
> *The BEP is more meaningful when broken down by the day, versus by month or year. It can be used as a motivator for staff, and the data become more meaningful.*

SUMMARY

Resolving financial problems is important to a successful school food and nutrition services program, because most programs are expected to be self-supporting. Revenue received needs to cover all expenses. The slim difference in revenue and expenses makes it unwise for management to guess at it or not be concerned. School food and nutrition services programs that involve federal reimbursements and USDA Foods are complicated businesses. The programs need to be treated as businesses.

The three important financial reports discussed in this chapter are balance sheet, statement of revenue and expenses (profit and loss statement), and budget. Because the food and nutrition service program should be treated as a business, it is considered an enterprise fund versus a budgetary fund. With an enterprise fund, it is important to determine the percentage of revenue being spent for food and labor (not the percentage of expenses).

If food and labor costs are increasing at a greater rate than the revenue, financial problem solving may be an ongoing challenge for management. A combination of increasing revenue sources and reducing labor costs are discussed in Chapter 11, "Resolving Financial Problems." Using the break-even formula can help management determine whether the problem can be solved and what needs to be done. It all starts with accurate financial reports provided on a timely bases.

QUESTIONS AND ANSWERS

1. The financial management of a local school's foodservice program is important to USDA.
   a. True
   b. False
2. To qualify for severe-need breakfast funding, the school must serve more than 40 percent of lunches at free and reduced prices.
   a. True
   b. False
3. A school district serving more than 60 percent of lunches free and reduced price will qualify for additional reimbursement.
   a. True
   b. False
4. The main sources of revenue for a lunch program serving more than 60 percent free and reduced price are:
   a. Student payment and value of USDA Foods
   b. Federal reimbursement and value of USDA Foods
   c. Student subsidy and a la carte sales
   d. Local and state subsidies
5. Food and labor costs should not exceed 60 percent of revenue.
   a. True
   b. False
6. Equity in school lunch pricing means the lunch prices are equal the breakfast prices.
   a. True
   b. False
7. The budget is a valuable planning tool.
   a. True
   b. False
8. A school foodservice program should be treated as an enterprise fund.
   a. True
   b. False
9. Break-even point is helpful in determining why a school foodservice program has a financial problem.
   a. True
   b. False

Answers: 1.b., 2.a., 3.a., 4.b., 5.b., 6.b., 7.a., 8.a., 9.a.

REFERENCES

Allison, G., Honegger, S., & Johnson, F. 2009. *Financial accounting for local and state school systems: 2009 ed.* National Center for Education Statistics, Institute of Education Sciences. Washington, DC: U.S. Department of Education.

Carter, J., Mann, N., & Conklin, M. 1999. *Financial management: A growing concern for child nutrition programs.* University, MS: NFSMI.

The Educational Foundation. 1992. *Basic accounting for food services.* Chicago, IL: National Restaurant Association.

The Educational Foundation, 1992. *Management accounting for food services.* Chicago, IL: National Restaurant Association.

Governmental Accounting Standards Board. 2000. *Guide to implementation of GASB statements 33 and 34.* Norwalk, CT: Author.

Martin, J., & Oakley, C. 2008. *Managing child nutrition programs: Leadership for excellence,* 2nd ed. Sudbury, MA: Jones & Bartlett Publishers.

Miller, J. & Pavesic, D. 1996. *Menu pricing and strategy,* 4th ed. New York: Van Nostrand Reinhold Company.

National Food Service Management Institute. 2010. *Financial management: A course for school nutrition directors.* University, MS: Author.

National Restaurant Association. 1996. *Uniform system of accounts for restaurants,* 7th ed. Washington, DC: Author.

OMB Circular A087. 2004. *Cost principles for state, local and Indian tribal governments.* Retrieved from http://www.whitehouse.gov/omb/circulars_a087_2004/.

Pannell-Martin, D. 2004. *Cost control manual for school foodservices,* 3rd ed. Santa Monica, CA: inTEAM Associates, Incorporated.

Pavesic, D. 1998. *Fundamental principles of restaurant cost control.* Upper Saddle River, NJ: Prentice Hall.

School Nutrition Association. 2011. *School nutrition operations report 2011: The state of school nutrition.* National Harbor, MD: Author.

USDA. 2008. *School lunch and breakfast cost study – II.* Washington, DC: Author. Retrieved from http://www.fns.usda.gov/-oame/menu/Published/CNP/FILES/MealCostStudy.pdf.

USDA. 2011. *Equity in school lunch pricing fact sheet.* Retrieved from http://www.fns.usda.gov/cnd/Governance/Legislation/Pricing_Equity_Facts.pdf.

Warner, M. 1989. *Break-even analysis and profit volume charting: Function and use by restaurant managers.* Presentation at the National Restaurant Association Convention, Chicago, IL.

ONLINE RESOURCES

Governmental Accounting Standards Board
http://gasb.org

National Center for Education Statistics
http://nces.ed.gov/pubsearch

NFSMI's Financial Management: A Course for School Food Service Directors
http://www.nfsmi.org/ResourceOverview.aspx?ID=63

USDA Rates of Reimbursement
http://www.fns.usda.gov/cnd/governance/notices/naps/naps.htm

U.S. Department of Education's Financial Accounting for Local and State School Systems
http://nces.ed.gov/pubs2009/2009325.pdf

Chapter 3

Nutrition and Menu Planning

STUDY QUESTIONS

1. What are the nutritional goals of menu planning for school children?
2. Why is the menu planning process so important?
3. How do planning menus for schools differ from planning menus for a restaurant or business?
4. When planning menus, what are the important factors to consider?
5. What steps are involved in planning a good menu?
6. What adjustments are made to menus for students with special needs?
7. What is a cycle menu?
8. What are the advantages of a cycle menu?
9. List three of the dietary guideline recommendations for school meals.
10. What does "offer versus serve" mean?

Chapter 3

"Celebrate Your Menu Flops" by Jean Ronnei, BS, SNS

Chief Operations Officer, Saint Paul (MN) Public Schools

How many times have you heard employees say, "Kids won't like it"? Well, they may be right! However, your students will not expand their food tastes unless you try new recipes and food products. So, go ahead and experiment with the understanding that there will be flops!

Twice each year, we invite vendors and staff to create new recipes to bring to a "taste test." We look at feasibility, nutritional analysis, and cost to determine what new items we will offer our students. That event may yield 40 or more potential new items. Generally, only 10 or so items make it to the next phase of recipe development and testing.

Over the past four years, we have introduced more than 50 new recipes such as Homemade Muffins, Buffalo Wild Rice Casserole, Veggie Lasagna, Roasted Harvest Vegetables, and Rice Bowls. Many have stayed a constant on the menu, while some come and go as featured or seasonal items. However, as the title suggests, we have had our share of flops!

One of our favorite flops was Veggie Loaf; a lentil loaf that we thought would be a nice alternative to our regular meatloaf. Did the kids take it? Absolutely not! No amount of marketing and taste testing had the students select it over regular meatloaf. We discovered that while students said they wanted vegetarian items, most were not "hard core."

Key learning from our flops:

- Eye appeal is critical—students may not even taste it if they do not like the look of the item.
- Market the heck out of a new item: PA announcements, signage, menus, and Facebook work.
- If you offer an alternative to the new item, offer just a soufflé cup's worth of the new item to students who choose not to take it.
- Have students, faculty, or other "celebrities" serve that item.

Employ three strikes and you're out rule!

- By having a three strikes rule, everyone knows that a flop will not stay on the menu forever!
- Feedback is critical—from students and cafeteria staff. Use surveys, word of mouth, and trashcan observations.
- Evaluate participation by free/reduced and full pay students. If participation dips below an acceptable level, take notice.

If you too have concluded that recipe flops are something to celebrate, then do so and keep up the risk taking! You will be rewarded when you see students loving new, healthy, and ethnically diverse foods.

Meeting nutritional goals through menu planning is the most challenging and important task of school foodservice personnel. Time spent planning a menu that is appealing to students, affordable, and nutritious is well spent and affects the quality of the program overall. This chapter reviews the nutritional goals and menu requirements for schools, as well as general menu planning best practices.

INTRODUCTION TO NUTRITION AND MENU PLANNING

Menu planning is the single most important influence on the success of a program and achievement of its mission to improve student health and prepare students to learn. Unfortunately, menu planning often does not get the attention that it needs to meet the goals of feeding the greatest number of students healthy meals while staying within the financial goals of the organization.

School menus must offer choices consistent with *Dietary Guidelines for Americans* (2010) (*Dietary Guidelines*). In the early years of the National School Lunch Program (NSLP), the Type A menu consisted of items from four food-based components: meat, vegetables/ fruits, grains, and milk. For over 30 years, menu requirements experienced few changes (Exhibit 3-1).

Until 1977, regulations required students to take all meal components resulting in a high amount of food waste. To address the waste, meal patterns that offer different serving sizes based on age groups replaced the Type A. A new initiative, "Offer Versus-Serve," allowed students to decline parts of the meal that they did not intend to eat.

In the 1990s, more emphasis was placed on meeting nutrient targets. Nutrient Standard Menu Planning (NSMP) was a new menu planning option. NSMP allowed personnel to plan menus to meet age-based nutrient targets. Although this allowed more flexibility in the type of items offered and in many cases lowered food cost, it also required menu planners to have computer software and extensive nutrition information for products served. One

Exhibit 3-1 NSLP Menu Planning Changes Occurred

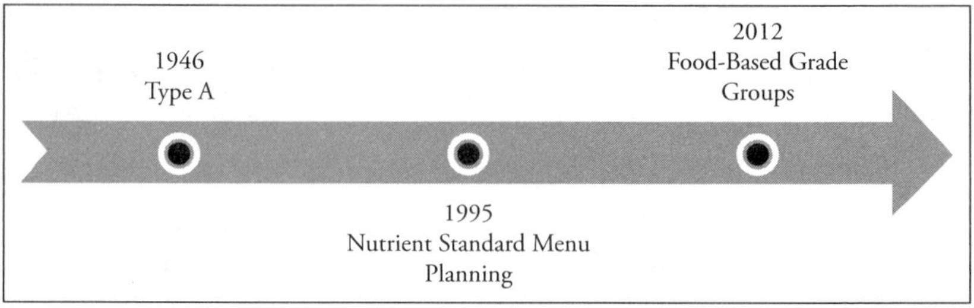

unintended consequence was a variety of products coming to market fortified with nutrients not normally seen in those products such as pastries fortified with nutrients normally found in fruits or vegetables.

In the Healthy, Hunger-Free Kids Act of 2010, new menu requirements replace nutrient-focused menus with menus planned using five food-based components (Exhibit 3-2). In many ways, the new menus resemble those of earlier years; however, they also address the age-based nutrition targets by including specific foods that are high in vitamins and minerals necessary for child development.

Exhibit 3-2 Food Components Used in Menu Plans

1. Meat or high-protein foods
2. Whole grains
3. Vegetables
4. Fruit
5. Fat-free or low-fat milk

The first step in effective menu planning is to determine how much revenue is available to spend on each meal. Additional considerations when selecting menu items are:

- Student preferences
- Nutritional goals

- Culinary skills of personnel
- Equipment

For new programs, plan the menu before purchasing equipment or hiring employees. In existing programs, the menu planner needs to work with the skill set of current employees and available equipment.

Plan meals to ensure students are interested enough to choose a meal. This means offering a variety of menu items familiar to students, as well as new items to broaden students' eating experiences. Some students may need special accommodation due to disabilities affecting their diets (e.g., celiac disease). In other cases, offering special diets may provide great customer service (e.g., accommodating students of certain religions). Extra foods or a la carte items can complement meals in programs that have the ability to offer this feature.

NUTRITIONAL GOALS

From the beginning of the NSLP, eliminating malnutrition was the goal in planning school meals. In nearly 70 years since the program began, the concern has shifted to obesity and prevention of disease, such as diabetes, heart disease, and certain cancers. The *Dietary Guidelines* and Dietary Reference Intakes are the basis for nutrition targets set for current school meals. Nutrient targets are used to determine menu patterns and not directly used for planning menus. Establishing food-based menu patterns rather than planning menus based on nutrient targets makes menu planning easier.

Dietary Guidelines for Americans

In 2010, the Institute of Medicine (IOM) made criteria recommendations for nutrient targets and meal standards for school lunch and breakfast. These recommendations reflected the latest nutritional research and the *Dietary Guidelines.* The goals of the *Dietary Guidelines* are to help individuals:

- Balance calories over time to achieve a healthy weight.
- Focus on consuming nutrient dense foods.
- Build healthy eating patterns.

The IOM recommendations for school meals were food-based rather than nutrient-based so that students could learn a pattern of combining food items that would lead to healthy eating habits. Specifying groups of foods with certain characteristics, such as whole grains and different types of vegetables (e.g., deep green), addresses the nutrients lacking in today's diet. Exhibit 3-3 lists the specific dietary guidelines.

Exhibit 3-3 Specific *Dietary Guidelines* Recommendations

- Control calorie intake to manage body weight.
- Reduce sodium to less than 2,300 milligrams (mg) per day.
- Consume less than 10% of calories from saturated fatty acids.
- Keep trans fatty acids as low as possible.
- Increase fruit and vegetable intake.
- Eat a variety of vegetables especially dark green, red, and orange vegetables, beans, and peas.
- Consume at least half of all grains as whole grains.
- Increase intake of fat-free or low-fat dairy products.
- Choose foods that provide more potassium, dietary fiber, and vitamin D.

Source: *Dietary Guidelines,* 2010.

Congress passed the Healthy, Hunger-Free Kids Act of 2010 that incorporated the IOM recommendations into new regulations for school menus. The new menu regulations include requirements for vegetable subcategories, whole grain-rich breads, fat-free or low-fat milk, and certain nutrient targets including calorie minimums/maximums, saturated fat, trans fat, and sodium. Exhibit 3-4 offers the nutrient targets.

Exhibit 3-4 Breakfast and Lunch Nutrient Targets for Grade Groups

	Breakfast			Lunch		
	Grades K–5	Grades 6–8	Grades 9–12	Grades K–5	Grades 6–8	Grades 9–12
Minimum-maximum calories	350–500	400–550	450–600	550–650	600–700	750–850
Saturated fat (% calories)	<10	<10	<10	<10	<10	<10
Sodium (mg)[1]	≤430	≤470	≤500	≤640	≤710	≤740
Trans fat	0	0	0	0	0	0

[1] Sodium requirements begin with the SY2015

Note: < means "less than" and ≤ means "less than or equal to"

Source: USDA, 2012.

District Wellness Policies

In 2004, Congress signed the Child Nutrition Women Infant and Children Reauthorization Act of 2004 requiring each local school district participating in the National School Lunch Program or other USDA meal programs to establish wellness policies. Nearly all schools now have policies with goals for physical activity and nutrition.

In 2010, the Healthy, Hunger-Free Kids Act passed additional regulations requiring districts to strengthen policies by adding (1) an implementation plan, (2) a method of evaluating effectiveness, and (3) a means to communicate progress to their communities. Requirements in 2013 for local school wellness policies include:

- Goals for nutrition education, physical activity, nutrition guidelines for all foods available on campus, and nutrition promotion.

- Involvement of all interested parties in developing, implementing, and evaluating the policies, including parents, students, school administration, school food authorities, school board, teachers in physical education, school health professionals, and community members.
- Notification of the public including parents, students, and other community members about the content and implementation of the local wellness policies.
- Assessment of the implementation plan including the extent that schools are compliant and how the policies compare to model policies.
- Designation of one or more district/school officials charged with the responsibility of ensuring the district/school meets the local wellness policies.

The intent of the local wellness policies regulation is to establish a healthy environment for students that is supportive of school nutrition program initiatives. Acceptance of food changes occurs when the school district focuses on instilling healthy habits.

Nutrition Education

Team Nutrition is a program developed by the USDA to promote lifelong healthy eating and physical activity habits in school children. Serving healthy school meals and setting a school climate is only part of the solution to instilling healthy habits in children. Students also need to learn about how the habits help them and why they should adopt lifestyle changes. In this regard, nutrition education is essential.

Team Nutrition provides schools with resources for training school nutrition personnel, children, and their parents. Many school districts have incorporated nutrition education objectives into the curriculum. In some cases, the classroom teacher includes nutrition education along with other subjects (e.g., health). Some districts utilize foodservice employees to provide nutrition information. Materials are readily available at no charge from USDA's Team Nutrition, many state agencies, the National Food Service Management Institute, and the School Nutrition Association.

Food marketing organizations also provide materials related to their products. The National Dairy Council, Produce for Better Health Foundation, and the Whole Grains Council provide materials designed for classroom teachers, foodservice personnel, and parents.

MENU PLANNING REQUIREMENTS

In order to meet nutritional requirements set forth in the *Dietary Guidelines*, school menus are planned using food-based meal patterns. Studies have shown that following meal patterns using specific food groups result in menus that achieve nutrient targets for school-age children. Three different grade groups are addressed.

Grade Groups for Menu Planning
Elementary (kindergarten–5)
Middle (grades 6–8)
High school (grades 9–12)

When school buildings contain more than one grade group (e.g., K–8 buildings) school nutrition managers must either plan menus that meet but do not exceed targets for both groups or plan different menus for each group. The Healthy, Hunger-Free Kids Act of 2010 specifies changes to school meals that increase the quantity of fruits, vegetables, and whole grains, controlled calories, and reduces the amount of sodium and trans fat.

In order to allow manufacturers time to make reformulated products available to schools, some requirements are being phased in. After July 1, 2014, all grain products must be whole grain-rich. Exhibit 3-5 shows sodium levels in meals implemented over several years. The Healthy, Hunger-Free Kids Act also separates fruits and vegetables into different components at lunch and specifies subgroups of vegetables to offer weekly.

Exhibit 3-5 Sodium Requirement Timelines for Breakfast and Lunch

Grade Group	July 1, 2014	July 1, 2017	July 1, 2022
School Breakfast Program			
Elementary	≤ 540 mg	≤ 485 mg	≤ 430 mg
Middle	≤ 600 mg	≤ 535 mg	≤ 470 mg
High	≤ 640 mg	≤ 570 mg	≤ 500 mg
National School Lunch Program			
Elementary	≤ 1230 mg	≤ 935 mg	≤ 640 mg
Middle	≤ 1360 mg	≤ 1035 mg	≤ 710 mg
High	≤ 1420 mg	≤ 1080 mg	≤ 740 mg

Note: ≤ means "less than or equal to"

Lunch

Lunches served under the NSLP offer five components:

1. Meat or meat alternate
2. Vegetable
3. Fruit
4. Bread or grain
5. Fluid milk

Students may decline two of the five meal components; however, they must take at least ½ cup of a fruit or vegetable. Exhibit 3-6 shows the specific quantities of each component.

Exhibit 3-6 Lunch Meal Patterns for Grade Groups

Components	Elementary	Middle	High
Fruits (cups/day)	½	½	1
Vegetables (cups/day)	¾	¾	1
Vegetable subgroups			
Dark green (cups/week)	½	½	½
Red/orange (cups/week)	¾	¾	1 ¼
Legumes (cups/week)	½	½	½
Starchy (cups/week)	½	½	½
Other (cups/week)	½	½	¾
Additional (cups/week)	1	1	1 ½
Grains (ounce equivalents/day)	1 (8/week)	1 (8/week)	2
Meat/Meat Alternate (ounces/day)	1 (8/week)	1 (8/week)	2
Fluid Milk (cups/day)	1	1	1

Source: USDA, 2012.

The menu planner should consider these additional requirements:

- Meat alternates include whole eggs, cheese, peanut butter or other nut butters, nuts, or seeds (e.g., pumpkin seeds), commercially processed tofu, yogurt, and legumes. Legumes count as either a meat alternate or a vegetable, but not both in the same meal. Nuts and seeds count for half the meat/meat alternate contribution.

- Fresh leafy green vegetables need twice the volume to count toward the contribution (e.g., one cup of fresh spinach is equal to ½ cup serving of dark green vegetables).
- Dried fruits need half the volume to count toward the contribution (e.g., ¼ cup of raisins is equal to ½ cup fruit).
- Fruits may be fresh, frozen, or canned in juice or light syrup.
- Only half of the fruit or vegetable servings may be 100% fruit or vegetable juice.
- Half of grain products must be whole grain-rich. Starting July 2014, all grain products must be whole grain-rich.
- No more than 2 ounce equivalents of whole grain-rich desserts (e.g., graham crackers) may be offered per week.
- If flavored milk is offered, it must be fat-free. White milk may be fat-free or 1% butterfat. Schools must offer at least two different choices of milk.

Definition of Whole Grain-Rich

- A product contains 50% or more whole grains, or
- Whole grain is the first grain listed in the ingredient list, or
- The product contains at least 8 grams of whole grain.
- Most grain products contain additional ingredients therefore serving sizes vary. To address this, common grain products are assigned to one of nine grain groups based on "ounce equivalents" or the equivalent of actual ounces of grain contained in the item.

Breakfast

Breakfast offered under the School Breakfast Program (SBP) consists of three components:

1. Fruit
2. Grains
3. Milk

Exhibit 3-7 shows specific quantities of each component for grade groups. In addition, four items must be offered and students may decline one. A double portion of a component counts as two items (e.g., large muffin containing two ounce equivalents of grain).

Exhibit 3-7 Breakfast Meal Patterns for Grade Groups

Items	Elementary	Middle	High
Fruits (cups/day)[1]	1	1	1
Grains (ounce equivalents/day)	1 (7/week)	1 (8/week)	1 (9/week)
Fluid Milk (cups/day)	1	1	1

[1]Fruit quantity for breakfast increases from ½ cup to 1 cup beginning —SY2015

The breakfast menus must meet the following requirements:

- Half of grain offerings must be whole grain-rich. Beginning with the SY2014, all grains must be whole grain-rich.
- Fruits may be fresh, frozen, or canned in juice or light syrup.
- If flavored milk is offered, it must be fat-free. White milk may be fat-free or 1 percent butterfat. Two types of milk must be offered.

- Protein is not a requirement but may be offered in place of grain if the minimum grain requirement is met.
- Vegetables may be substituted for fruit.

Other Meals

The USDA website offers menu planning requirements for other school meals such as Child and Adult Care Food Program, after-school snacks, and supper. Daily requirements for the NSLP After-school Snacks include two of the following four components:

- Fluid milk
- Meat or meat alternate
- Whole-grain or enriched bread or cereal
- Fruit or vegetable

MENU PLANNING BASICS

Menu offerings must entice students and at the same time be nutritious, cost-effective, follow program requirements, effectively utilize labor and equipment, as well as result in a pleasant blend of color, texture, and shapes on each plate. In order to achieve these results, menu planning requires an organized approach.

Factors to Consider When Planning Menus

Before planning menus, consider several factors. The skills of food-service personnel, equipment, and budgets can differ greatly from one school district to the next. Getting menu ideas from other districts can speed up the menu planning process; however, menus will then need review against the needs of the district.

- **Available revenue:** Programs with a high number of low-income students have fixed revenues that dictate how much may be spent on menus. In districts with more affluent families, higher meal prices may allow the menu to offer selections that are more expensive.

- **Cost of food and supplies:** Some items may be too expensive to offer and packaging costs may add too much for some types of service such as grab-and-go choices.
- **Labor:** Cooking with convenience foods (e.g., proof and bake breads and boil-in-bag sauces) may be a necessity in some districts due a lack of employees with cooking skills or the high cost of labor.
- **The availability of USDA Foods in useable forms:** Planning menus with USDA Foods can lower food costs, however, customer acceptance is important to consider so that participation does not suffer.
- **Number of serving areas:** The fewer the serving lines the fewer items offered. If there are only two serving lines offer no more than five items. Otherwise, service will be slow while students make selection decisions.
- **Regional or ethnic favorites:** Incorporate the cultural preferences of students into the menu. For example, if large numbers of students do not eat certain foods (e.g., pork), offer the item less frequently. Religious holidays such as Lent may also affect menu choices during certain seasons.
- **Facilities and equipment:** Some schools may have limited space and equipment for meal preparation and/or service. The oven space and cooking temperatures may prohibit two different entrees to be prepared at the same time (e.g., pizza and chicken nuggets).
- **Frequency of deliveries:** Some items, such as fresh produce, have limited shelf life. Planning to serve these items a day

or two after delivery will ensure that produce is still at peak quality. Planning an easier menu on delivery days will also help balance the workload.

Menu Planning Steps

Like most other tasks in the nutrition program, developing a menu requires a standardized procedure to guarantee a good outcome. Simplify some steps by using software that makes new items available to bids, orders, inventory, recipes, and menus without duplicating data entry. To help the menu planner meet all requirements, it is helpful to create a menu planning template (Exhibit 3-8).

Eight Menu Planning Steps:

1. Evaluate menu items and ingredients for component contributions, nutritional guidelines, student acceptability, and estimated cost. Add items meeting all criteria to a list for menu planning.
2. Determine how to present or package the product.
3. Develop a standardized recipe for the menu item including packaging information and precost.
4. Develop menu cycle that balances program requirements, color, texture, temperature, equipment and personnel usage, and serving space.
5. Determine a la carte price for each menu item.
6. Add ingredients and supplies to inventory form.
7. Add ingredients and supplies to order form.
8. Add menu/ingredient items to production record.

Once implemented, evaluate menus to make sure that participation is consistently good. It is also important to evaluate the workload balance for employees and equipment. Making small adjustments to the menu to address problems creates less stress on the program than total menu overhaul.

Exhibit 3-8 Sample Elementary Menu Template

	Monday	Tuesday	Wednesday	Thursday	Friday
Meat/Meat Alternate	Hamburger	Pepperoni pizza	Chicken tenders	Burrito	Fish taco
Vegetables					
Orange/ Red		Baby carrots	Baked sweet potato tots		
Deep Green		Spinach salad			Garden salad
Legumes	BBQ beans			Black beans	
Starchy	Roasted potato			Corn	
Other			Green beans		Veggie dippers
Grains	Whole-grain bun	Whole-grain crust	Whole-grain roll	Whole-grain tortilla	Corn taco shell
Fruit	Mandarin oranges	Fruit mix	Peaches	Grapes	Cinnamon apples
Milk	Low-fat white Fat-free chocolate	Low-fat white Fat-free chocolate	Low-fat white Fat-free chocolate	Low-fat white Fat-free chocolate	Low-fat white Fat-free chocolate

Cycle Menus

A menu cycle is a set of menus that repeat (e.g., every two or three weeks). The length of the cycle correlates to the number of daily entrée choices. In a program that offers many choices, the cycle can be short, even one week. When offering a single entrée daily, the cycle needs to be longer in order to offer enough variety to make the menu interesting. The goal should be to build a cycle that offers enough choice to maximize participation. Using a cycle menu provides many benefits.

- Production records can be utilized for forecasting future production.
- Inventory is reduced because products turn over quickly.
- Employees can be more productive because they are producing the same products every few weeks.

- Work methods can be developed and standards set for production time.
- Procurement forecasting is more accurate, usually resulting in fewer out-of-stocks and lower bid prices.
- Receiving practices improve because the person receiving knows what products to expect each week and learns to recognize quality issues.
- Issues with theft are easier to spot when sales and inventory figures are not following an expected pattern.
- Less time is spent on the menu-planning steps, allowing more time to merchandise and market the menu offerings.
- Employees can become creative with presentation around themes and holidays.

Menu Costing

Determining the cost of menus is a critical but potentially overlooked step in the planning process. Knowing the planned menu cost provides a standard to measure how well the site personnel is managing food cost. The site manager cannot improve the food cost beyond the planned cost. Menu costing uses two different approaches.

One method is to establish target costs for each component (e.g., entrée is 45–50¢, vegetables 20–25¢, etc.). The total of each component is equal to the food cost goal for the meal. This method is best used when choices are not offered and students are not allowed to decline menu items (e.g., when offer versus serve is not implemented).

A second method uses the forecasted number of servings for each item on the menu and multiplies it times the cost of each menu item. After totaling the weighted cost of each item, divide the sum by the total projected meals. The calculated value is the projected food cost per meal (Exhibit 3-9).

Exhibit 3-9 Sample Precosted Elementary Menu for 200 Meals

Component	Menu Item	Serving Size	Forecast	Cost per Serving	Total Cost of Menu Item
Meat/Meat Alternate	Hamburger	1 patty	200	$0.35	$70.00
Grain	Whole grain bun	1 each	200	0.15	30.00
Vegetable	Broccoli Roasted potatoes	½ cup ½ cup	50 150	0.15 0.12	7.50 18.00
Fruit	Mandarin oranges	½ cup	100	0.25	25.00
Milk	White 1% Fat-free chocolate	1 carton 1 carton	50 100	0.21 0.22	10.50 22.00
Condiments	Catsup Mustard	2 packs 1 pack	150 100	0.10 0.05	15.00 5.00
Average Food Cost per Meal					$203 ÷ 200 = $1.015

A la Carte Offerings

Many school districts offer extra food items in addition to the school meals. These items are a la carte items or nonprogram food items. Selling a la carte items meets several goals:

- Provides foods to supplement meals for students requiring extra calories.
- Provides items to build a lunch students prefer.
- Provides food items for students who prefer to bring their meals from home.
- Offers snack items not included in meals.
- When priced correctly, increases the revenue for school meal programs.

Too often a la carte items are an afterthought for menu planners. Without careful planning, a la carte items can compete with school meal programs reducing both the nutritional quality of the program and profits.

A la carte items should be planned and priced so that students still get the best price by selecting a meal. A la carte choices can complement meals (e.g., offering baked chips with sandwiches) and priced so that total sales are round numbers and easy for students to buy (e.g., $2.50 meal plus a $0.50 chip).

As with meals, the selection of a la carte items or nonprogram food items should be no more than what is required to increase sales. If an item does not sell at least 25–50 units a day, drop it from the menu. The exceptions may be for healthier items that are shelf stable such as granola bars.

USDA has new regulations effective July 1, 2014, addressing nutrition standards covering all food and beverages sold anywhere on school campus throughout the school day. The regulations include food sold as fundraisers and those sold by departments outside of foodservices. Below is a summary of criteria:

- Must have as a first ingredient a fruit, vegetable, dairy product, or protein food, or
- A grain product with at least 50 percent whole grains, or
- A combination product that contains at least ¼-cup fruit or vegetable.

In addition, the product must:

- Contain 10% of the daily value of a nutrient cited as a public health concern by the *Dietary Guidelines* (calcium, potassium, Vitamin D, or fiber). After July 1, 2016, these criteria may no longer be used.
- Calories for a snack product must be 200 kcal or less, for an entrée 350 kcal or less.

- Sodium for a snack must be 230 mg or less per portion as packaged, for an entrée 480 mg or less per serving. After July 1, 2016, the sodium level must be 200 mg or less for snack foods.
- Total fat must be less than 35% of kcal, saturated fat less than 10% of kcal, and no trans fat.
- Total sugar cannot exceed 35% of total weight.
- Only low-fat white milk, fat-free flavored milk, 100% juice, or plain unflavored water (with or without carbonation) is available in elementary and middle schools. Elementary may not exceed 8 ounces and middle and high schools may not exceed 12-ounce portions of milk and juice. Make available any amount of plain water.
- High schools may sell a limited amount of other beverages (e.g., without added sweeteners, with or without carbonation).

Many states have nutritional requirements (e.g., calorie or fat targets) that a la carte items must meet before they can be offered. Check with state agencies for all current requirements for a la carte foods.

SPECIAL NUTRITIONAL CONCERNS

Most school districts have special needs students that require changes to their diet. The decision to accommodate these students with menu modifications depends on the district's philosophy and whether the student is classified as having a disability.

Students with disabilities requiring modifications to their diet are, by law, eligible to receive a special diet at no additional cost. A district may choose to accommodate nondisabled students. Many districts consider the accommodations as good customer service and try to honor the diet requests.

If the student is disabled, the modification is not required to follow the NSLP or SBP requirements even though the menu planner should attempt to do so to the extent possible (e.g., milk allergy). If the student is not disabled, the menu modifications must still meet program requirements.

Allergies

Food allergies affect one in every 13 children under the age of 18 years (Food Allergy Research and Education, 2012). Eight foods contribute to 90 percent of all food allergies: peanuts, tree nuts, soy, milk, egg, fish, shellfish, and wheat.

Since January 2006, these eight food sources of allergens are on food packaging lists due to the Food Allergen Labeling and Consumer Protection Act. Labels help menu planners identify foods containing allergens and help with planning menu substitutions.

Because students may not be able to determine the ingredients in foods served at school, it is important for personnel responsible for purchasing, writing recipes, and planning menus to identify foods with allergens known to affect students in the school. If the school has a student with an allergy, it is important to become familiar with "hidden" sources of the allergen. Several online resources listed at the end of this chapter provide information about reading ingredient lists and finding these sources.

Communicate this information to students, parents, and school health professionals by posting information on the district website or indicating on menus the foods containing allergens. Most point-of-sale systems have diet alerts programmed to notify cashiers when a student has special needs.

Most allergies and food intolerances are not considered to be disabilities. Students with a severe allergy, considered anaphylaxis, are usually classified as disabled because their condition can be life threatening.

Modified Diets

Students may also require modification to the consistency of their food. Physical disabilities commonly affect students' ability to chew or swallow. Most menus will include foods that can be ground or pureed in a blender for these students.

Diabetics and students with celiac disease may also require menu modifications. Celiac disease is an autoimmune disease that requires a gluten-free diet. Gluten is in wheat, rye, and barley. A gluten-free diet is restrictive and may necessitate schools to purchase products not typically on the menu (e.g., bread made with potato or rice flour).

Children with diabetes often require insulin. It is important to provide information on the carbohydrate content of menu items to both the student and the school nurse so that they can plan a balance between carbohydrate intake and insulin. It usually is not necessary to provide menu modifications for diabetics because schools participating in federal school meal programs already provide a balanced diet appropriate for most diabetics.

Religious and Cultural Preferences

Religious or cultural preferences are optional considerations, but if large populations of students in the community follow the same practice, it is wise to adjust menus to meet their needs. Provide

Cultures and Prohibited Foods

Islam/Muslims	– Pork
Seventh Day Adventist	– Pork, shellfish
Judaism	– Pork
Buddhist	– Meat (especially beef) or fowl
Hindu	– Beef and pork

Source: *Food for Fifty*, 2011.

foods on the menu that they can eat, and identify foods on the menu that their culture prohibits.

SUMMARY

In schools, the nutritional needs of school-aged children drive the menu-planning process. The Dietary Reference Intakes for student age groups and the *Dietary Guidelines* are the basis for school menu requirements.

Menu planning for schools is different from planning a menu for a restaurant. Schools must adhere to program regulations requiring certain nutrient targets, portion sizes, and types of food offered.

The menu directs many aspects of the school meal program including nutritional quality of the meal, food cost, needed employee skills, and equipment requirements. Several different factors affect menu planning, such as:

- Revenue available
- Cost of food, supplies, and labor
- Student preferences
- Equipment
- Time available for students to be served
- Skill of employees

Menu planning involves several steps. It is important to:

1. Evaluate the nutritional contribution, cost, and ease of preparation for menu items under consideration.
2. Precost recipes and menus to ensure menus fit the budget. Evaluate final menus for compliance with regulations, eye

appeal, student preference, and capacity of equipment and personnel.

3. Revise inventory, ordering, and production records to include new menu items.
4. Evaluate and modify menus for students with special needs, which may include allergies, intolerances, certain diseases, and conditions affecting the ability to chew or swallow.

QUESTIONS AND ANSWERS

1. The menu determines:
   a. Employee skills required
   b. Food cost goals
   c. Nutritional quality
   d. All of the above
2. Menus for schools include:
   a. Targets for fiber
   b. A requirement for fresh produce
   c. Targets for Vitamin C
   d. Calorie ranges for three grade groups
3. Nutrition goals for school meals are based on:
   a. Recommended Dietary Allowances
   b. *Dietary Guidelines for Americans*
   c. Recommendations from the American Pediatric Association
   d. Recommendations from the Academy of Nutrition and Dietetics
4. When planning school menus, which factors are important to consider?
   a. The cost of food, labor, and supplies
   b. Locally available products
   c. The availability of organic products
   d. The cost of utilities
5. Schools are required to adjust menus for special dietary needs when the student has:
   a. An allergy
   b. Religious beliefs affecting food choices
   c. A certified disability that requires a diet modification
   d. Food intolerance
6. District wellness policies are to contain:
   a. An assessment component
   b. Policies that address nutrition
   c. Policies that address physical activity
   d. All of the above
7. At lunch, students are required to take at least one fruit or vegetable in order to claim reimbursement for the meal.
   a. True
   b. False
8. All milk served with school meals must be unflavored.
   a. True
   b. False

9. An important factor to consider when planning menus includes:
a. Seniority of employees
b. Income level of the student household
c. Employees' preferences
d. Student preferences

ANSWERS: 1.d., 2.d., 3.b., 4.a., 5.c., 6.d., 7.a., 8.b., 9.d.

REFERENCES

Food Allergy Research and Education. 2012. *Facts and statistics.* Retrieved from *http://www.foodallergy.org/facts-and-stats.*

Institute of Medicine. 2009. *School meals: Building blocks for healthy children.* Washington, DC: National Academies Press.

Martin, J., & Oakley, C. (Eds.). 2008. *Managing child nutrition programs: Leadership for excellence,* 2nd ed. Sudbury, MA: Jones & Bartlett.

Molt, M. 2011. *Food for fifty,* 13th ed. Upper Saddle River, NJ: Prentice Hall.

NFMSI. 2006. *Handbook for children with special food and nutrition needs.* University, MS: Author.

Pannell-Martin, D. 2005. *inTEAM food system.* Santa Monica, CA: inTEAM Associates, Inc.

USDA and U.S. Department of Health and Human Services. 2010. *Dietary guidelines for Americans,* 7th ed. Washington, DC: U.S. Government Printing Office. Retrieved from *http://www.cnpp.usda.gov/DGAs2010-PolicyDocument.htm.*

USDA Federal Register, 7 CFR Parts 210 and 220. 2012. *Nutrition standards in the National School Lunch and School Breakfast Programs: Final rule.* Washington, DC: U.S. Government Printing Office.

ONLINE RESOURCES

Alliance for a Healthier Generation
http://www.healthiergeneration.org/schools.aspx

Dietary Guidelines for Americans
http://www.dietaryguidelines.gov/

Food Allergy Research & Education
http://www.foodallergy.org/home

Model School Wellness Policies
http://www.schoolwellnesspolicies.org/index.html

National Dairy Council Child Nutrition Health Education
http://www.nationaldairycouncil.org/ChildNutrition/Pages/ChildNutritionHealthEducationKit.aspx

NFSMI Meal Pattern Training
http://www.nfsmi.org/ResourceOverview.aspx?ID=425

Produce for Better Health Foundation
http://www.pbhfoundation.org/pub_sec/edu/

School Nutrition Association Local School Wellness Policies
http://www.schoolnutrition.org/Content.aspx?id=8504

USDA Dietary Reference Intakes
http://fnic.nal.usda.gov/dietary-guidance/dietary-reference-intakes

USDA Healthy Meals Resource System: Menu Planning Tools
http://healthymeals.nal.usda.gov/menu-planning/menu-planning-tools

USDA Nutrition Standards for School Meals
http://www.fns.usda.gov/cnd/Governance/Legislation/nutritionstandards.htm

USDA Team Nutrition Resources A to Z
http://www.fns.usda.gov/tn/library.html

Whole Grains Council
http://www.wholegrainscouncil.org/resources/educational-materials

CHAPTER 4

FOODSERVICE MANAGEMENT SYSTEMS AND FACILITIES

STUDY QUESTIONS

1. What is a food production system?
2. When should a school district select the conventional approach to food production over convenience?
3. When should a satellite system be considered?
4. State reasons for a school district to consider building a central kitchen.
5. What are the trends in facility planning?
6. Who should be involved in a new facility planning?
7. List five of the physical characteristics that should be planned into a new kitchen.
8. Why is menu important to purchasing equipment?
9. Describe a serving area that would improve speed of service.
10. How should a new manager or new director go about writing specifications for a major piece of kitchen equipment?

Chapter 4

"Serving in Half the Time" by Jana Landrum, BS, SNS

Director of Food and Nutrition Service, San Benito [TX] Consolidated Independent School District

Managing comes with many challenges. One of the challenges I faced came six years ago with a phone call from the newly appointed high school principal, announcing she was changing the lunch schedule. School was starting in 30 days with one 40-minute lunch period for 1,900 students—what was she thinking? I immediately went into defense mode, called the superintendent, and set up a meeting with the principal. I gave her all the reasons why it would not work. The one lunch period stood. Defeated, but not discouraged, it was time to go into action with limited time, budget, and staff to create six more serving lines.

Six serving lines had to be expanded to 12 to serve all the students in one lunch period. We walked the campus to see where we could set up lines in order to spread the service throughout the campus to minimize congestion and manage flow. The menu was dissected to create 12 destination stations. No longer were multiple entrée options served on one line. Each line became a specialty station featuring an entrée, such as Mexican, Italian, burgers, pizza, Asian, artisan sandwiches, chef salads, potato line, and daily specials.

Now that the menu was ready, we needed the equipment. Purchasing serving counters was not an option due to time and budget restraints. The stations were created throughout the school using wrought-iron shelving, screens, and artificial trees from local stores. Marketing support from vendors, such as countertop merchandisers, signage and packaging were used to identify the unique spaces. We did purchase heated and refrigerated slide merchandisers for a just-in-time installation.

The staff had to be rescheduled to meet this new lunch period and way of serving. There was no time for batch cooking. Everything had to be ready to go at one time. One of my biggest concerns was losing student participation from serving 80 percent the previous year, but it only increased.

Having one lunch period and serving throughout the hallways with the existing staff required another very important adjustment. All food items would have to be pre-portioned for self-service. This was critical to the timing of service and to maintain efficiency. Pre-portioning of food helped control waste in food and labor. A map was created of the school with all the serving areas identified. Students enjoyed the destination stations and quickly adapted.

This experience changed the serving approach in all schools, including the elementary schools. We found this system of service to be so effective and efficient that we applied the pre-portion self-serve system PreK–12th grade. Serving lines in all schools are built to utilize countertop merchandisers and free-standing and drop-in refrigeration. The design requires less floor space by having multilevel heated and cold merchandising units. School staff has commented that it is more student friendly: "It looks like food served at Disney World." Our meals per labor hour (MPLH) range in average of 20–26 throughout the district and participation averages 95 percent district-wide.

Which comes first—the menu, the food system, or the facility and equipment? Ideally, the menu comes first, followed by adopting a foodservice management system, and finally the facility and equipment. In reality, many directors begin working in school districts with kitchen/cafeteria facilities built years ago. The system is "just the way it is done." The menus are planned to fit the facilities and equipment.

FOODSERVICE MANAGEMENT SYSTEM

A foodservice management system is comprised of an arrangement of related and connected elements. These elements include planning menus, purchasing, receiving, storing, issuing, preparing, cooking, serving, and cleaning up.

The type foodservice management system is based on the degree to which food used is processed. The categories of systems discussed in the chapter are:

- Conventional food production system—food preparation takes place on site.
- Convenience food production system—food is partially prepared or fully prepared and requires minimal preparation on site.
- Satellite food production system—production is done at one location for service in another site(s).

A standardized approach or system of managing school foodservice will aid in financial control regardless of the system used to produce the food. When a standardized approach is used successfully, more uniformity in food served throughout the school district is the typical result. For example, in Hammond (IN), the menu is the same in all elementary schools, with a standardization of food products purchased, the recipes, and portion size. As in many school districts, a different portion size and menu are served in the middle and high schools.

FOOD PRODUCTION SYSTEM

Conventional Food Production System

The conventional, or on-site, food production system is the most prevalent and is used by 82 percent of the schools across the country. This system may mean cooking and baking foods from raw ingredients, often referred to as "cooking from scratch." This system is not prevalent in many inner-city and large urban school districts.

In recent years, this system has changed to a mix of convenience foods (partially prepared) and raw foods that are prepared on site. Rural school districts usually use this system of preparing and serving food because of geographic location, tradition, and need for full-time jobs.

The advantages of the conventional foodservice system have changed somewhat over the past 20 years. More processed foods are used as the quality and variety improve. In addition, the USDA Foods are available in different degree of preparedness.

Advantages of the conventional food system:

- Allows management to determine the ingredients used (e.g., sodium, additives, and preservatives)
- Provides more jobs that are full time
- Allows for more individual school preferences
- Offers more flexibility

Disadvantages of the conventional food system over convenience:

- Reduces productivity
- Requires more skilled employees
- Needs more preparation equipment and larger facilities

Convenience Food Production System

As labor costs and turnover increase and skilled labor shortages plague the industry, the convenience foodservice system has become a more attractive option. A convenience foodservice system can vary greatly from little to no preparation on site. It may involve simply thawing and serving a sandwich, as well as other parts of the menu.

Advantages of the convenience foodservice system:

- Provides more consistency in quality
- Increases productivity and lowers labor costs
- Reduces need for skilled employees and training

Disadvantages of the convenience foodservice system:

- Results in higher food cost
- Requires more refrigeration/freezer storage space
- Provides fewer full-time jobs

On the other hand, it may mean the assembling of sandwiches on site using bakery bread, presliced sandwich meats, and cheeses.

The degree of convenience varies greatly in this system. The convenience foods may be purchased in single servings or in bulk quantities. Today it is possible to purchase high-quality frozen menu items that require no preparation or cooking, just simply preheating or thawing to a desired serving temperature. The number of fully prepared foods on a school's menu has increased slowly. In this system, the pieces of cooking equipment (e.g., steamers) have become storage cabinets in some school kitchens.

Definitions:

BASE OR PRODUCTION KITCHEN—A kitchen where meals are prepared for serving on-site and for one or more other locations.

CENTRAL PRODUCTION KITCHEN OR COMMISSARY—A kitchen where food is prepared to be served for a number of other locations.

COOK-CHILL/FREEZE SYSTEM—Food is prepared, chilled, or frozen, and reheated and served at a later time.

FINISHING KITCHEN—A kitchen that receives partially prepared foods that need heating, finishing off, or reconstituting before serving.

RECEIVING KITCHEN—The school kitchen receives food ready to serve. The food may be delivered in bulk or in individual servings.

SATELLITE FOOD PRODUCTION SYSTEM (SATELLITING)—Food is prepared at one location for serving at another.

Satellite Food Production System

The satellite food production system means simply "food is prepared somewhere other than where it is served." A number of different approaches are used to obtain the prepared food.

Transporting Food Ready-to-Serve

Food may be transported ready-to-serve in a hot or cold state. The challenge is to maintain the food at a safe serving temperature. It is probably the oldest and most common means of satellite food. The food is usually transported within two to three hours following preparation. Timing is important to maintaining quality and safety of the product.

Well-insulated and electrically heated food carriers are usually used. At the receiving schools, students are served from a serving line—cafeteria-style—picking up their trays, food, milk, silverware, and napkins. This system requires little labor and equipment at the receiving school.

Cook-Chill/Freeze Food Production System

Cook-chill or cook-freeze preparation system is a time-tested and USDA-approved approach. Food production occurs on site or in commissaries. Many commercial foodservices and successful chain restaurants use this system. With this system, food products are cooked "somewhere" in a large quantity and poured into polyethylene bags while still hot (180° F). The bags are closed and chilled in an ice water bath or tumbler chiller to drop the product temperature from 180° F to 36–38° F in 30–45 minutes. (The time required will depend on the food product's viscosity.) USDA requires reducing the temperature within two hours. The product may be refrigerated for up to 30 days.

Some kitchens take the extra precaution of freezing rather than chilling the finished product. Freezing makes transporting the finished product to the service sites safer and easier; however, it may require a change in some recipe formulations to assure product quality.

When and Why the Satellite Food Production System

In the early 1970s, the school lunch program participation increased overnight, and federal funding increased substantially. This funding increase was primarily because of the Child Nutrition Act of 1966. Student population was increasing faster than new buildings. To meet these needs, schools came up with alternative ways of producing and serving food at school. One of those approaches was a satellite food production system with a central kitchen.

Corpus Christi (TX) built one of the first central kitchens. In recent years, a more automated kitchen replaced the central kitchen. The kitchen provides some baked products for all the district schools and all the food for the satellite schools. The labor and food cost controls in place have served this school district well over the years.

Reasons for using a satellite system are many. Some of the main advantages are:

Reduces	→ cost of food and supplies
	→ initial cost of construction
	→ equipment needed
	→ number of labor hours needed
	→ cost of labor
	→ inventory at each school site
	→ energy (electricity, gas, and water) used
	→ number of delivery sites for vendors
Increases	→ productivity
Improves	→ standardization
	→ quality and quantity control

Some disadvantages or concerns with a satellite include the following:

Increases	→ potential of foodborne illness
	→ cost of large equipment
	→ specialized maintenance
Decreases	→ menu flexibility
	→ number of full-time jobs available
Problems	→ traffic/congestion and weather
	→ maintaining good quality
	→ maintaining the correct temperature

Central Kitchen and Receiving Kitchen

In the last five years, several long-time central kitchens have closed, for example, Portland (OR), Arlington (VA), and Norfolk (VA). At the same time of closing some central kitchens, new central kitchens are opening, for example, Dallas (TX) and Palm Springs (CA). Orange County (FL) has a central kitchen on the drawing board.

Some larger high school kitchens are now mini-central kitchens. These schools are receiving raw foods, prepping, assembling, and distributing foods for nearby schools, for example, Fairfax County (VA) and Orange County (FL). Howard County (MD) built schools with this plan in mind and realized significant capital outlay savings.

Some directors reason that the improvement in convenience foods has made the central kitchen obsolete. Perhaps the central kitchen of today needs to be more for assembling, repackaging, and distributing just the right quantities to the satellite schools. The savings from controlling inventory would make it worthwhile.

Manufacturers are processing USDA Foods into convenience foods at competitive prices. USDA is responding to schools' needs and has made it less necessary for a district to produce food from "scratch" or "raw ingredients." The emphasis on fresh foods has made assembly of food more the approach than "cooking."

Productivity increases by five to eight times over the conventional system production rate. On the average, an on-site production system can produce 14 to 18 meals per labor hour (MPLH), whereas the central kitchen can produce 50 to 75 meals per labor hour. Suggested MPLH are provided and discussed further in Chapter 5, "Personnel and Staffing."

These large central kitchens resemble factories. It takes expert management and highly skilled labor to operate a "food factory." The central kitchens in Palm Springs (CA) and Jefferson County (KY) are examples of this type of operation, but once fully operating should provide impressive productivity. The shorter-hour employees needed at the receiving school kitchens may be more difficult to obtain than longer-hour employees used in a central kitchen.

What works best for one school district may not be the best for another. The distance to transport, traffic routes, the volume of food production, the source of employees, and the goals of the school district affect the decisions. Some argue that so much is lost when food is not cooked on site (e.g., the smell of rolls and cookies baking).

Additional points in locating a central kitchen include distance to transport between central kitchen and receiving kitchen, problems related to large equipment and vehicle breakdowns, expansion needs, and accessibility to primary traffic routes for deliveries.

Pre-Plated Meals

Pre-plated meals come (1) ready to serve, and (2) ready to reheat and serve. Timing is especially important when using a ready-to-serve pre-plated meals system.

The pre-plated meals heated and served on site give more flexibility. Those that come ready to serve have a short window of time between cooking and serving. This method does not work well for large operations.

The Indianapolis (IN) Public School District delivers chilled pre-plated meals in baskets at night. The drivers not only deliver the food, but also they check that schools are secure (partly a security role), deliver mail, and pick up used baskets. The advantages to combining jobs and working during the night include reduced labor costs, no children on playgrounds, and less traffic.

TRENDS IN FACILITY PLANNING

The conventional production kitchen is one of the most expensive spaces in a school. The kitchen should be planned for the next

10–20 years. Foodservice management should encourage using construction funds wisely. The results should be an efficient kitchen that uses only the space needed. The philosophy of the school district and the federal regulations have the greatest impact on facility and equipment trends.

Over the past 10 years, the emphasis tended toward employing chefs, reducing fat in foods, and increasing the use of fresh fruits and vegetables. As a result, many school districts are going back to basics. Today school kitchens contain fewer deep-fat fryers, more ovens, and more refrigeration. Some school kitchens are moving more to cooking from raw products. The federal equipment stimulus money of 2009 helped some school districts afford new equipment for preparing fresh fruits and vegetables. Exhibit 4-1 discusses recent trends affecting school facilities.

Exhibit 4-1 Trends for School Nutrition Programs

- Increased emphasis on health and wellness
- Food security and emergency preparedness
- Alternate food production systems
- Smaller and more mobile equipment
- Equipment with new or blended technologies
- Labor-saving options
- Better ventilation
- Increased emphasis on food safety
- Incorporation of electro-processors and computers into equipment
- Changes in refrigeration/freezer needs
- E-commerce for small wares, tabletop or small pieces of equipment, and tracking deliveries
- Display cooking
- More colorful and/or less-expensive construction materials
- Environmentally friendly
- Changing student customer and service systems
- Growth of culinary science as a career

Source: NFSMI, 2009.

Many school districts find these changes back to basics harder to sell to the customers. The food choices may be unfamiliar, the quality of food harder to maintain, and costs higher than some school districts can afford.

The leaders in the school market 10–15 years ago did not necessarily plan for today's changes. The challenge for a facility planner, then and now, is to plan flexible foodservice facilities that can be adapted to the needs of the future. School kitchens, and particularly dining areas, are being used today for more than just school children's lunches. This trend will continue.

Nontraditional serving areas are the biggest new trend in schools today. Makeovers and reimaging efforts are turning dull institutional serving areas into beautiful, bright, new food courts or "mock food courts." The school facilities built in the 1970s need to be replaced or drastically remodeled. Some school districts have done this very creatively, such as San Benito (TX), Newport News (VA), and Palm Beach (FL). Chapter 10, "Marketing," discusses this topic in greater detail.

BASIC FACILITY PLANNING

Knowledgeable people, who understand the foodservice operation and the menu, need to be involved in the planning of the foodservice facilities. Foodservice management must insist on being a part of the planning team for a new school. If a new facility is in the planning, the director or staff member should read the excellent publications by National Food Service Management Institute (NFSMI) on the subject. To be a "trusted advisor" requires being an informed,

> *"Bigger is not necessarily better"* when planning kitchen space. Enough space, but not too much, is the first requirement for an efficient kitchen. The second essential element is a good flow in the layout.

knowledgeable advisor, which includes understanding the architect's blueprints.

The local and state health departments, state department of education, and fire department should be consulted during the early planning stages as well. Occupational Safety and Health Administration (OSHA) regulations must be adhered to. The emphasis on Hazard Analysis & Critical Control Points (HACCP) influences the policies of the local and state health departments.

Facility planning factors include the following:

- Capacity of the school and number meals to be served at one time
- Potential future expansion
- What meals will be prepared and served
- Menus
- Age of the children
- Type of food production system to be used
- Type of utilities to be used
- Water and drains needed
- Type of equipment needed
- Number of staff, facilities, and amount of office space needed

Exhibit 4-2 provides an example of space planning for a conventional on-site production kitchen. It is conservative in space allotments, and if funds are available, the space could be increased. Over the past 10 years, the demand for refrigeration/freezer space has increased with use of more fresh fruits and vegetables and frozen convenience foods. See NFSMI website for guidelines.

Architects and kitchen planners may tend to overequip a kitchen, particularly if paid based on the dollars spent. A competitive

Exhibit 4-2 Example of Space for a School Foodservice Facility with Conventional On-site Production Kitchen and Dining Areas

Area	Up to 400 Meals/day	401–800 Meals/day	801–1200 Meals/day	1201–1500 Meals/day
Receiving area	60 sq ft	75 sq ft	85 sq ft	100 sq ft
Dry storage				
Food storage	200 sq ft	400 sq ft	500 sq ft	600 sq ft
Nonfood storage*	50 sq ft	75 sq ft	85 sq ft	100 sq ft
Office/employee space				
Office	70 sq ft	100 sq ft	130 sq ft	150 sq ft
Lockers and toilet for employees	200 sq ft	200 sq ft	225 sq ft	250 sq ft
Kitchen				
Preparation	600 sq ft	700 sq ft	800 sq ft	1000 sq ft
Refrigeration	300 sq ft	400 sq ft	400 sq ft	600 sq ft
Serving/holding	300 sq ft	800 sq ft	1200 sq ft	1400 sq ft
Dishwashing/pot washing	200 sq ft	300 sq ft	400 sq ft	500 sq ft
Maintenance area				
Janitor area	50 sq ft	75 sq ft	95 sq ft	100 sq ft
Garbage/trash area*	50 sq ft	75 sq ft	100 sq ft	150 sq ft
Total kitchen and serving areas (approximately)	2,080 sq ft	2,640 sq ft	3,115 sq ft	3,640 sq ft
Dining area (based on 2–3 seatings)				
Elementary-age students	1,600 sq ft	2,400 sq ft	3,200 sq ft	3,600 sq ft
Secondary-age students	2,400 sq ft	3,200 sq ft	3,600 sq ft	4,500 sq ft
Total kitchen, serving, and dining areas				
Elementary-age students	3,680 sq ft	5,040 sq ft	6,315 sq ft	7,240 sq ft
Secondary-age students	4,480 sq ft	5,840 sq ft	6,715 sq ft	8,140 sq ft

*Size is based on washing dishes and eating utensils. If disposable products are used the size will need to be doubled, but space for dishwashing area in kitchen can be reduced.

Adapted from *Space allocation for school nutrition facility design, Fact Sheet, by NFSMI, 2011.*

bid process usually results in prices that are more competitive and with more service for the money. Buyers are tempted to buy from the Internet, but full-service dealers often offer extras that are valuable.

Physical Considerations

School districts often aim to achieve the U.S. Green Building Council's Leadership in Energy and Environmental Design (LEED) for Existing Buildings: Operations & Maintenance designation. The results are LEED certification for an energy-efficient building and a better physical environment.

The American with Disabilities Act and OSHA standards and requirements must also be met. These include, for example, width of aisles, height of tables, and accessible dining area and dining tables for wheelchairs.

The foodservice areas general requirements and considerations of most concern for the architect include:

- Menu to be served
- Type of food production system to be used
- Enrollment anticipated and percentage of that to be served at one time
- Age of students
- Kitchen location
    - Near a back loading dock
    - On the first floor or ground floor
    - Adjoining the dining room
    - Can be secure and accessible
- Dining room seating capacity
    - Ability to seat ⅓ to ½ of the student body at one time
    - Accessible/convenient to classroom areas
    - A combination of round and rectangular tables or booths

- Trash area: influenced by use of disposables or dishwashing
- Dish washing located adjacent to dining area
- Waste disposal handy for students
- Physical conditions desired
  - Adequate lighting (type)—warm white fluorescent lights in serving area
  - Bright-colored accents to be included in the décor; light wall and ceiling color without glare
  - Good air circulation and ventilation with change of air every five minutes
  - Ergonomic design: safe, efficient, and productive
  - Air conditioning (kitchen included)—68° to 78° F; relative humidity at 40–45%.
  - Adequate hot water supply (140° F all year round, with booster to raise the temperature to 180° F, if needed for sterilization)
  - Electrical outlets and water and drains where needed; the electrical voltage matches equipment
  - Entrance/exterior door into the kitchen large enough for equipment to pass through
- Kitchen layout
  - Planned around work centers
  - Manager's office enclosed with glass panels 3–4 feet above floor level with clear view of production area
  - A secure place for counting money
  - Restrooms with employees' lockers off kitchen

- Serving area
  - Scramble, straight line, food court, window service, speed lines, vending machines
  - Located near kitchen
  - Appropriate number of serving lines/stations
  - Good acoustics

When planning a facility, the planner should consider ergonomics. Ergonomic design is one that is the safest, most efficient, and productive. For example, the depth of sinks may be too deep for shorter employees and worktables may be too high or too low.

Standardizing menus, facilities, and equipment in all schools in the school district will result in a savings, particularly if the school district has "in-house" repair and maintenance. Stocking of repair parts and training of repair staff is standardized and therefore simplified.

Production Area

One of the latest trends is the smart kitchen, which monitors and controls temperature and timing, and is more efficient. Regardless of smart kitchen or traditional kitchen setup, the work centers should maintain a flow of work that is natural and logical and follows the sequence of food processing (Exhibit 4-3).

Normally the flow of food processing is from receiving to storage, to pre-preparation to preparation areas, to service, and to cleanup without crisscrossing or backtracking. The emphasis needs to be on using as little space as required, having efficiencies built in, consideration for labor shortage, and the need for convenience.

Exhibit 4-3 Flow of Work

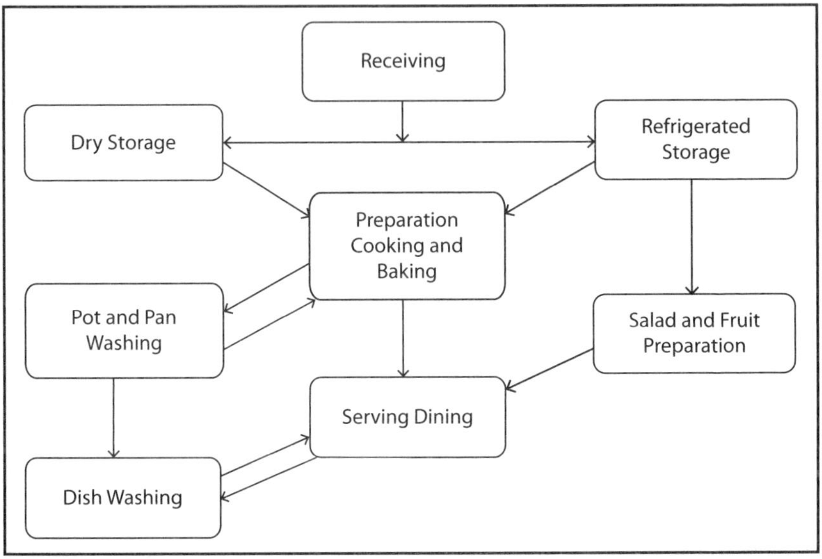

Serving Area and Dining Room

Atmosphere becomes important in the serving area and dining room. Atmosphere is one of the prime inducements for people to want to dine out, and this factor applies not only to adults, but also to students at school. In a Maryland company, the management changed the color of carts from bright orange to battleship gray and the flowered cups of orange and yellow to plain white. Within six weeks, the food sales dropped 40 percent.

The atmosphere has an effect—negative and positive—on behavior in the dining room. It can be an unpleasant place or a fun place. Today's facility and equipment should promote an expanded menu and upbeat décor in the production, serving, and dining areas. The results are increased participation and greater satisfaction with food at school.

The flow of traffic in the serving area will improve speed of service and enhance the atmosphere. For example, a scramble system will encourage more free flow and allow more students to be actively involved in serving themselves at one time. The straight line may be less confusing for small children but is less interesting.

San Benito (TX) has done an excellent job with makeovers in older schools. The director realizes the importance of color and convenience. The addition of service "stations" at little cost has resulted in increased participation and improved student satisfaction.

Colors can have a significant impact on foodservice customers. According to studies, colors promote different feelings, moods, and mental associations.

Yellow	Sunny, warm, cheerful, inspiring, high-spirited; boosts morale and enhances food
Orange	Bright, warm, jovial, lively, forceful, energetic, enhances food; most stimulating color to the appetite
Green	Clear, cool, quieting, refreshing, low-spirited, sells more salad
Blue	Transparent, cold, subduing, melancholy; least stimulating to the appetite
Purple	Deep, cool, dignified, mournful
Red	Brilliant, hot, exciting, active, intense

See Exhibit 4-4 for examples of what remodeling can do for the school foodservice program. The Newport News (VA) and Palm Beach (FL) websites show the school dining room renovations with before and after pictures. Palm Beach (FL) calls it reengineering. Chapter 10, "Marketing," discusses this further.

Multiple points of service make it more interesting to students. This format involves and empowers the student in the decision making. In addition, the student does not stand in line as long.

Exhibit 4-4 Remodeling Resulted in Increased Participation

Newport News (VA)	10% increase
Palm Beach (FL)	25% increase
San Benito (TX)	15% increase
Greenwich (CT) High School	15% increase

LARGE EQUIPMENT

The American Recovery and Reinvestment Act of 2009 provided some needed equipment money, but the needs were much greater than revenue available.

Labor cost, labor shortages, and food safety issues influence equipment trends. The need for flexibility and energy savings also play into use of automation and available technology. Some of the new automated equipment may increase the learning curve and require more training. The use of computer technology has many advantages, which makes it worth the time it takes for training users.

The NFSMI provides some of the best information on purchasing equipment, and it is available free in online course form. When money is available to purchase equipment, the challenge is to use the money wisely.

The menu should drive the equipment purchases. With the menu and food production system planned for a school, next comes a list of equipment needs. Exhibit 4-5 provides an example of one menu and the equipment needed. If a piece of equipment has use for only one menu item, another way of cooking/preparing the item may be necessary. A detailed template and checklist is available in the Online Resources at the end of chapter.

Equipment Design

Purchasing equipment is generally for one of the following reasons:

- Improve sanitation
- Reduce labor costs

Exhibit 4-5 Example of Menu Guiding Equipment Decisions

Menu Items	Convection Oven	Combi-Oven	Steamer	Mixer	Refrigerator
Roasted chicken	X	X[1]			
Mashed potatoes				X	
Fresh raw veggies					X
Steamed broccoli			X[2]		
Fruit cup					X
Roll	X[3]			X[3]	
Milk					X

[1]Depends on volume and resources.
[2]Can cook in combi-oven.
[3]If bakery bread is used, the mixer and oven will not be used.

- Provide new technology
- Maintain nutritional value of foods
- Reduce food costs
- Add appeal and variety to menus
- Increase productivity and efficiency
- Replace old equipment
- Reduce energy usage

Trends are toward smaller, more mobile, and more versatile and flexible equipment. Advice from experienced foodservice directors is to put equipment on wheels and avoid getting too specialized. When money is available to replace or purchase a new piece of equipment, it is important to look at what is new on the market, trying to upgrade and use technology where available. The cook's advice may be "just like what I have." Taking that advice, the staff may miss new technology and improved pieces of equipment.

Some of the popular, newer pieces of equipment to be considered include the combination convection and microwave ovens, highly automated combi-ovens, and induction cooking. With emphasis on food safety and improving the quality and taste, the holding and serving areas are getting more attention. These service areas should include both refrigerated and heated aspects.

The NFSMI provides a checklist and matrix for determining equipment needs, which can be particularly helpful for a new director when the school district is building a new facility. A variety of questions needs to be asked. For example: How often will each piece of equipment be used—daily, weekly, or monthly? How many worktables, pans, utensils, and so on will be needed?

The National Sanitation Foundation (NSF) provides standards for foodservice equipment. The equipment will bear the NSF seal. In addition, much of the equipment will be Energy Star–rated and carry that label. This distinction will be important to new "green" school designs.

Writing Equipment Specifications

A requirement for obtaining needed and wanted features is to write precise specifications. Good specifications are essential to competitive prices and can save money in the end. For example, if the kitchen needs six racks in a refrigerator, the specification includes six racks (not the typical four).

Before writing the equipment specifications, some basic physical restrictions need to be checked. For example, the capacity of the utilities, size of door openings, and state/local requirements are considerations. The equipment selected should meet the goals today, as well as for the next 10 years. Exhibit 4-6 offers some basic elements of specifications.

Restaurant equipment trade shows, as well as the associations' annual convention exhibits, will provide valuable information to managers and directors. The manufacturers' representatives can also answer questions about equipment. Other excellent sources of

Exhibit 4-6 Basic Equipment Specifications

1. Generic names: what it is (e.g., oven, grill, steamer, milk cooler)
2. Quantities: number of items
3. Description: not detailed but sufficient to describe what is wanted to a supplier
   a. Size: length, width, height, number of gallons, etc.
   b. Utility requirements: gas, electric, plumbing
   c. Seals of approval: Underwriters' Laboratories (UL), National Sanitation Foundation (NSF), American Gas Association (AGA)
   d. Accessories (e.g., number of bowls for the mixer or shelves for the refrigerator)
4. Other requirements
   a. Demonstration/training: on-site demonstration and training
   b. Adjustments (e.g., calibration)
   c. Service within 50–70 miles
   d. Manuals: number (1 for school, 1 for maintenance, 1 for office)
   e. Warranty: one-year parts and labor if the equipment has working parts (If it is an expensive piece of equipment, the specification should provide for service.)
5. Delivery date: specify a range of dates
6. Price FOB: price delivered to a specified location

information on equipment and planning facilities are in the "Online Resources" section.

Federal regulations do not require formal bidding for purchases of $150,000, or less. Before making an equipment purchase, however, it is important to check the state and local government purchasing requirements. Even though a formal bid is not required, the informal bid process can save a considerable amount of money. *Procurement in the 21st Century* (NFSMI, 2013) is a source of information on competitive purchasing.

SUMMARY

This chapter includes discussion on three different subjects that support the production and service of food to school students:

1. System of management
2. Facility design
3. Equipment needs

All three influence the foodservice program; however, they should not drive the results. The menu should drive the system and, ideally, determine the facility and equipment. The facility and equipment should not control the program.

In the past 10 years, the push has been to use more "scratch cooking" and less processed foods. Scratch cooking does not necessarily mean better quality and food that is more nutritious. Many new employees do not cook at home and have little or no experience. School foodservice will have to train them in whatever skills are necessary to do the job.

The planner, user, and buyer should evaluate the trends and try to build in flexibility. The school food and nutrition service program is always changing. With the Internet, a novice can become an informed planner, user, and buyer.

QUESTIONS AND ANSWERS

1. The most common food production system is:
   a. Satellite production system
   b. Convenience production system
   c. Conventional production system
   d. Central kitchen production system
2. A kitchen should be planned to meet the needs:
   a. Today and next year
   b. The next 10–20 years
   c. The next 30–40 years
   d. Forever
3. Planning a new school's kitchen should be done by:
   a. School foodservice staff
   b. A team of knowledgeable people
   c. The school board
   d. Foodservice consultant
4. Equipment specifications should be:
   a. Written by the manufacturer
   b. Adequate to get the piece of equipment needed
   c. Written in great detail
   d. Written so different manufacturers' products can be bid
5. The serving style that will offer greatest speed is:
   a. Window approach
   b. Straight line
   c. Scramble
   d. Family style
6. A school kitchen should be located:
   a. Near the front office of the school
   b. Close to the loading dock
   c. On the second floor
   d. In the basement
7. The main goals for kitchen design should be:
   a. Safety, security, and efficiency
   b. Lowest cost possible and for today's use
   c. Esthetics and showy
   d. As large as possible with a lot of equipment

8. Dry and refrigeration storage should be located:
   a. Near the delivery dock
   b. Where the delivery goes through the preparation area
   c. Near the dining room
   d. By the front office of school

ANSWERS: 1.c., 2.b., 3.b., 4.d., 5.c., 6.b., 7.a., 8.a.

REFERENCES

Gregoire, M. 2012. *Foodservice organizations: A managerial and systems approach,* 8th ed. Upper Saddle River, NJ: Prentice Hall, Inc.

Gryder, S. 2012. Pop quiz! *School Nutrition*, 66 (1), 18–26.

Martin, J., & Conklin, M. (Eds.). 2008. *Managing child nutrition programs: Leadership for excellence,* 2nd ed. Sudbury, MA: Jones & Bartlett Publishing.

Maryland State Department of Education. 1996. *Design manual.* Baltimore, MD: Maryland State Department of Education, Nutrition and Transportation Services Branch.

McLaren, P. 2012. Kitchen open or kitchen closed? *School Nutrition,* 66 (1), 42–52.

NFMSI. 1997. *The new design handbook for school foodservice.* University, MS: Author.

NFMSI. 1998. *A guide for purchasing foodservice equipment.* University, MS: Author.

NFMSI. 2009. *Equipment purchasing and facility design for school nutrition programs.* University, MS: Author.

NFMSI. 2009. *School nutrition professional; Involvement in the equipment purchasing and facility design process.* University, MS: Author.

NFMSI. 2011. Templates and checklist. Retrieved from *http://www.nfsmi.org/ResourceOverview.aspx?ID=273.*

NFSMI, 2013. *Procurement in the 21st Century.* University, MS: Author.

Pannell-Martin, D. 2004. *Cost control manual for school foodservices,* 3rd ed. Frankfort, KY: Kentucky Department of Education, Division of School and Community Nutrition.

Schweitzer, D. 2010. *Planning & designing innovative and modern school kitchens and dining rooms.* Hammond, IN: AuthorHouse.

Scriven, C. & Stevens, J. 1999. *Food equipment facts: A handbook for the foodservice industry.* New York: Van Nostrand Reinhold.

ONLINE RESOURCES

Food Service Technology Center (Fishnick)
http://www.fishnick.com/

National Sanitation Foundation (NSF) Energy Star Program
http://www.nsf.org/business/energy_testing/

North American Association of Food Equipment Manufacturers (NAFEM)
http://www.nafem.org

NSF Food Equipment Certification
http://www.nsf.org/business/food_equipment_services/index.asp?program=FoodEquSer

NFSMI Templates and Checklist
http://www.nfsmi.org/ResourceOverview.aspx?ID=273

OSHA Information
https://www.osha.gov/

U.S. Green Building Council's LEED for Existing Buildings: Operations and Maintenance
http://www.usgbc.org/leed/rating-systems/existing-buildings

USDA Hazard Analysis & Critical Control Points
http://www.fda.gov/Food/GuidanceRegulation/HACCP/

Chapter 5

Personnel and Staffing

STUDY QUESTIONS

1. What is the line of authority from the federal government level to the local school food level?
2. Describe the difference in centralized and decentralized school food and nutrition services.
3. What makes up a job description?
4. Define *span of control.*
5. How is productivity measured in school foodservices?
6. Define *meal equivalent* and *meals per labor hour.*
7. Describe the difference in a conventional preparation system and a convenience preparation system.
8. Explain how to determine the number of labor hours needed at a school's foodservice program.
9. What factors affect meals per labor hour?
10. What are the advantages of a work schedule?

Chapter 5

"Not Enough Employees to Do the Job"

by Julia Bauscher, BS, SNS
Director, School and Community Nutrition Services, Jefferson County (KY) Public Schools

What do you do when you do not have enough employees to prepare lunch? For 95,000 students? Well, that is what we were faced with in the 1990s. The Louisville area was blessed with low employment rates, which was not good for us. It was impossible to recruit enough 3-hour and 4-hour staff members to prepare and serve meals every day in all cafeterias.

The first thing that happened when short staffed was we would change the menu. It was unlikely that yeast rolls and other made-from-scratch menu items could be prepared. Ultimately, menu changes had an overall negative impact on school meal participation, which affects the bottom line.

In 1996, the department raised the minimum hours worked for all Nutrition Service assistants to five hours, which meant they were also eligible for benefits. That change improved the availability of workers because many worked for benefits alone, but the number of workers still seemed to be insufficient. And, the bottom line was feeling the increased cost.

A concurrent rising problem was the lack of skilled workers who understood, for example, the nuances of yeast breads and some other basic food preparation techniques. The department began exploring the possibility of building a central kitchen. From Nutrition Service's perspective, a central kitchen would reduce the number of assistants necessary to prepare meals at the site level and would increase the food safety and nutrition integrity of the products served in the school meal program.

We broke ground on the Nutrition Service Center (NSC) in 1998. Through retirements and attrition, the number of nutrition assistants at the site level was reduced to appropriate levels.

The quality and quantity of products available in the school meal program improved and increased, and so did customer satisfaction and participation. In addition, the NSC offers 8-hour per day jobs for many workers.

Today, the NSC continues to help the department keep direct labor expenses below 40 percent. It has also been a valuable resource in making healthier menu items available to students (e.g., whole grain yeast rolls, lower-sodium recipes for popular items like taco meat and spaghetti meat sauce, and locally sourced produce for school meals). The ability to adapt and adjust recipes quickly has helped the department to maintain school lunch participation at 62,000 students despite required meal pattern changes and paid-lunch price increases.

An automated substitute placement program was implemented in 2013. This has increased the number of substitutes available to the program and the number of vacant positions filled daily.

A leading personnel problem for school food and nutrition service programs is lack of skilled employees. This issue remains despite the fact that unemployment rates have increased. Since the early 2000s, the emphasis on cooking from raw ingredients has required labor that is more skilled. Many school districts had to increase their hourly wages and extend labor hours to attract enough skilled employees to do the jobs.

PERSONNEL MANAGEMENT

Personnel are instrumental to the success of school food and nutrition service programs—they make the difference. The management of personnel includes a wide range of functions. Many college courses are devoted to aspects of managing, motivating, and personnel satisfaction. This text is limited to the uniqueness of the programs and services provided. The uniqueness begins with the line of authority and its importance to management.

Exhibit 5-1 Line of Authority for Federal Child Nutrition Programs

Line of Authority

U.S. Department of Agriculture
↓
Seven Regional Offices
↓
State Department of Education
Or
State Department of Agriculture
↓
Local School Food Authority
(School District)
↓
Superintendent
↓
Business Department or Support Services
↓
Food and Nutrition Services Director
↓
(School Principal)
↓
Food and Nutrition Services Manager

Line of Authority

The USDA administers the National Child Nutrition programs at the federal level. At the state level, the program may differ from state to state. In most states, the department of education administers the child nutrition programs (Exhibit 5-1). In some states, child nutrition programs are under the state department of agriculture. The USDA

Foods program (formerly known as commodity program) is usually administered at the state level under either the department of agriculture or education.

USDA and state agencies refer to the school district as the School Food Authority (SFA) or Local Education Agency. Little uniformity is imposed on what the local district calls the SFA. The line of authority also differs from one district to another. The school principal may have a lot or little authority in decisions for the foodservice program at the school level. However, it is important for the manager to know to whom to report. It may be both principal and foodservices director.

Positions and Job Descriptions

Once the basic plan of an organization is established and the line of authority is set, a job description is needed for each position. A good job description provides a definition of the position to give management and an employee an understanding of what a job entails. A number of job descriptions are available on school districts' websites.

In a small school, the person responsible for running the "cafeteria" is usually called the *manager* or *cook-manager*. In a satellite school or finishing kitchen, the position may be referred to as the *lead person*.

In the 1970s, job titles included head cooks and head bakers, even assistant head cooks and assistant lead bakers. Jobs were departmentalized, which is no longer the case. The trend now is toward less management—not more—and toward giving more responsibility to the staff.

Though some school districts are using products "directly from the farm," most school districts use considerable quantities of convenience foods. As ready-to-serve foods, such as ready-to-serve entrées, raw vegetables and fruits, and bakery products are used, the questions become:

- Does the "head cook" really cook or "reconstitute" or heat ready-to-serve foods?
- How many days a week does the baker bake?
- How much do the baked products really cost?
- Should staff employees have titles and be paid accordingly, or should all staff be paid at the same rate?

The answers often point to more general titles and pay scales. For example, "staff employee assistant" and "food and nutrition service assistant" could refer to positions with a pay scale that differs by years of experience. In a small to medium-size kitchen (10 or fewer employees), the manager needs the flexibility to cross-train and move employees around to different jobs. In this situation, different pay levels and distinct titles can be a problem. Establishing titles for job purposes, without pay differences at the staff level, gives more flexibility, which is especially valuable with high absenteeism.

LOCAL FOODSERVICE ADMINISTRATION

Centralized Versus Decentralized

The two basic ways of administering a food and nutrition service program in a school district are **centralized** and **decentralized**. Though the trend in school districts in the 1990s was toward site-based management (as far as school administration was concerned), most school districts have centralized their food and nutrition service management. In some states, the trend is toward merging two or more small school districts under one director to reduce administrative costs. The need for a qualified director has increased with stricter and more complex federal guidelines. Merging districts allows for sharing the director's skills and costs.

When the school district has a decentralized foodservice operation, each school controls its own foodservice. This control may involve menu planning, purchasing, implementing federal and state regulations, financial and personnel management, and preparing state reports. State agencies require one claim for the entire school district or SFA. The USDA Foods distribution is to the SFA (not to the individual schools).

In large school districts, the line of authority often has foodservice responsibility under general services, support services, or business managers. Centralized management means different things to different school districts. In some districts, it means little more than doing the accounting work and the monthly state claims at one location. In other districts, it means centralized menu planning, purchasing, warehousing, accounting, fiscal control, and hiring personnel.

Centralized administration, with the responsibility for all the various jobs related to the school food and nutrition service operations, has the following advantages:

- The district can afford a more-qualified person in the leadership role.
- More purchasing power is possible.
- Principals spend less time on food and nutrition service matters.
- More consistency in service exists among schools.

In a small school district, a director and one or two clerical people make up the staff. The clerical staff becomes knowledgeable about the school food and nutrition service programs.

Food and Nutrition Service Director or Supervisor

At the district level, the most common title for the person in charge of school food and nutrition services is *director*; however, some use *supervisor, general manager,* or *executive director.*

> According to the School Nutrition Association Certification Committee *"the director is one who plans, organizes, directs, administers the foodservice program in a school system according to policies established by the Board of Education."*
>
> Source: SNA, 2002.

The School Nutrition Association (SNA) established the School Nutrition Specialist (SNS) Credentialing Program in 1997. Many states have established their own certification. These certification programs have improved and helped standardize the profession; however, they may be replaced by the new USDA's Food and Nutrition Service (FNS) certificate program.

The Healthy Hunger-Free Kids Act of 2010 requires USDA to establish professional standards for school nutrition personnel. These proposed standards were released in early 2014. They are expected to be effective beginning in July 2015, when all new school nutrition program (SNP) directors hired are to meet a minimum educational requirement or be working toward meeting the requirements.

Exhibit 5-2 summarizes the "proposed" requirements of the professional standards at the local educational agency (LEA). There are requirements for state directors, LEA directors, managers, and staff. These will affect every state and local school district participating in the federal nutrition programs. See the "Online Resources" and state agencies for current and detailed information on requirements, which ultimately will have a very positive impact on the SNP.

Exhibit 5-2 Summary of SNP Proposed Professional Standards for LEA by Size

Minimum Requirements for Directors	Student Enrollment 2,499 or less	Student Enrollment 2,500–9,999	Student Enrollment 10,000–24,999	Student Enrollment 25,000 or more
Required Minimum Education Standards (new directors only)	High school diploma or equivalency	Associate's degree or equivalent educational experience.	Bachelor's degree or equivalent educational experience	Bachelor's degree or equivalent educational experience
Preferred Minimum Education Standards (new directors only)	Associate's degree or equivalent educational experience	Bachelor's degree or equivalent educational experience	Master's degree or willingness to work toward master's degree	Master's degree or willingness to work toward master's degree
Required Minimum Training Standards (new directors only)	At least 8 hours of food safety training in prior 3 years of starting date or completed within 30 days of employee's starting date			
Annual Continuing Education Training	15 hours in topic related to program accountability (meal claiming, application processing, verification, and meal counting) as well as other topics determined by FNS			

The FNS certificate program consists of four core areas: nutrition, operations, administration, and communications/marketing. There will be a shortage in people meeting these professional standards for many years.

Span of Control

In the business world, the span of control recommended is one supervisor for five to seven employees. This ratio results in layers of management. The trend today is toward a broader span of control and holding each employee responsible for the total job he or she has done. When budgets are reduced, "delayering" or "right-sizing" often occurs, usually through reducing middle management.

The span of control will depend on what the director/ supervisor/manager is responsible for and the training and skill level of the people supervised. The following questions will help in making that decision.

Questions to be asked are:

- How many schools can one person supervise?
- When does a director need another supervisor?
- When does a supervisor need an assistant?
- How many employees can one person manage?
- What other responsibilities will the person have?

Exhibit 5-3 provides a suggested guideline for staffing at the administrative/supervisory level. The positions are the equivalent of a director, assistant director, and supervisor, but the titles may differ from school district to school district. The use of technology should expand the span of control, but it has been offset by the additional federal requirements placed on the Child Nutrition Program.

Exhibit 5-3 Administrative Staffing Guide for District

Number of Schools[1]	Director	Assistant Director	Supervisory Staff
Up to 10	1		
11–20	1		1
21+	1	1	1 for every 20 schools

[1]Schools in this chart are those with on-site preparation.
Source: Author, 2013.

In addition to supervising the schools, the director/assistant director/ supervisory and office staff are assigned numerous other responsibilities. For example, the director and staff are responsible for the following:

- Menu planning, special diets
- Purchasing, handling of bid process and orders
- Technology
- Marketing

- Training, particularly with many new requirements
- Hazard analysis and critical control points
- Wellness program and the assessment of the program
- Free and reduced-price meal applications
- Required community and student input
- Monthly claims for federal and state reimbursement
- Distribution and accountability for USDA Foods
- Free and reduced-price meal applications

The central office may also have responsibility for maintenance of equipment, hiring personnel, payroll, and accounting.

San Benito (TX) Consolidated Independent School District is a good example of a foodservices using technology to increase span of control. Each manager is equipped with an iPad and transmits pictures of their food just before service begins. They use standardized procedures in schools, and cross-train office and school staff. With a small office staff, this district carries out all the many requirements. The district has 22 schools and serves an average of 16,700 meals per day. The central office is staffed with a director, assistant director, and four other people. Their titles and main responsibilities are listed here.

1. Director—Program administration and compliance, equipment and facilities, personnel, menu, budget
2. Assistant Director—Production records, nutritional analysis and standardized recipes, nutrition education, campus monitoring (21 schools), employee training, special diets
3. Secretary—Monthly reimbursement claim report, edit checks, time cards, substitutes, communication with all campuses, website maintenance

4. Ordering Clerk—Inventory master-file and order guides maintenance, weekly orders and weekly produce bids, campus shortages/add-ons/hot shots, as needed, monthly physical inventory reconciliation with perpetual
5. Maintenance and Equipment Supervisor—All point-of-sales equipment maintenance for all schools, kitchen maintenance reporting as needed to district maintenance or contract services, delivery truck driver as needed, and monthly inventory reconciliation
6. Accounts Payable Clerk—Invoice reconciliation with orders/pricing, create purchase orders, bank deposits verification, tracking commodity processing

Larger school districts may have a staff that is more specialized. Supervision of schools is usually not a full-time job. The person who supervises schools is often assigned other responsibilities that affect all schools, for example, marketing, nutrition education, menu planning, and ordering. If the school managers and staff are well trained and turnover is low, close supervision by the central office is not needed.

STAFFING INDIVIDUAL SCHOOLS

Food and Nutrition Service Manager

The person in charge of school food and nutrition service at the school level may be called a *manager*, *assistant manager*, or *lead.* Exhibit 5-4 provides an example of what is included in a Denver (CO) manager job description. One manager may be responsible for two or more schools, which is working effectively for many school districts, such as Jefferson County (CO) and Orange County (FL).

Exhibit 5-4 Example of Job Description for School Food and Nutrition Services Manager

Summary of Position:
Monitors and participates in the preparation and service of school meals for students and adults.

Duties and Responsibilities:
- Monitors and participates in the preparation, cooking, and service of food for students and adults.
- Ensures that meals served conform to planned menus, or that emergency substitutions comply with meal pattern requirements.
- Supervises the food service staff by preparing work schedules, assigning and directing work, training, enforcing work production standards, evaluating work performance, and recommending disciplinary action if necessary.

Qualifications:
- High school diploma or GED preferred.
- Meets department's performance standards or excels in a related field.
- Demonstrates excellent attention to detail.
- Demonstrates excellent organizational skills.
- Has the ability to perform math computations and basic bookkeeping skills.
- Demonstrates the ability to supervise others.
- Demonstrates financial management skills.
- Willing to work in any area of the city as needed.
- Completion of Manager Training Program.
- Ability to provide on-the-job training in equipment use and care, food production, sanitation, safety, record keeping to staff members and newly assigned employees.
- Adaptable to new and unusual situations.
- Knowledge and application of marketing principles and procedures.
- Demonstrated ability organizing and assigning work.
- Demonstrated ability in delegation of authority and responsibility.
- Demonstrated interpersonal skills with lunchroom and school staff.
- Must have the ability to interact well with students, principals, parents, and all customer groups.
- Must be able to work in a team-oriented environment.
- Evaluations—must have scored average or above in all categories.
- Must be able to speak, read, and write in the English language.

Source: Food & Nutrition Services, Denver, CO, 2013.

Considerations When Staffing Individual Schools

Labor availability, cost of a labor hour (wages of school- based labor hour plus benefits and related cost), and desired productivity rates should be considered together. The goal is to keep labor costs at 40 percent of the revenue (or lower). When the cost is at or above 45 percent, the program will probably experience financial problems.

> *Foodservices at the school level will need someone in charge, regardless of how many or few meals the school serves.*

An accurate assessment of the work to be accomplished is needed to determine the number of labor hours to assign. To arrive at the number of labor hours, a guideline that works is helpful in answering the question: What productivity rate is reasonable in a school food and nutrition services? The emphasis since the early 1980s has been on increasing productivity. Productivity rate is a way of measuring how much work an employee produces in an hour.

Management companies frequently use percentage of revenue to help determine how many labor hours to use. This method drives many restaurants' staffing. One of the problems with using percentage of revenue for schools is the differences in cost of a labor hour. For example, in a school district in the Northeast, the average cost of a labor hour may be as high as $35 (wages plus benefits), whereas in the Southeast as low as $12 (wages plus benefits). These school districts' revenues may be fairly equal, if the districts are depending on the federal government for 60 percent or more of the revenue. The workload will be similar in both districts.

Many studies have focused on a method to arrive at the best way to determine labor hours needed. The staffing formulas in this chapter are based on research and experience of the authors. Studying productivity in other industries and in thousands of schools has been a part of the recommendation. The goal should always be to exceed the productivity rates of the guideline and keep labor costs under 40 percent of the revenue.

Following the staffing formula is no guarantee of financial success. If the cost of a labor hour is very high, it may be very hard (or impossible) to generate enough revenue or productivity to be financially successful. That is when school districts have to make hard decisions and changes.

Meal Equivalents and Measuring Productivity

When using a staffing formula, it is essential to know the average number of meals served for breakfast, snacks, and lunch/supper, and the average dollars in other sales. These different meals/services are not equal in amount of work required, thus an equivalency rate is needed.

Meal equivalent (MEQ) and *meals per labor hour* (MPLH) are terms most frequently used to measure productivity in school food and nutrition services.

A MEQ is recommended to determine MPLH or productivity rate. Many different approaches can be used to determine meal equivalents. The goal is to arrive at equivalent work involved in the different services provided. The one that follows is based on the work required to produce and serve a lunch, because it is the usually the largest service provided. This MEQ is easy to remember and the results may not be too different from the more complicated approaches.

1 lunch or supper	= 1 MEQ
2–3 breakfasts	= 1 MEQ
3–4 snacks	= 1 MEQ
\$3–\$4 a la carte sales	= 1 MEQ

All services are converted to MEQs and divided by the number of labor hours to determine productivity. A number of equivalency rates are used to arrive at the MEQ for breakfast, snacks, and a la carte (extra food) sales. For example, the National Food Service Management Institute (NFSMI, 2005) recommends:

1 lunch = 1 MEQ

3 breakfasts = 2 MEQ

3 snacks = 1 MEQ

Dollar amount in sales of nonreimbursable food ÷ Free lunch reimbursement rate + USDA Foods value = 1 MEQ. (The formula changes annually.)

Examples of MEQs in use in SY2014:

Dade County (FL)

1 lunch = 1 MEQ

2 breakfasts = 1 MEQ

3 snacks = 1 MEQ

$2.33 of a la carte sales = 1 MEQ

Dallas (TX)

1 lunch = 1 MEQ

3 breakfasts = 1 MEQ

3 snacks = 1 MEQ

$3 a la carte sales = 1 MEQ

Hammond (IN), San Benito (TX), and Jefferson County (KY)

1 lunch = 1 MEQ

3 breakfasts = 1 MEQ

4 snacks = 1 MEQ

$3 a la carte sales = 1 MEQ

Alabama (state)

1 lunch = 1 MEQ

2 breakfasts = 1 MEQ

4 snacks = 1 MEQ

$3 a la carte sales = 1 MEQ

The decision on which MEQ to use depends on the answers to the following questions:

1. What is being served?
2. How much preparation is needed?
3. How long does it take to serve?
4. How much cleaning time is required?

Comparing the time it requires to prepare and serve a lunch with a breakfast, the questions are:

Is it ⅓ the time? (3 breakfasts equal 1 lunch)

or

Is it ½ the time? (2 breakfasts equal 1 lunch)

Formula for Determining Productivity Rate of a School Foodservice

Output ÷ Input = Productivity

Output = Total Meal Equivalents Served

Input = Total Labor Hours

Productivity Rate is the Meals per Labor Hour (MPLH)

The same questions apply when determining MEQ for snacks and a la carte sales. When a school district contracts with a food-service management company, the MEQ becomes important in determining the cost of the contract. Productivity rate has little relationship to what the federal reimbursement rates are. Productivity rates do not change when the federal reimbursement rates change (usually annually). However, as more school districts depend on federal reimbursement for most of the revenue, the rates are more significant. The formulas used in this text are easy to apply and do not change often. The $3-$4 MEQ for non-reimbursable food sales should be changed as the revenue and equivalent work changes.

Number of Meal Equivalents (output) ÷ Number of Labor Hours (input) = Productivity Rate or Meals Per Labor Hour (MPLH)

Example: 425 lunches, 150 breakfast, 175 snacks, $85 a la carte sales

Staffed with 32 labor hours

Lunch	425 MEQ	
Breakfast (150 ÷ 2)	75 MEQ	or (150 ÷ 3 =) 50 MEQ
Snack (175 ÷ 3)	58 MEQ	
A la carte ($85 ÷ $3)	28 MEQ	
Total Output	586 MEQ	

586 MEQ (output) ÷ 32 Labor Hours (input) =
18 MPLH (productivity rate)

Is 18 MPLH (in the preceding example) a good productivity rate? This question is discussed next.

Staffing for On-Site Production

Staffing school foodservices in the past may have been based on "we need more help." A number of guidelines apply for staffing on-site production in schools, but the guide in Exhibit 5-5 is widely used.

Exhibit 5-5 Staffing Guidelines for On-Site Production

Number of Meal Equivalents[1]	MEALS PER LABOR HOUR (MPLH) FOR LOW AND HIGH PRODUCTIVITY			
	Conventional System[2] MPLH		Convenience System[3] MPLH	
	Low	High	Low	High
Up to 100	8	10	10	12
101–150	9	11	11	13
151–200	10–11	12	12	14
201–250	12	14	14	15
251–300	13	15	15	16
301–400	14	16	16	18
401–500	14	17	18	19
501–600	15	17	18	19
601–700	16	18	19	20
701–800	17	19	20	22
801 and up	18	20	21	23

[1]Meal equivalents include breakfast and a la carte sales. Three breakfasts equate to one lunch. A la carte sales of $3-$4 equate to one lunch.
[2]Conventional system is preparation of some foods from raw ingredients on premises (using some bakery breads and prepared pizza and washing dishes).
[3]Convenience system is using maximum amount of processed foods (e.g., using all bakery breads, precooked chicken, ready-to-serve raw fruits and vegetables, proportioned condiments, and washing only trays and using disposable dinnerware).
Source: Pannell-Martin, 1999.

Using the staffing guidelines in Exhibit 5-5 includes the following steps:

1. Determine the average MEQ.
2. Determine whether a conventional or convenience system of food preparation is used.
3. Select the recommended productivity rate.
4. Divide total meal equivalents by productivity rate.

The staffing guidelines in Exhibit 5-5 are for a **conventional system** and a **convenience system**. The conventional system of on-site production uses some convenience foods, such as bakery-made hamburger and hot dog rolls, prepared pizza, and some disposable dishes. The convenience system uses maximum amount of prepared foods and disposable plates and eating utensils. The number of MPLH should be higher for a satellite food system. Exhibit 5-6

Exhibit 5-6 Example of Determining Staff Hours Needed Using Staffing Guidelines

Average Breakfast Served	325 ÷ 3 = 108 Meal Equivalents
Average Snacks Served	120 ÷ 3 = 40 Meal Equivalents
Average Lunches Served	930 ÷ 1 = 930 Meal Equivalents
Average $s Extra Sales	224 ÷ 3 = 75 Meal Equivalents
Total Meal Equivalents	1,153

Total Meal Equivalents ÷ Productivity Rate = Labor Hours

1,153 Total Meal Equivalents ÷ 19 MPLH = 61 Labor Hours
(low, conventional)

1,153 Total Meal Equivalents ÷ 21 MPLH = 55 Labor Hours
(high, conventional)

1,153 Total Meal Equivalents ÷ 22 MPLH = 52 Labor Hours
(low, convenience)

provides an example of determining MEQ and using the staffing guidelines in Exhibit 5-5.

Other Factors to Consider

No magic formulas can be applied to staffing all schools foodservice programs. Many factors influence the hours needed, such as:

- Production system (on-site production or satellite)
- Service provided (breakfast, lunch, snacks, etc.)
- Amount of convenience food used versus using more raw ingredients directly from the farm
- Menus (number of choices)
- Total number of meal equivalents served
- Skill level, training, and experience of employees
- Facility, equipment, and use of automation
- Disposable service items or washing dishes
- The custodial work of cleaning the dining room

San Benito (TX) Independent School District has obtained an average of 23 MPLH, 33 percent of revenue for labor, and 95 percent participation in the lunch program. This productivity rate is the result of planning a short menu cycle, standardizing procedures, and providing good training.

Staffing Based on Sales

When schools are not participating in the federal Child Nutrition Programs, their services may be very different. In these cases, the question may be, "How much time does it take to sell $700 worth of food?"

The previous factors should be considered along with the following:

- Number of items offered
- Amount of preparation involved
- Time required when sales occur

Two methods that are frequently used for staffing based on sales are:

1. Percentage of revenue budgeted for labor (35–40%) at the production and service sites are by multiplying by desired percentage. For example:

   Sale of $300 x .40 (40%) = $120 Labor Cost

   Divide $120 by the average hourly cost of a labor hour (e.g., $17 including benefits = 7 labor hours).

2. Convert sales to equivalent meals and use guidelines in Exhibit 5-5:

   For example, $300 in sales using the $3 equal to one lunch ($300 ÷ 3 = 100 MEQs), based on 14 meals per labor hour, would allow 7 labor hours.

A more exact method would be to determine the actual time and motion required for preparing and serving various foods.

STAFFING CENTRAL KITCHEN AND RECEIVING SCHOOLS

The number of large central kitchens in operation has stayed about the same for the past 20 years. Some districts have converted back to on-site production while other districts have built new central kitchens, such as Dallas (TX) and Jefferson County (KY). Many school districts are transporting food produced in one site to several other locations for serving, such as Orange County (FL) and Fairfax

County (VA). Exhibits 5-7 and 5-8 provide some examples of how school districts are staffing their central kitchens and the schools receiving and serving the food.

Definition of terms used in Exhibits 5-7 and 5-8:

BULK COLD—Food is cooked, then chilled or frozen (e.g., cook-chill system) and transported for finishing off in the receiving (finishing) school.

BULK HOT—Food is cooked and maintained hot through transporting and serving at the receiving (serving) school.

PRE-PLATED COLD (BAG) —Food is prepared and bagged or pre-plated ready for distribution at the receiving (serving) school.

PRE-PLATED FROZEN—Food is prepared, portioned, and frozen, and then transported ready for heating for service.

PRE-PLATED HOT—Food is prepared, portioned, and transported on the day of service, hot food hot (and cold food cold) ready-to-eat.

The research by Hanna (2012) has influenced changes in the guidelines in Exhibit 5-8 from the fifth edition of *School Foodservice Management for the 21*st *Century*. Establishing a staffing guideline for a central kitchen is difficult because MEQ and MPLH may not apply.

On-site production requires the most labor and has a lower productivity level than efficient satellite systems. Increasing productivity 2–3 MPLH will result in a financial savings. Other factors should to be considered before making the changes in systems.

Exhibit 5-7 Staffing Guidelines for Production of Meals for More than One School

Number of MEQ	MPLH AND NUMBER OF LABOR HOURS BY TYPE OF PREPARATION SYSTEM[1]				
	Bulk Cold[2]	Bulk Hot	Pre-Plated Cold (BAG)[3]	Pre-Plated Frozen[1,2]	Pre-Plated Hot[2]
	MPLH	MPLH	MPLH	MPLH	MPLH
200–500	25–30	27–32	21–26	22–27	20–25
501–1,000	30–35	30–35	30–35	37–42	40–45
1,001–2,000	50–55	45–50	50–55	55–60	60–65
2,001–3,000	65–75	60–70	100–110	120–130	130–140
3,001–5,000	75–85	70–80	110–120	120–130	130–140
5,001–10,000	110–130	110–120	110–120	120–135	130–150
10,001– up	150–160	120–130	120–130	120–135	130–150

[1]Does not include transporting of food or preparing/serving at the receiving school. Transporting of food should be figured. The amount of time will depend on number of stops, distance, number of meals, and type of menus; however, the cost of delivering should be included in total food cost.
[2]Requires heating at site before serving.
[3]Should be highly automated when more than 20,000 food items are prepared per day.

Exhibit 5-8 Staffing Guidelines for Satellite Schools and Finishing Kitchens

Number of MEQ	MPLH AND NUMBER OF LABOR HOURS BY TYPE OF PREPARATION SYSTEM				
	Bulk Cold[1] (FK)	Bulk Hot (FK)	Pre-Plated Cold (BAG)	Pre-Plated Frozen[2]	Pre-Plated Hot
	MPLH	MPLH	MPLH	MPLH	MPLH
Up to 75	16–20	17–22	75–80	30–35	50–55
76–100	18–23	19–23	75–80	30–35	50–55
101–200	20–25	21–26	100–110	50–55	75–80
201–300	22–27	24–29	100–110	60–65	75–80
301–400	26–31	26–31	100–110	60–65	75–80
401–500	26–31	28–33	100–110	60–65	75–80
501–700	28–33	30–35	100–110	60–65	75–80
701 up	30–35	32–37	100–110	60–65	75–80

[1]Needs heating, portioning, and serving.
[2]Needs heating and serving.

SCHEDULING AND PLANNING WORK HOURS

After assigning the number of labor hours to a school, the next step is to determine the number of employees. Scheduling a combination of part-time and full-time employees is usually the most efficient way to staff a foodservices program. The one-meal-a-day foodservices programs of the 1960s–1990s did not need employees to work seven to eight hours a day. In recent years, more schools are offering breakfasts, lunch, and snack programs and may need more of the "full-time" employees.

The productivity of foodservices workers is greatest during the first six hours of work and declines after that. When breaking down the labor hours and distributing the hours, the number of employees needed for serving time should be decided (Exhibits 5-9 and 5-10).

The 31 labor hours are divided among tasks. The number of employees is determined by the number needed at lunchtime. To serve 475 on one serving line will require careful scheduling on behalf of the school principal and speed on behalf of the foodservices employees (10 lunches served per minute). Five to six employees could cover the tasks (e.g., cashier, server, dish machine operator, backup/cook, and manager; the manager could serve or back line during lunch, keep food on line).

Exhibit 5-9 Staffing an Elementary School Foodservice with On-Site Production Operating Dish Machine

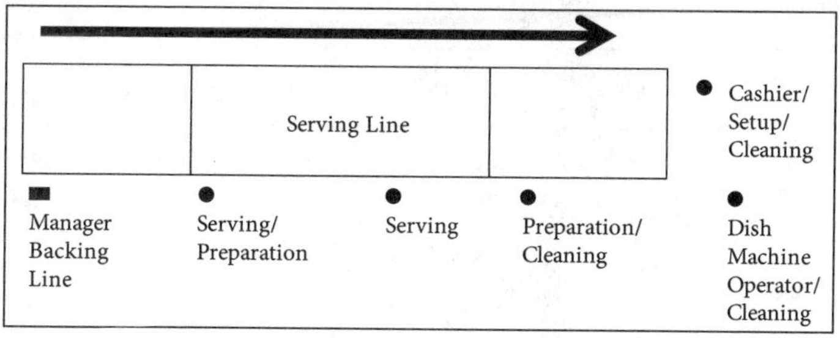

Task	Hours
Preparation/setup	10
Serving	8 ½
Cleaning/dish washing	4
Cashiering/cleanup	3
Management work/ accountability	4
Breaks	1 ½
TOTAL HOURS	**31**

Sample of Hours Assigned	
Manager *	7.5
Staff Assistant 1 *	5.5
Staff Assistant 2 *	5.5
Staff Assistant 3 *	5.5
Staff Assistant 4	4.0
Staff Assistant 5	3.0
Total Hours	**31.0**

*½ hour break included

Labor Assigned:	31 hours
Productivity rate:	17 MPLH
Total MEQ:	530
Breakfast served:	125 (125 ÷ 3 = 42 MEQ)
Lunches served:	475 (475 MEQ)
A la carte:	$40 ($40 ÷ 3 = 13 MEQ)

Exhibit 5-10 Staffing a High School Foodservice with Two Serving Lines and Salad or Extra Sales Station and Three Lunch Periods

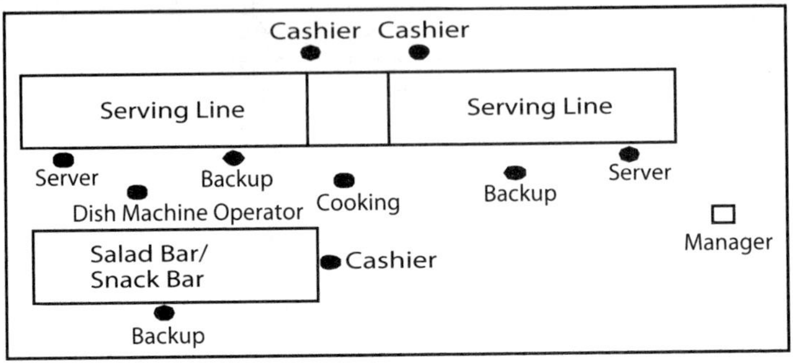

Assigned:	45 hours
Productivity rate:	20 MPLH
Breakfasts served:	120 (120 ÷ 3 = 40 MEQ)
Lunches served:	750 (MEQ)
A la carte:	$320 ($320÷ 3 = 107 MEQ)
Total MEQ:	897
	897 ÷ 20 MPLH = 45 hours

Staff/Tasks	Time	Hours
Manager	7:30–3:00*	7.5
Preparation	8:00–1:30*	5.5
Assistant/Backup	9:00–2:30*	5.5
Assistant/Cashier	8:30–2:00*	5.0
Cashiers (2 x 3½ hours each)	10:00–1:30	7.0
Salad/Backup	9:00–1:30*	5.0
Dish machine/Cleaning	10:30–2:00	3.5
Servers (2 x 3 hours each)	10:00–1:00	6.0
TOTAL		**45.0**

* break included

The hours are divided among the positions/tasks and the number of positions depends on the number of meals served. The employees' hours are scheduled according to when the tasks need to be done.

When planning the work schedule, the manager should determine assignments with menus and each person's abilities in mind.

WORK SCHEDULES

Planning a work schedule can take time, but if cycle menus are used, work schedules are reused. Cycle menus are discussed in Chapter 3, "Nutrition and Menu Planning." The purpose of a work schedule is to inform employees concerning the specific tasks for the day, their individual responsibilities, and the sequence for each of their duties, and the time it should take to do the job.

Work schedules should be in writing and available to each employee or on an easy-to-see board. Small foodservice operations need schedules that are more detailed, whereas the larger operation may assign people to do much the same things every day (e.g., prepare salads and make sandwiches). In such a case, a large board can show the schedule.

Some of the advantages of work schedules include:

- Saves time and energy; prevents employees from waiting for someone to tell them what to do next.
- Distributes the workload evenly and informs the staff as to who is responsible for each job.
- Helps the kitchen run more smoothly and more efficiently; helps increase employee efficiency by setting deadlines.
- Makes it less likely that a job will not be done or will not be completed in time.
- Helps the staff feel more secure, knowing that the job can be done within the time available.
- Makes employees more accountable for their assignments.

Parkinson's Law, which states "Work expands so as to fill the time available for its completion," is illustrated at an overstaffed workplace without work schedules and time limits on tasks. One hour of work can be stretched out to fill two hours. Time needs to be managed and some employees have to be motivated to be efficient and time-conscious.

Exhibit 5-11 provides a sample work schedule for a small elementary school serving 400 lunches and breakfast. In a large school

Exhibit 5-11 Sample Work Schedule for a Small Elementary School Offering Three Choices (Wednesday – Week 1 of Cycle Menus)

POSITION	Position 1 - MANAGER	Position 2	Position 3
# of HOURS	**7 Hours**	**6 Hours**	**6 Hours**
7:00-7:15	Unlock; pick up money; count. Prepare computer for breakfast.	Set out cereal and set up milk in cooler. Put cinnamon rolls and blueberry muffins in heated cabinet.	
7:15-7:30	Set out trays, napkins, and sporks.	Prepare sausage and toast. Prepare French toast.	
7:30-7:45	Set out juice, fruit, and trail mix.		
7:45-8:00	Setup serving line with hot food.		
8:00-8:15	Cashier	Serve breakfast.	Prepare lettuce for salad. Slice cucumbers and shred carrots for chef salad. Shred cheese for week's menu. Dice tomatoes, chop onions for tacos. Cook eggs for chef salad.
8:15-8:30			
8:30-8:45	Count breakfast money. Complete breakfast production record.	Put away breakfast. Clean serving line. Clean tables.	
8:45-9:00	*Set up juice and fruit cup. Label breakfast and refrigerate.	*Pan sliced ham, cover with plastic bag and refrigerate. *Prepare egg mixture for Wednesday.	*Wrap and pan apple cinnamon muffins, coffee cake, and English muffins. Cover with plastic and refrigerate. Label.
9:00-9:15	*Set up 10 cereals.	Portion shredded cheese, onions, & tomatoes. Prepare Garlic bread. Prepare spaghetti and meat sauce. Prepare meat and beans for tacos.	Prepare chef salads.
9:15-9:30	Prepare computer and money for cashier.		
9:30-10:00	Portion applesauce. Mix tossed salad and portion.		

*Prepare for next day.

(*Continued*)

POSITION	Position 1 - MANAGER	Position 2	Position 3
# of HOURS	7 Hours	6 Hours	6 Hours
10:00-10:15	EAT LUNCH	EAT LUNCH	Portion croutons. Wash pots and pans.
10:15-10:30			
10:30-10:45	Wash fresh fruit and display. Place utensils and condiments on serving line.	Set up steam table. Check temperatures of food and steam table.	
10:45-11:00			
SERVE LUNCH 11:00 - 1:00			
11:00-11:15	Check line; batch cook; keep food on line. Backup. Observe and communicate with customers. Portion more fruits and fixings as needed.	Serving Line (Wash pots and pans during break in service).	Cashier: Spot check line for cleanliness, debris on floor, condiments needing replacement.
11:15-11:30			
11:30-11:45			
11:45-12:00			
12:00-12:15	Supervise money counting. Determine food used for 1st hour.		
12:15-12:30	Backup line.		
12:30-12:45	Place daily orders.	Count food left/ portions; record.	
12:45-1:00			
1:00-1:15	Supervise money counting. Close out computer.	Clean serving line. Cart canned items to be used following day. Check for following day's items.	Count money. Prepare reconciliation form.
1:15-1:30	Determine food used for 2nd hour Check production record for food usage. Adjust next day's record for leftovers. Complete production record.		EAT LUNCH
1:30-1:45			
1:45-2:00			Wash pots and pans. Wipe tables and seats. Store food in storeroom. Clean storeroom.

district, a supervisory staff person with a few managers can plan work schedules for schools with the same physical setup. Standardization of the physical plant, menus, and staffing will encourage greater efficiency.

LABOR SHORTAGES AND TURNOVER

Shortage of service employees at the low end of the pay scale and high turnover of short-hour employees were two of the most challenging personnel problems of the late 1990s and early 2000s. Jefferson County (KY) Schools built a central kitchen to reduce the need for as many employees, reduce labor cost, and improve standardization and food quality.

The increased use of raw foods, along with an increase in the number of breakfast and snack programs, has increased the need for more five-hour to six-hour employees. The stability of the school-based job and the six- to seven-hour jobs have resulted in the positions being attractive to more experienced employees and even trained chefs.

When the turnover rate is 10 percent or higher, it is difficult for management to keep trained employees in each position. The turnover rate is the ratio of the number of workers that must be replaced in a given time period to the average number of workers. To figure the turnover rate the following formula can be used:

$$\frac{\text{Number of Separations from Job During Year x 100}}{\text{Number of Employees at Midyear}} = \text{Turnover Rate\%}$$

Example: $$\frac{\text{105 Employees Resigned x 100}}{\text{1075 Employees}} = 17\%$$

The turnover of qualified school foodservice directors was felt in the early 2000s, when nearly 50 percent of the directors in some states reached retirement age.

LABOR COSTS

In 2013, the federal minimum wage was $7.25. However, many cities and states have a higher minimum wage. For example, in 2013 Washington State's minimum wage was $9.19, and city of San Francisco, $10.55. Congress is considering raising the federal minimum wage to $9.25 per hour. The starting pay in many school districts is above even their states' minimum wage. Exhibit 5-12 provides an example of starting pay scales in some school districts.

Exhibit 5-12 Example of Different Starting Pay in 2013 for School Food and Nutrition Services Employees

School District	Starting Pay[1]
Dade (FL) Schools	$9.20
Dallas (TX) Independent Schools	$13.00
Denver (CO) Public Schools	$9.82
Jefferson County (KY)	$9.90

[1]Not including benefits.

The hourly wage is just a portion of the cost of a labor hour. To determine the real cost of a labor hour, all the costs have to be included (e.g., the number of paid holidays and sick days; the employer's share of taxes, Social Security, and Medicare; worker's compensation; retirement benefits; uniforms; health and life insurances; etc.). The beginning may be minimum wage ($7.25 per hour in 2013), but it may average costing as much as $15 to $20 per hour when the real costs are considered.

According to NFSMI, the average cost of labor varies greatly from district to district. To determine the cost of a labor hour, all cost associated with employees have to be recognized.

In 2007, the cost of a school lunch ranged from $1.66 to $3.55, with an average of $2.24. At that time, the average cost of labor per lunch was $1.02, based on a study of 534 school districts in Florida, Mississippi, and Texas. Labor cost consumed an average of 44 percent of the revenue, and food costs were 35 percent (NFSMI). By 2011 many school districts' food cost increased by 10-15 percent.

Personnel Policy on Use of Social Media

A school district probably has a personnel policy regarding the use of social media and cell phones while on the job. These policies need to be addressed during orientation of employees and enforced.

Restrictions on use of cell phone and social media devices are particularly important in work areas when using equipment and working with food. Although occasional personal phone calls may be allowed, use needs to be limited to nonwork time whenever possible. Drivers of foodservice vehicles should not be allowed to use cell phones while driving.

Social media "can be beneficial" in the workplace, as many district offices communicate with the school manager via of emails and Facebook. The use of the office computer for personal reasons needs to be limited or disallowed.

SUMMARY

Labor costs together should consume no more than 40 percent of the revenue (not a percentage based on expenses, but based on revenue). In recent years, some school districts have gone back to cooking with more raw ingredients and decreased the amount of convenience foods used. This shift has increased the need for more labor hours, and in many cases increased food costs. These issues will have to be dealt with in coming years. Chapter 11, "Resolving Financial Problems," provides suggestions for reducing labor costs.

QUESTIONS AND ANSWERS

1. The federal Child Nutrition Program is administered by:
   a. U.S. Department of Education
   b. U.S. Department of Agriculture
   c. U.S. Department of Health and Human Services
   d. U. S. Department of the Interior
2. The abbreviation SFA refers to:
   a. State food authority
   b. State & federal administration
   c. School food association
   d. School food authority
3. Centralized school food and nutrition services usually have the advantage of:
   a. Greater responsibility on the principal
   b. More consistency in meals served in schools
   c. Less purchasing power
   d. Different menus in every school
4. What percentage of revenue should be spent for labor?
   a. No more than 20%
   b. No more than 40%
   c. No more than 50%
   d. No more than 60%
5. What is a breakfast meal equivalent?
   a. 1 breakfast = 1 meal equivalent
   b. 2 to 3 breakfasts = 1 meal equivalent
   c. 4 breakfasts = 1 meal equivalent
   d. 5 breakfasts = 1 meal equivalent
6. How do you measure the productivity of foodservice employees?
   a. Divide average meal equivalents by number of lunches served
   b. Divide total labor hours worked by number of employees
   c. Divide average meal equivalents by number of labor hours
   d. Divide number of employees by total labor hours worked
7. A meal equivalent is not the same for lunch, breakfast, snacks, and a la carte sales.
   a. True
   b. False
8. What factors influence meals per labor hour?
   a. Number of meals served
   b. Length of serving period(s)

   c. Use of convenience foods and disposable dishes
   d. All of the above

9. Span of control has been changing to require each person to take more responsibility and less supervision.
   a. True
   b. False
10. The manager should never assist on the serving line or backing up the serving line.
   a. True
   b. False

Answers: 1.b., 2.d., 3.b., 4.b., 5.b., 6.c., 7.a., 8.d., 9.a., 10.b.

REFERENCES

Carr, D. & Cross, E. 2008. Vending reimbursable lunches to high school students: A study of two successes. *Journal of Child Nutrition and Management*, 1. Retrieved from *http://docs.schoolnutrition.org/newsroom/jcnm/08spring/carr/index.asp*.

Cater, J. 2005. *Financial management information system (FMIS): A guide to program evaluation and analysis*. University, MS: NFSMI.

Cater, J., Cross, E., & Conklin, M. 2000. Productivity indices of school foodservice operation. *Journal of Child Nutrition and Management*, 24, 49.

DeMicco, F., Oh, H., Maurice, W., McElwain, P., & Boss, D. 1997. In search of school food service leaders: The next millennium. *School Food Service Research Review*, 21 (1), 2–4.

Denver Public Schools Food & Nutrition Services Enterprise Management. 2009. Hourly Manager Job Description. Retrieved from *http://foodservices.dpsk12.org/hmjobdescription.html*.

Hanna, E. 2008. *An assessment of performance measures in child nutrition program*. (Unpublished doctoral dissertation). Iowa State University, Ames, IA.

Hwang, J. & Sneed, J. 2004. Benchmarking financial performance in school foodservice. *Journal of Child Nutrition and Management*, 28. Retrieved from *http://docs.schoolnutrition.org/newsroom/jcnm/04spring/hwang/*.

Martin, J., & Oakley, C. (Eds.). 2008. *Managing child nutrition programs: Leadership for excellence*, 2nd ed. Sudbury, MA: Jones & Bartlett Publishing.

Mayo, C. 1981. *Variables that affect productivity in school food services*. (Unpublished doctoral dissertation). Virginia Polytechnic Institute and State University, Blacksburg, VA.

Meier, K. & Bokte, J. n.d. *Span of control and public organizations: Implementing Luther Gulick's research design*. College Station, Texas: Texas A & M University.

NFSMI. 2007. *Financial management benchmarks for school nutrition programs*. University, MS: Author.

NFSMI. 2010. *Competencies, knowledge and skills for district-levels school nutrition professionals in the 21st century*. University, MS: Author.

NFSMI. 2011. *Financial management: A course for school nutrition directors*. University, MS: Author.

Pannell-Martin, D. 1995. *Controlling costs in the foodservice industry.* Alexandria, VA: inTEAM Associates, Inc.

School Nutrition Association. 2011. *School nutrition specialist (SNS) credentialing exam handbook.* National Harbor, MD: Author.

Sherrin, A., Bednar, C., & Kwon, J. 2009. Labor productivity standards in Texas school foodservice operations. *School Nutrition,* 33 (1). Retrieved from *http://www.schoolnutrition.org/Content_Aspx?id.*

Tart, R. & Taylor, R. 1997. Optimizing school foodservice employee scheduling. *School Food Service Research Review*, 21, 24–27.

ONLINE RESOURCES

National Center for Education Statistics: State Education Data Profiles
http://nces.ed.gov/programs/stateprofiles/

National Food Service Management Institute
www.nfsmi.org

Professional Standards
www.federalregister.gov
www.regulations.gov

School Nutrition Association
www.schoolnutrition.org

USDA Child Nutrition Programs
www.fns.usda.gov/cnd

USDA Professional Standards
www.13ProfStandardsBrochure.pdf

Chapter 6

Procurement and Inventory Control

STUDY QUESTIONS

1. What does supply chain mean?
2. What restricts competition in the bid process?
3. Why is it important to set goals as a basis of the purchasing process?
4. When forecasting, what factors determine the quantities to order?
5. Who is responsible for procurement in school foodservice programs?
6. Who should be involved in writing specifications?
7. Why use a CN-labeled product?
8. What information should be in a bid document?
9. What criteria should be used to evaluate a bid response?
10. What processes are used to manage food and supply inventories?

Chapter 6

"Checking-In" by Barry Sackin, BA, SNS

President of B. Sackin & Associates, LLC

As foodservice director for a residence complex at University of California–Davis, I was required to purchase meat from the vendor the company I worked for had selected. Every week we would receive hundreds of pounds of products to serve the 1,200–1,500 students who dined in my cafeterias.

One of the many important parts of the procurement cycle is receiving, or making sure that you actually get what you ordered. I had my order and also had a commercial scale in the kitchen that I had the State of California certify. Every time the meat shipment arrived, I counted and weighed everything. And every time there was a shortage somewhere. It was always a case missing here, a few pounds shy there. The delivery person would make the changes on the receipt and we paid only for what we actually received.

After several weeks of checking every item on every delivery, amazingly the receipt and the shipment started matching. After several more weeks, I stopped checking every item. Then I stopped checking every shipment. But I still checked most orders and several items from each. Lo and behold, accurate deliveries and receipts.

The moral of this tale? Good receiving practices save money!

"Purchasing Pointers" by Claudie Phillips, MA

Director of Food & Nutrition Services, School District U-46, IL

Every successful business must have standards in order to achieve excellence. I learned early on that food and service are the most important ingredients in a successful foodservice operation. Developing clearly defined specifications was the first step in purchasing food for our program. Student focus groups that represent our customer base were instrumental to developing those specifications.

My staff does the research to make sure we maximize the dollar. Our industry partners assist us in identifying products in the foodservice industry that will meet our needs. They develop products for specific target groups. We use multi-year contracts when at all possible. This gives our vendors enough time to obtain pricing for our bids. It promotes competitive bidding, and, as a result, we get good pricing.

Our student focus groups test new products. We survey our customers often to identify products that we should remove from the menu cycle. For example, the YAC Groups in the elementary schools "taste buds" did not like Teriyaki Chicken. It was because of their feedback that we removed it from the menu.

We take advantage of all promotions, rebates, and bargain buys. But, we have learned that a bargain is only a bargain if you can use the product before the expiration date. We are careful to menu produce that is in season in order to maintain a good food cost. The most challenging for the managers is forecasting how much product they need for any given period. Cycle menus are very important in forecasting the needs and maintaining good inventory levels.

Last but not least, understanding the meal pattern requirements and commodity processing are basis to our developing good purchasing practices. Keeping up with the menu pattern changes in FY2014 and training the staff in the requirements has been a challenge for management.

Food purchases in school food and nutrition service programs are big business representing $8.5 billion in SY2010 (USDA, 2013). In 2008, food costs, including USDA Foods, consumed 46 percent of school food and nutrition services revenue (USDA, 2008).

OVERVIEW OF MARKET

New regulations, effective in 2012, increased the amount of food required for school lunch. Although no studies have been conducted to measure the result of these changes, it has likely increased the percentage of program revenue spent on food. With food purchases taking such a large slice of the food and nutrition services budget, it is important that personnel responsible for purchasing practice efficient and effective procurement methods. The goal is to obtain high-quality foods for the best overall cost.

> A Supply Chain
>
> *"A set of three or more organizations directly involved in the upstream or downstream flow of products, services, finances, and/or information from a source to a customer."*
>
> Source: Mentzer, 2001.

A modern approach to purchasing includes an awareness that businesses no longer operate as individual entities, but rather in partnership across a supply chain. In school food and nutrition services, the supply chain is complex, including not only producers, manufacturers, and distributors but also various governmental agencies involved in the procurement of food.

Traditional procurement focuses on product selection and then solely on the price of an item. When a supply chain approach is used, the operator considers the costs and value added to the product from the point produced until it is served or discarded. The operator then works with members of the supply chain to reduce costs where they do not add value. The goal is to identify ways that the operator can reduce the district and/or vendor expenses that in turn will result in reducing the overall cost of items purchased, not just the price.

Legal consequences must be considered in addition to financial consequences if fair and open competition is not incorporated into the purchasing process. School food and nutrition programs should abide by U.S. government regulation, 7 CFR 3016, when purchasing. Some key provisions contained in these regulations related to school food and nutrition services include:

- Maintain a written code of conduct for individuals engaged in the purchasing process.
- Prohibit award of bid based on cost plus percentage (%) of cost.
- Prohibit award of contract to those involved in the development of contract specifications.
- Maintain full and open competition.
- Use a publicly advertised sealed bid process for procurement of goods and services valued at more than $150,000 (use state or local threshold, if it is less).

Of these, one of the most important provisions is establishing a "Code of Conduct" for those involved in the purchasing process. The National Institute of Government Purchasing has developed suggested guidelines for ethical procurement that includes the following elements:

- Avoid real or perceived conflict of interest.
- Conduct with vendors must be fair and transparent.
- Have no engagement in or toleration of corruption.
- Do not allow soliciting or accepting of gifts, money, entertainment, or favors.
- Embed ethics practices in all policies and procedures.
- Ensure compliance by implementing monitoring procedures.

Purchasing practices are an important factor in establishing the quality and financial stability of a school food and nutrition services program. It is not possible for production staff to improve the quality or cost when a low-quality product was purchased at an inflated price. Specifying desired quality of items, accurately estimating how much of each item you will use, and following fair and open purchasing processes will help the operator get the best quality for a good value.

Situations That Restrict Competition

- Placing unreasonable requirements on firms in order for them to qualify to do business (e.g., state or local preferences other than as allowed or encouraged by federal regulations)
- Requiring unnecessary experience and excessive bonding
- Organizational conflicts of interest
- Specifying only a "brand name" product instead of allowing "an equal" product to be offered and describing the performance of other relevant requirements of the procurement

The National Food Service Management Institute (NFSMI) offers an excellent course for school foodservices program purchasing agents. A link to *Procurement for the 21st Century,* the manual used in this course, is in the Online Resources section at the end of this chapter.

DETERMINING WHAT TO PURCHASE

An important step in the procurement process is to establish goals that the foodservice operation expects to achieve. These goals may include achieving a target food cost percentage, reaching a nutritional target such as reducing sodium, and using more locally grown produce. Thinking about the goals of the organization will help identify the types of products that are needed. Having a written list of goals that can be communicated to prospective vendors will help to engage vendors in focusing on products and services most important to your program.

The menu and food production system adopted are the basis of purchasing food and supplies. It requires menus planned far enough in advance to allow time for product descriptions, forecasting quantities to purchase, bid document preparation, and other steps in the purchasing process to be completed.

Factors Influencing Purchasing

School districts have many differences affecting the purchasing process. Differences in customer tastes, employee skills, equipment, and budgets make it difficult for districts to purchase the same items or even follow the same purchasing practices. Some of the factors that influence the purchasing process include:

- **Customer Acceptability**—Smart buyers realize it is what the customers like that really matters. Much can be learned about food preferences by talking with students and watching plate waste.
- **Menu and Nutritional Content**—A menu is the blueprint for purchasing, and a manager should buy for the menu rather than planning the menu around what has been purchased. The menu is planned to meet certain nutritional requirements.
- **Food Budget**—The food budget will determine to a large extent what is on the menu and consequently what to purchase. On the average, 30–50% of the budget is spent on food. In school districts with unusually high labor costs, food costs need to be closer to 30% for the program to break even. Approximately 22% of the food dollar is going to

Exhibit 6-1 How School Districts Spent Food Dollars in SY2010

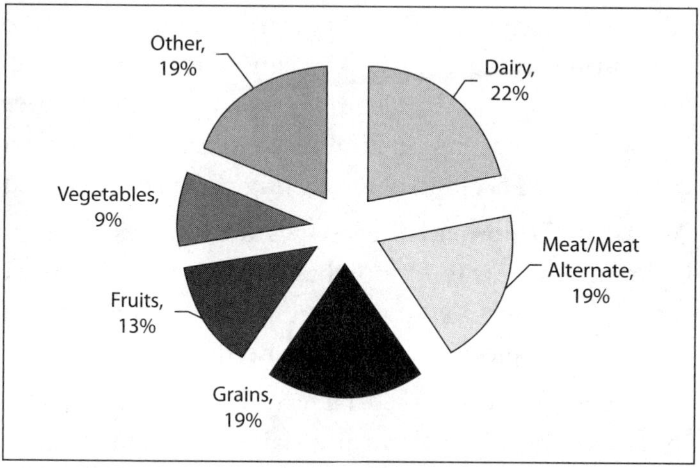

Source: USDA, 2012.

milk and dairy products (Exhibit 6-1). Fruits and vegetables require 13% and 9%, respectively.

- **Labor Costs and Skills of Personnel**—The labor available, skills of the employees, and the cost of labor are considerations by a foodservice program. (Chapter 5, "Personnel and Staffing," discusses this in more detail.)
- **Season and Availability of Foods**—The season and availability of foods affect the price and quality of foods. For instance, purchasing fresh green bell peppers in January will mean higher costs in most parts of the country. Drought and other factors can have an impact on availability and prices, particularly for produce.
- **Storage**—The type, quantity, and availability of storage should be carefully considered. Many products can be purchased in canned, fresh, and frozen states. The amount of freezer space available may determine how the product will be purchased. Storage capacity will also affect the frequency of delivery.

- **Numbers of Meals Served**—The numbers of meals served and other services offered will determine quantities needed. Forecasting with accuracy, especially when choices are offered, is one of the challenges for managers. If cycle menus are used, the food production records kept daily by managers can be used in accurately forecasting the quantities needed.
- **Available Equipment**—The types and amounts of available equipment affects foods purchased. In some cases, it may be more economical to purchase an item already prepared than to purchase a piece of equipment needed to prepare it.
- **Federal Regulations**—Federal regulations that affect school foodservice programs are many. Major regulations can be found in Federal Office of Management and Budget Circular (OMB A-102), Volume 7 Code of Federal Regulations (7 CFR) Part 3016.36, and 7 CFR 210.21. Some additional regulations address product standards and others, such Federal Trade Commission Act of 1914, address antitrust laws. The NFSMI's *Procurement for the 21*st *Century* manual has an excellent chapter devoted to the regulatory environment affecting school food and nutrition services programs.

Schools are required to "Buy American" products when possible. When buying a processed food, 51 percent or more of the ingredients must come from the United States.

- **USDA Foods and Processing Contracts**—Food received by schools from USDA will continue to make a considerable difference. USDA Foods account for 19% of the total food used by most school districts. USDA Foods affect the menus, in some cases immediately (e.g., when a product is fresh produce). Exhibit 6-2 shows the impact of USDA Foods to foodservices programs.

Exhibit 6-2 Source of Food Used in School Foodservices in SY2010

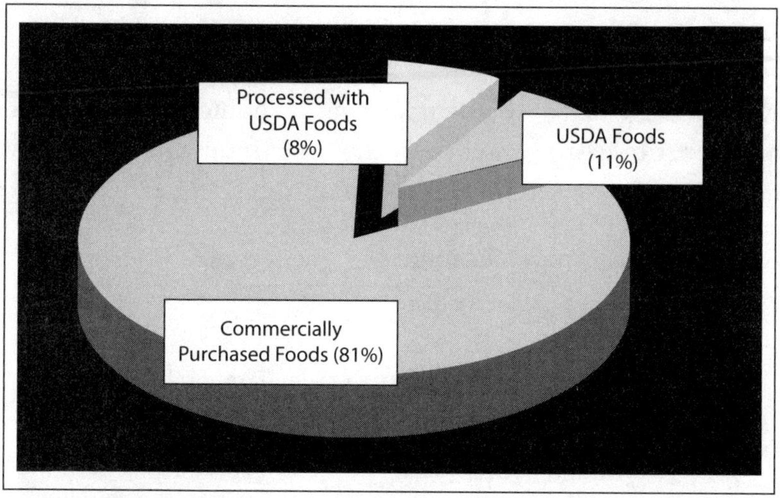

Source: USDA, 2012.

Using USDA Foods as ingredients in processed foods has become very popular. Nearly 42% of the foods issued in 2012 by the USDA for schools went to companies for further processing. State processing contracts are being used in most states (USDA, 2012).

The buyer should be aware that for some items, processing is no bargain. The cost of processing should be added to the value of the USDA Foods to determine whether it is a good deal. In some cases, it may cost more to process raw ingredients than to purchase the product outright when the cost of storage, delivery, backhaul, and state handling fees are included.

True cost of processed USDA Foods includes:

- Fair market value
- State fee
- Administrative fee
- Distribution fee
- Processing fee
- Storage costs

Product Evaluation and Selection

One of the most important functions of purchasing is the development of product description or specifications. A specification is a precise description of the desired item. It should list the product's characteristics in a manner mutually understandable to the buyer and potential sellers as shown in Exhibit 6-3.

Exhibit 6-3 Specification Example

SPECIFICATION EXAMPLE	
Item name:	Beans, green
Description:	Canned, 1- to 1½-inch long school cut, dark green, Blue Lake variety, 3 sieves
Grade:	Grade A
Pack size:	6/10 cans per case
Net drained wt.:	60 ounces
Approved brands:	Comstock, Code Red Label, or approved equal
Purchase unit:	Case

The specification should communicate to the bidder or seller what is wanted, so when evaluated the bid is the lowest price on the product wanted, not on an inferior product. Many people use brands to identify products; however, the specification should state the approved brands (two to three at minimum) and "approved equal."

Procedure for Approving Products

1. Obtain nutritional information and product formulation statements from manufacturer. Does the product fit nutritional and component requirements for the target grade groups?

(*Continued*)

2. Obtain cost information from current distributor or manufacturer's representative/broker. Does this product fit your budget?
3. Can this product be processed using USDA Foods, and has it been approved by the state agency for processing?
4. Test small batch of product using equipment available in the district. Can you produce, hold, and serve the product and meet quality standards?
5. Taste test products using a panel of students. Students should be asked to indicate which products are acceptable rather than ranking all selections.

Some school districts, and especially cooperatives, screen products and restrict bidding to "prior approved brands." In other words, testing is done before the specifications go out to bid. It is important to select more than one brand in order to obtain competitive pricing. It is dangerous to get into a situation where only one company provides the product wanted. No one should limit competition to the point that the bid process results in higher prices being paid.

If products are required to be evaluated and approved in advance, the product description can contain less detail (e.g., Global Trade Item Number [GTIN]) as shown in Exhibit 6-4 and product name. GTINs are unique product identification numbers obtained through GS1. GS1 is a not-for-profit organization that assists businesses implement GS1 product identification standards for improving product safety and supply chain efficiency. Chapter 8, "Food Safety," contains more information on the use of GTINs.

Exhibit 6-4 Global Trade Item Number Example

The GS1 Identification Key is a unique 14-digit number used to identify products, such as a specific brand, unit of measure, and product code. The key is comprised, at a minimum, of a GS1 or GS1 US UPC company prefix and an item identification number (GS1, 2009 February).

0 00 38000 03665 1

(01) 1 0049485 052507 (10) 10036

1 00 18000 27852 4

Source: NFSMI, 2012.

When products are not preapproved, it is important to include enough detail to describe the product desired, including quality indicators (e.g., Grade A). Depending on the products, a specification can include the following:

> *A standard of identity outlines what ingredients a product must contain, which ingredients it may contain, and any requirements of manufacturing.*

- Name of item (When available, the official Standard of Identity should be listed for processed food products such as mayonnaise, ketchup, and peanut butter.)
- Ingredients of processed items having no standard of identity
- Quality or official grade

Foodservice GS1 U.S. Standards Initiative

The ability to identify a product and its unique properties has become critical in school operations. The Foodservice GS1 U.S. Standards Initiative contains three components.

1. Global Location Number identifies a company, shipping location, or billing address.
2. Global Trade Item Number identifies a product in a standardized manner, allowing companies to share information about the product.
3. Global Data Synchronization Network is a network of standardized data pools that all members of the supply chain can use to share information about a product, such as nutritional information, ingredients, and marketing information.

It is important for schools to understand and begin to use GTINs when purchasing products because it is a reliable way to know that the product you ordered is the product you received. GTIN bar codes used with scanners can increase efficiency in receiving and inventory processes. More importantly, they serve a role in the effective tracking of products in the event of a recall or other food-related incident. More information about Foodservice GS1 U.S. Standards can be found in the "Online Resources" section of this chapter.

- Class, kind, style, and/or variety
  - Class refers to the sex of and type of animal
  - Kind refers to types of food, such as flour (e.g., whole grain)

  - Variety refers to specifics for such foods as fruits and vegetables (Red Delicious, Jonathan, and Winesap apples)
  - Style generally refers to how a product is processed (canned green beans may be cut, whole, or French style)
- Size of product (refers to weight [18- to 20-pound turkey], number per container [125 per box], can size [Number 10], and count [8 per pound])
- Origin (Is the product domestic or imported?)
- Package unit (e.g., crate, carton, box, retort pouch, bag barrel, or case)
- Special instructions (i.e., may spell out other types of restrictions; e.g., on processed canned foods, this year's pack may be required, and for frozen foods, the products must be delivered at 0°F or below)

Child Nutrition Labels

The Child Nutrition (CN) Labeling Program, instituted in 1984, provides buyers assurance of a product's contribution toward meal components. Originally, entrée and fruit juice products were evaluated for CN labels indicating the amount of protein and fruit/vegetable component contributions. In 2013, the program was updated to cover only entrées and expanded the meal component contributions to include:

- Meat/meat alternates with a minimum of 0.5 ounce
- Grains in a minimum of 0.25 ounce equivalents
- Vegetables in a minimum of ⅛ cup and identified by subgroup: red/orange, dark green, legume, starchy, and "other"

The CN label is easily identified by the CN border, a six-digit identification number, the USDA/Food Nutrition Service authorization statement, and the month and year of approval (Exhibit 6-5). The new labeling program also includes Agricultural Marketing Service or National Marine Fishery Service review and approval of the Manufacturers Quality Control Program and inspection of manufacturing processes to ensure quality and compliance.

Exhibit 6-5 Sample Child Nutrition Label

Chicken Stir-Fry Bowl

Ingredient Statement:
Chicken, brown rice, broccoli, red peppers, carrots, onions, water, olive oil, soy sauce, spices

CN

099135

Each 4.5 oz. Chicken Stir-Fry Bowl provides 1.5 oz. equivalent meat, 1.0 oz eq Grains, ¼ cup dark green vegetable, ¼ cup red/orange vegetable, and ½ cup other vegetable for Child Nutrition Meal Pattern Requirements. (Use of this logo and statement authorized by the Food and Nutrition Service. USDA XX/XX).

CN **CN** **CN**

Source: USDA, 2013.

Although schools are not required to purchase CN-labeled products, doing so will provide a warranty that the product provides the meal component contribution indicated on the label. It is important to obtain product formulation statements on the manufacturer's letterhead for processed products that do not contain a CN label. Sample product formulation statements for meat/meat alternate, vegetable, fruit, and whole grain are available on USDA's website. A link is provided in the "Online Resources" at the end of this chapter.

RESOURCES FOR DEVELOPING SPECIFICATIONS

Although developing a clear specification for products can seem daunting, many resources are available to help. Links to the following items are located in "Online Resources:"

- Standards of Identity
- Grade Standards
- Commercial Item Descriptions
- *Food Buying Guide*
- Food Connect
- USDA Foods Fact Sheets
- Produce Safety Fact Sheets

DETERMINING HOW MUCH TO PURCHASE

Determining the amount to purchase takes knowledge of the foodservice operation. It is easy to order too much, which can mean a lot of waste. Several factors need to be considered when determining amounts to purchase.

- **Forecasting Need**—Manufacturers base their pricing on the volume needed. Determining accurate quantities is important in order to take advantage of volume discounts. Once menus are planned, forecasts estimate the number of servings of each menu item. A spreadsheet used for forecasting is available in the School Nutrition Association Purchasing Toolkit referenced in the "Online Resources" at the end of the chapter.
- **Distribution Considerations**—The bidder should be provided with the number and location of delivery sites. Foodservices programs can choose to have products delivered

to each serving site, only a few sites, or a single warehouse. Although the purchase price is less when products go to a single site, the cost to the program to store and deliver products for more than one school is important to consider.

In order to calculate a "per case" cost of delivery, add the annual expenses (see the following list) and divide by the total number of cases that will be stored and distributed from this location annually:

- Annual maintenance, fuel, and insurance of vehicles
- Price of vehicles amortized over the life expectancy of the truck
- Labor costs of drivers, including benefits
- Labor cost of warehouse staff, including benefits
- Cost of utilities
- Equipment costs (e.g., freezers, coolers, forklift)
- Shrinkage and loss

The cost of warehousing and delivering products calculated on a per-case basis should be added to the case price. This figure can then be compared to the price of the same product delivered directly to serving sites. This calculation can help determine whether true savings are realized in warehousing products versus direct delivery to serving sites

PLANNING A PURCHASING PROCESS

Methods of Procurement

The two basic procurement methods—formal and informal—both require written specifications in order to communicate what is needed. The informal procurement method generally used for small purchases is a Request for Quote. A quote is solicited from at least three sources and then the product is ordered by telephone, fax, or online. The formal methods are either an invitation for bid (IFB) or request for proposal (RFP). They require publicly advertising the purchasing requirements, receiving a sealed bid by a specified date, and awarding a contract.

Federal law requires school districts to use a formal purchasing method when the total annual purchase from a vendor exceeds the "simplified acquisition threshold" (currently $150,000). State laws may have lower purchasing thresholds, so it is best to check with the state agency overseeing school meal programs to ensure requirements are met.

Most school districts use the formal bid for all major purchases and the informal quotes on items such as produce. The larger the school district, the more that is purchased through a formal bid contract.

Common Types of Formal Bids

Invitation for Bid (IFB) —An IFB describes in great detail the services or products required and awards the contract to the lowest responsive, responsible bidder. For example, IFB is used for canned and staple foods.

Request for Proposal (RFP) —A RFP describes in a general way what is needed and requests that vendors submit a proposal for serving the needs of the district. RFPs can be awarded based on the merits for the proposal using an evaluation process specified in the bid document. Terms and prices may not be firm and can be negotiated after the contract is awarded. RFPs are used when selecting a group purchasing organization (GPO), a prime vendor when value-added services are expected, or when buying computer software.

Pricing Methods

The three pricing methods most frequently used are:

1. **Fixed Price.** A price quoted is for a period of time: onetime buy, over three months, six months, or a year. It is a contractual agreement. Most school districts use fixed pricing on the major items (e.g., canned and frozen foods). Companies often have trouble holding prices for long periods of time. A large school district or cooperative bid may involve the distributor obtaining a guaranteed price from the manufacturer or processing company.
2. **Fixed Price with Escalator or Market-Based.** This method is used mostly with produce, milk, bread, poultry, and eggs. This system allows for long-term contracts on items that otherwise require frequent bidding, such as produce. When using this method, information from a third party is important.
3. **Cost-Plus-Fixed-Fee.** For this written contract, the fee for service is added to the price the vendor paid for the product plus freight. Some refer to it as "formula pricing," "fee for service," or "cost reimbursable contract." The fee covers the cost of warehousing, delivery, sales, overhead costs, and profit.

As the market becomes more complicated and vendors learn new ways of "sheltering income," the cost-plus-fixed-fee purchasing becomes more risky. It requires detective work on behalf of the purchaser, and it may be difficult to audit and keep people honest. Sheltered income is in the form of discounts, promotional allowances, and so on.

Because the reimbursable cost-plus-fixed-fee method usually prevents companies from having to take a risk of prices changing, using this method of pricing allows bids to cover longer periods of

Some of the sources of this type information can be obtained from:

Food Institute Report (weekly) from American Institute of Food Distribution, Inc., is available for canned fruits and vegetables, frozen fruits, and juices.

Federal market news reports (USDA/AMS) is produced for different parts of the country (referred to as the "terminal markets")—for produce in particular.

Producer Price Index has been established for several categories of food including cereal and bakery products.

Urner Barry's Price-Current, National Provisioner Yellow Sheet, and HRI-Buyer's Guide are other examples.

time. It may ensure that a school district will get a product even if the cost has increased. School districts must constantly monitor and audit companies when using cost-plus-fixed-fee.

Purchasing Calendar and District Profile

The first step in the procurement process is to develop a calendar of purchasing activities. Although a district may only solicit bids once a year, the activities involved with developing the bid usually take place throughout the school year. A calendar will ensure that enough time has been allocated for each step in the process and that all tasks are completed by the date needed. Start with the date the first deliveries are needed and work backwards. Exhibit 6-6 provides a sample calendar.

A district profile tells the prospective vendors information about the district that will help them determine the purchasing process and how best to work with the district.

Exhibit 6-6 Sample Purchasing Calendar

Purchasing Task	Date
Plan menus and determine list of products to purchase.	4th week in November
Distribute product list to vendors.	2nd week in December
Pre-bid meeting.	3rd week in January
Evaluate products for nutrient content, components, costs, preparation, and student acceptability.	3rd week in March
Advertise and distribute IFB or RFP.	1st week in April
Bid opening.	1st week in May
Evaluate responses and make recommendations for award.	3rd week in May
Notify successful vendor.	1st week in June
Receive first deliveries.	2nd week in August

Typically, the profile contains:

- Statistics such as contact information, number and types of schools, number of meals served, programs offered, purchasing budget, distribution, production type
- How products are evaluated
- Purchasing schedule and pricing-type for product categories (escalator/de-escalator)
- Sales call policy
- Special requirements (e.g., nutrition targets)

The district profile is included in the bid document but can also be provided during pre-bid meetings and posted on the district website.

RESPONSIBILITY FOR PROCUREMENT

Many different solutions exist for assigning responsibility for purchasing for school foodservice programs. The district needs to consider the time and expertise available in-house when deciding which option is best for them.

Centralized Versus Decentralized Purchasing

Most school districts use direct purchasing methods for at least some of their food and supply purchasing. Direct purchasing may be carried out at the school or district level. Direct purchasing gives the district complete control over the methods of procurement, pricing, and product qualities.

With centralized purchasing, the central office purchases for a number of schools. Decentralized purchasing allows each manager to meet with sales representatives from the companies and determine the products that will be purchased.

The advantages of centralized purchasing include the following:

- Time is saved.
- Buying power is greater, and prices are usually better.
- Competitive bidding processes can be used.
- Person handling purchasing can specialize.
- Product purchases are standardized.
- Better budgetary control is achieved.
- Federal regulation compliance can be better controlled.

Collective or Cooperative Purchasing

When multiple organizations participate as a group to make purchasing decisions, it is collective or cooperative purchasing. Collective purchasing increases buying power, saves time, and usually lowers the price of products.

Three types of collective purchasing typically used by schools:

1. State or regional purchasing cooperatives or buying groups
2. Group purchasing organizations (GPOs)
3. Interagency agreements

In SY2010, more than half of the public school districts participated in cooperative purchasing, buying nearly 74 percent of their foods using this method (USDA, 2012). Schools with enrollments under 1,000 are less likely to participate in cooperative purchasing even though small school districts in particular can profit from this method (USDA, 2012).

Utilizing cooperative purchasing results in lower food prices in most cases; however, the difference is typically 10 percent or less compared to direct purchasing (USDA, 2012). To arrive at specifications that all the directors/supervisors can agree upon may be the biggest challenge in the process. It requires being flexible and accepting some change.

The state agency administering school food and nutrition services in some states, (e.g., Iowa, Mississippi, Montana, and Texas) are purchasing on a statewide contract. Mississippi's state cooperative prices and services were evaluated. The study verified a savings to school districts in that state (Boudreaux and Oldenquist, 1996). All but nine school districts in the state of Mississippi (140 out of 149) use the state cooperative for purchasing food and supplies, making Mississippi a

Potential advantages to state purchasing
- Centralized expertise
- Increased buying power
- Guaranteed better prices
- Reduced workload and paperwork

large-volume bidder. The smaller the school district, the greater the advantages. With this approach, the school districts do give up some individuality and authority over the food quality and variety.

Group Purchasing Organizations

A group purchasing organization (GPO) or buying organization is a regional or national organization formed to increase the buying power of its members. Typically, the organization charges a fee to join and offers rebates based on the dollar volume of purchases. Many types of goods in addition to food may be purchased through GPOs and may include equipment, technology, and furniture.

Schools must use competitive purchasing practices and follow all other federal and state regulations when procuring services of a GPO. The fact that a GPO utilizes a competitive bidding process to secure contracts does not relieve school foodservice programs from following government procurement standards.

Intergovernmental Agreements

Some states allow schools to "piggyback" on a bid contract awarded by another school district or governmental agency. This process is facilitated by joint power laws at the state level. Both the initiating district and the vendor must agree to the arrangement. The district that is piggybacking must accept the terms of the bid as written.

Many states have a purchasing agent who puts into place a contract for food and supplies for state institutions such as jails, hospitals, and universities. Most states (e.g., Virginia, Tennessee, and Arizona) allow public schools to use the state purchasing service. The state may be purchasing in large enough quantities and have enough clout to obtain better prices than even a large school district, particularly for staple items such as canned goods, supplies, and chemicals.

COMMUNICATE REQUIREMENTS

Whether using an informal quote, a formal bid, or a request for proposal, clear written information provided to the prospective vendors is a critical step in receiving the product and services expected. Although this section applies to formal purchasing, the need for accurate information applies to all forms of purchasing.

Formal bids may contain many references to legal requirements. Still, it is important to use straightforward language understandable to vendors as well as district staff engaged in the purchasing process.

> A bid document contains four sections:
> 1. Instructions to the bidder
> 2. Terms and conditions
> 3. Product descriptions
> 4. Evaluation criteria

Instructions to the Bidder

Bidders need information related to what to include in the bid response:

- Date due
- Eligibility criteria
- District contact information
- Date and place of bid opening

In addition, information about the district can be included to help the vendor understand the scope of the procurement, the district profile, and the department goals (e.g., improving nutritional quality of meals).

Terms and Conditions

Once awarded, the bid becomes a contract with the school district. Terms and conditions should include a form for the vendor to complete indicating the product, GTIN, manufacturer's item code, price, fees, and any changes in the purchase unit of measure. This form may be paper or electronic (e.g., spreadsheet). If a spreadsheet is used, any fields containing formulas should be locked with password protection.

Terms and conditions include but are not limited to:

- Effective dates, including provisions for renewal in subsequent years
- Conditions for early termination
- Statements related to seller's responsibility for providing goods specified including handling of substitutions
- Statements related to the district's responsibility for payment
- A statement clarifying the district's right to purchase more or less than the estimated quantities or to purchase similar products from another source (e.g., local produce for a farm to school program)
- Insurance and certification requirements
- Warranty provisions, nonperformance, and remedies
- Access to vendor records
- Liability and insurance
- Signature page with any required affidavits

Specifications

General and specific product descriptions and specifications clarify the product and service requirements. The earlier section, "Product Selection and Evaluation," discusses the components of a clear product description. In addition, general requirements apply, such as:

- Deliveries and receiving
- Food safety
- Nutrition
- Quality control
- "Buy American," geographic or local definition
- Recalls and product tracking
- Ordering methods (e.g., online)

Requirements should be specific enough to ensure the quality of the program, but not so specific that competition is restricted.

Evaluation Criteria

Sharing evaluation criteria with vendors is an important, but often overlooked, section of the bid. An invitation for bid response may only be evaluated and awarded based on the lowest price from a responsible bidder. It is important to indicate whether the value of the bid will be determined based on:

- Each line item
- By category
- Bottom line

Awarding a bid based on the lowest price for each line item may result in more vendors than the district desires. Although this method may deliver the lowest *price* per item, the actual *cost* of this method may be higher due to additional staff time spent on ordering and receiving.

Evaluation of a RFP response uses multiple criteria. A fair evaluation of an RFP can be difficult unless objective criteria are established in advance. An effective method is to use a point system. Points may be assigned to categories such as:

- Total cost (e.g., price, fast-pay discounts)
- Minority, women-owned, or labor excess area businesses
- Geographic preferences (within legal boundaries)
- Value-added services
- Ability to service the account (e.g., references, fill rates, delivery minimums, handling of rebates, and commodity inventory information)

Geographic Preference Specification

A geographic preference can be specified for locally grown or raised agricultural products that are unprocessed or minimally processed.

The school district may define "local" in any manner that does not restrict competition.

Source: 7 CFR Part 210.21 (g) (2).

CONTROLLING FOOD AND SUPPLY INVENTORY

Knowing the value of the inventory plays an important part in accurately determining the cost of goods sold and maintaining inventory control. Inventory can make or break a foodservice operation. Proper storage is essential to safe, good-quality food, as well as product turnover. In moving inventory, it is important to control aging of products by following the "first in, first out" principle.

Managing inventory involves:

- Accurate receiving
- Proper storing in an organized facility
- Accountability for items in storage
- Timely removal from storage

Using technology can save time in the ordering, receiving, and inventory tasks. Exchange of information between supply chain members uses GTINs as a common identifier for products. Scanning bar codes reduces redundant data entry, making the processes faster and more accurate. (Chapter 9, "Technology," discusses this topic in more detail.)

Proper Receiving and Storage

The individual checking in deliveries needs to be knowledgeable about the order and the specifications of the products. Before the person receiving the order signs a delivery ticket or invoice, it is important to verify the following:

- Items ordered and GTIN
- Quantity ordered
- Quality specified
- Correct prices and extensions
- Specifications of products

The person receiving a product does not need a detailed specification, but at a minimum—the brand, code number, pack, and price.

If products ordered are in the delivery in the correct quantity, without damages, at the proper temperature, and meet the specifications, the receiving person can safely sign the delivery ticket. The receiving person writes the date on the cases. If a shortage of a product occurs and it appears on the delivery ticket, the next step is to write a request-for-credit memo and send it with the delivery ticket to accounts payable (within the school district). A copy of the memo goes to the driver delivering the product, and a copy is kept on file at the school.

Organized and clean areas are essential for safe-guarding inventory. Shelving should provide good air circulation, and products should be kept at least six inches off the floor. Steps to good storeroom organization and practices are as follows:

1. Arrange storeroom areas in assigned groupings.
2. Store heavy items at waist height or lower.
3. Store light items on upper shelves.
4. Store detergents/chemicals separately from food.
5. Store least-used items in less accessible areas.
6. Label areas with group names and shelves with item names.
7. Date all cases before placing them on shelves, and rotate stock.
8. Store goods in cases with identifiable labels visible.
9. Do not store items on the floor.
10. Empty cases as they are opened.
11. Schedule cleaning of storage areas.
12. Assign one employee the duties of "storekeeper."
13. Limit hours during which items can be obtained from the storeroom.

Ideal Storage Temperatures	
Dry storage	50° to 70° F
Refrigerated storage	32° to 40° F
Freezer storage	Below 0° F

14. Record where food leaving the storage area went using the food production record or snack bar/a la carte records.
15. Lock storerooms.

Preventing theft and pilferage is a major concern. According to the National Retail Security Survey (2009), shrinkage in the United States is calculated at 1.5 percent of sales. Shrinkage is the cost of loss due to waste, theft, spoilage, and other loss. It is estimated that 44 percent of shrinkage in retail operations is due to employee theft and 35 percent due to shoplifting. The remaining 21 percent can be attributed to spoilage, damage, shipping errors, misplaced product, and vendor fraud.

Accountability for Items in Storage

For a large operation, an in-house requisition records the product removed from inventory. The daily production record and snack bar/a la carte records provide audit trails that account for the use of food and supplies. This production record is particularly important for the kitchen where requisition records are not available to provide the audit trail.

Inventory Records

An important part of inventory management is good records. Many school districts maintain perpetual inventories, and some state agencies, such as Louisiana, require them in an effort to strengthen accountability. All managers should be taking a physical inventory, at a minimum monthly. In the past, USDA Foods and commercial products were separately stored and tracked.

Tracking Inventory

Perpetual Inventory — An up-to-date, running record of each item on hand in the storeroom that provides ready information to a manager for placing orders. Tracking manually is time-consuming; however, with the use of computers, scanners, and GTINs, it can easily be maintained.

Physical Inventory — An actual count of goods in stock. If a perpetual inventory is not being kept, a "mini" physical inventory will have to be taken before placing orders—if ordering is going to be done accurately. An accurate physical inventory should be taken monthly, at the end of the month.

Today, many USDA Foods are processed into commercial products, making it difficult to distinguish between them; therefore, a school foodservice program uses only a single inventory. Counting and valuing physical inventory is essential to determining the cost of food used. If a perpetual inventory is maintained, the physical inventory should be compared and reconciled. Any difference should be evaluated by management.

Following are some general rules for taking inventory:

- Take inventory with two people, one to count, and one to record.
- Inventory items by location, in order stored.

- Leave cans in cases until needed. Remove from cases once opened.
- Observe consistency. If counting food "in process," do the count consistently (particularly at large production sites).

The quantity of food and supplies in inventory should be considerably low at the end of the school year.

SUMMARY

Traditional purchasing practices aim at reducing the price paid for products and services. In recent years this approach has been replaced with a supply chain orientation in which the cost of doing business for each business partner is examined to identify and reduce areas of cost that do not add value. Eliminating unnecessary costs for any member of the supply chain will lower costs for the end user.

Menu planning prior to purchasing helps with more accurate forecasting of product quantities. Providing prospective vendors with realistic estimates will help obtain volume discounts to lower product prices. If the district purchases less than anticipated, future discounts will likely be eliminated or reduced.

Districts may elect to purchase directly or collectively. Increasing "buying power" or the quantities of items purchased will lower price in many cases. An effective purchasing process may not result in achieving food cost and quality goals unless it is combined with an effective inventory management system. Receiving, storage, issuing, and accountability systems ensure that purchased products retain maximum quality and value.

QUESTIONS AND ANSWERS

1. What factors should be considered during the purchasing process?
   a. Customer preferences
   b. The food and nutrition services budget
   c. Nutritional content and the menu
   d. All of the above
2. What information is contained in a good product specification or description?
   a. Menu
   b. Cost of the product
   c. Package unit
   d. Shipping location
3. The invitation for bid and a request for proposal are the same thing.
   a. True
   b. False
4. Who may be responsible for procurement in school food and nutrition services program?
   a. The school district
   b. The state agency
   c. A cooperative buying group
   d. Any of the above
5. What information is contained within a bid document?
   a. Current product prices
   b. Product specifications or descriptions
   c. A fax number for returning bid information
   d. Names of personnel
6. What criterion is not used to evaluate a bid response?
   a. Value-added service
   b. Total cost
   c. Ability to service the account
   d. Uniforms provided
7. What processes are used to manage food and supplies?
   a. Effective receiving
   b. Proper storage
   c. Inventory management
   d. All of the above

ANSWERS: 1.d., 2.c., 3.b., 4.d., 5.b., 6.d., 7.d.

REFERENCES

Bartlett, S., et al. 2008. *School lunch and breakfast cost study-II: Executive summary.* P. McKinney & J. Endahl (Project Officers). Alexandria, VA: USDA.

Boettger, J. 2009. *Effects of organizational attributes on adoption of technology for supply chain management in large school nutrition programs.* Retrieved from Graduate Theses and Dissertations, *http://lib.dr.iastate.edu/etd/10516/.*

Boudreaux, L. J., & Oldenquist, J. A. 1996. The effectiveness of the Mississippi State Department of Education purchasing programs for Child Nutrition Programs. *School Food Service Research Review,* 20 (1), 13–18.

GS1. 2009. *GS1 standards document: Business process and systems requirements for full chain traceability (1.1.0).* Retrieved from *http://barcodes.gs1us.org/dnn_bcec/Documents/tabid/136/DMXModule/731/Command/Core_ViewCollection/Default.aspx.*

Mentzer, J., DeWitt, W., Keebler, J., Min, J., Nix, N., Smith, C., et al. 2001. Defining supply chain management. *Journal of Business Logistics,* 22 (2), 1–25.

NFSMI. 2001. *Choice plus: A reference guide for food and ingredients.* University, MS: Author.

NFSMI. 2012. *Inventory management and tracking reference guide.* University, MS: Author.

NFSMI. 2013. *Procurement in the 21st century.* University, MS: Author.

Public Health Law Center. *Collective purchasing for food and federal school nutrition programs.* Retrieved from *http://publichealthlawcenter.org/sites/default/files/resources/Collective%20Purchasing%20of%20Food%20for%20Federal%20School%20Nutrition%20Programs.pdf.*

Rice, B., et al. 2010. Comparison of cooperative and noncooperative purchasing in school nutrition programs. *Journal of Child Nutrition and Management,* 34. Retrieved from *http://www.schoolnutrition.org/Content.aspx?id=14754.*

Sadler, S. 2008. *Managing child nutrition programs.* J. Martin & C. Oakley (Eds.). Sudbury, MA: Jones & Bartlett.

School Nutrition Association. 2006. *Supply chain roundtable.* Retrieved from *http://www.schoolnutrition.org/uploadedFiles/SchoolNutrition.org/News_&_Publications/Tuesday_Morning/SNA-USF%20Supply%20Chain%20RoundTable%20Summary%20-%20for%20SNA2.pdf.*

7 CFR Part 210.21 (g) (2). *Cost reimbursable contracts* and *geographic preferences.* Retrieved from *http://www.gpo.gov/fdsys/pkg/CFR-2013-title7 vol4/xml/ CFR-2013-title7-vol4-sec210-21.xml.*

7 CFR 3016. *Uniform administrative requirements for grants and cooperative agreements to state and local governments: Procurement.* Retrieved from *http:// www.ecfr.gov/cgi-bin/text-idx?c=ecfr&tpl=/ecfrbrowse/Title07/7cfr3016_ main_02.tpl.*

Young, N., et al. 2012. *School food purchase study-III.* J. Endahl (Project Officer). Alexandria, VA: USDA.

ONLINE RESOURCES

Commercial Item Descriptions
http://www.ams.usda.gov/AMSv1.0/getfile?dDocName=STELPRDC5088490

Foodservice GS1 U.S. Standards Initiative
http://www.gs1us.org/industries/foodservice/foodservice-initiative

National Institute of Governmental Purchasing's Public Procurement Practice: Ethical Procurement
http://principlesandpractices.org/wp-content/uploads/2013/04/Ethical.pdf

NSFMI *Inventory Management and Tracking Reference Guide*
http://www.nfsmi.org/documentlibraryfiles/PDF/20121114100354.pdf

NFSMI *Procurement in the 21st Century*
http://www.nfsmi.org/documentlibraryfiles/PDF/20130820034348.pdf

SNA School Nutrition Procurement Toolkit
http://procurement.schoolnutrition.org/

Standards of Identity for Animals and Animal Products
http://www.gpo.gov/fdsys/pkg/CFR-2012-title9-vol2/xml/CFR-2012-title9-vol2-part319.xml

USDA CFR–Code of Federal Regulations Title 21
http://www.accessdata.fda.gov/scripts/cdrh/cfdocs/cfcfr/CFRSearch.cfm

USDA Food Buying Guide for Child Nutrition Programs
http://www.fns.usda.gov/tn/resources/foodbuyingguide.html

USDA Food Connect
http://www.foodconnect.usda.gov/fcc/index.aspx

USDA Food Facts
http://www.fns.usda.gov/fdd/foods/healthy/Professional.htm

USDA Fruit and Vegetable Market News Users Guide
http://www.ams.usda.gov/AMSv1.0/getfile?dDocName=STELPRDC5048679

USDA National Weekly Pricing Report
http://www.ams.usda.gov/AMSv1.0/foodserv

USDA Quality Standards
http://www.ams.usda.gov/AMSv1.0/standards

USDA Sample Product Formulation Statement
http://www.teamnutrition.usda.gov/resources/smi_appendixl.pdf

Chapter 7

Managing Ordering, Food Production, and Service

STUDY QUESTIONS

1. Describe the forecasting process.
2. List at least three functions of food preparation.
3. What is a standardized recipe?
4. What are some steps to quality control?
5. What is the purpose of a production record?
6. What are the advantages of batch cooking?
7. Describe portion control.
8. What influences "eye appeal" of food?
9. Why is the temperature of food important?
10. Why is the attitude of employees important to the serving of customers (students and teachers)?

Chapter 7

"Relighting the Pilot Light" by Cyndie Story, PhD, RD, CC

President, Culinary Solution Centers, LLC

The year was 1989. I had just landed my first nutrition services director position at a small hospital in Atlanta, Georgia. At the time, no jobs were available in child nutrition, because then you had to wait until someone retired. Each workday, I entered the kitchen as though I knew everything about everything. Looking back, maybe my attitude was due to being fresh out of school and filled with enthusiasm. At least weekly, I was giving orders that caused major changes in food production, even though I had never relit a pilot light or sautéed vegetables in a tilting skillet.

Approximately one month into my new position, I was scheduled to work the evening shift for the supervising chef. To my shock and horror, all but one of the entire evening staff decided to call in sick. There we were, two people attempting to prepare the dinner meal (and of course, the pilot light was out). The events of that evening are too painful to recall. However, the experience taught me several great lessons:

- You must have a supportive staff to operate a successful kitchen. You are only as good as your most challenged employee.
- You should consider yourself a member first, to effectively direct the team. Ultimately, many final decisions are yours to make, but when possible ask questions and risk being vulnerable by not always knowing the answer or being perfect.
- You should know how to operate all of the equipment (small, large, electronic, etc.) in your kitchen(s). Most school nutrition employees have great respect for a director who knows how to re-light the pilot light, or comes to the rescue when needed. Nonskid shoes that match your dress pants come in handy.
- Be familiar with the individual tasks of the team; the forest is important, but so are the trees. The success of your operation is in the details.

My final words of wisdom are "get out of your office and into the kitchen as often as possible." Management by awareness (MBA) allows you to see the system procedures you have developed and implemented come to life. Take time to connect with your customers for immediate feedback. Eat lunch with a student or educator. Observe the foods on the serving line for freshness and appeal. Remember, no great recipe was ever developed and prepared while sitting in a chair staring at the computer screen.

The chapters that precede this one discuss the initial essential elements in producing and serving food at schools. After the menus are planned to meet the federal requirements, personnel are employed, and the food bids put in place, the school-level staff can do their jobs. The manager and staff in each kitchen determine the success of the food and nutrition services program.

ORDERING JUST ENOUGH JUST IN TIME

Well-planned menus, standardized recipes, and food production records are vital to ordering just enough for delivery just in time for use. If the menu is a short-cycle menu (e.g., one- to three-week cycle), the staff can become more efficient and improve the processes.

Forecasting

Exhibit 7-1 shows the steps to use when forecasting and ordering. The following information will be required: menus, recipes, previous production records, inventory, and order forms. This aspect may be the most difficult job for a new manager. The fear of "running out" will weigh heavy at first. The more standardized the procedure, the easier it becomes.

Fresh produce has a short shelf life and the waste can be substantial. Ordering the correct amount—not overstocking or running out—should be the goal. Doing this task accurately can make the difference in the food cost, consuming less or more than 40 percent of the revenue. It is not a simple job, but an important job.

Some school districts have software packages that aid in determining what to order, when to order, and how much to order. For any of these aids to be effective, standardized processes are essential. Bad data entry (or lack of data entry) can result in bad experiences.

Exhibit 7-1 Forecasting Flowchart

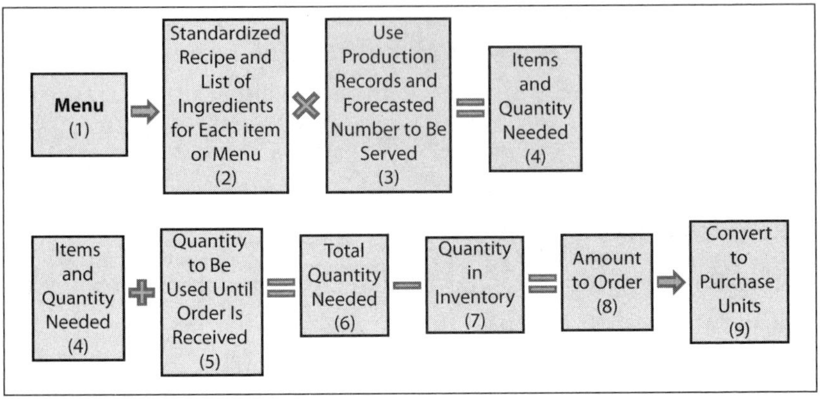

Source: Pannell-Martin and Applebaum, 2005.

FOOD PREPARATION

Some say food production is an exact science and others argue that it is a "love affair." Perhaps it is a little of both—which is the approach in this chapter. The exact science starts with standardized preparation procedures and the control aspect of the process; the "love affair" is with the beautifully presented finished products.

In the past 10 years, the federal child nutrition programs have had many changes in regulations that aim to control menus and food preparation. An emphasis on reducing fat has met with some success. In recent years, school food and nutrition services managers have seen increases in the use of raw fruits and fresh vegetables. Some refer to this approach as "back to basics." For a successful change, "back to basics" requires:

- Revenue to cover cost
- Skilled employees
- Preparation equipment
- Customers/students accepting the changes
- Manager ordering just enough just in time

These changes are difficult for many school food and nutrition services programs to manage within the budget and with the skill level of the staff. This chapter will provide steps to help one succeed regardless of the changes in regulations and emphasis.

Whether the food is prepared from raw ingredients or convenience foods, standardized recipes or clearly written directions are necessary. This first step helps to make it possible—even easy—for the novice to turn out good products.

The manager and assistants or staff must be able to read and understand directions. The manager must be skilled in scheduling the staff, as well as food preparation. The people portioning/serving must be creative enough and care enough to present the food in an attractive, appetizing, and interesting way.

Convenience Foods Versus Raw Ingredients

Convenience foods have improved and are commonly used, better accepted, and more reasonably priced. The quality of convenience foods has improved to the point where the quality may be better than "made from scratch" items. It may not be necessary to prepare food from raw ingredients.

As labor costs have increased and the lack of trained employees has grown in the 2000s, it has become harder to rationalize preparing certain foods from raw ingredients. In the 1970s, pizza took days to prepare. Today most school districts purchase prepared, frozen pizza that requires only 10 minutes in the oven before serving, or they use pizza kits that turn out excellent pizza with a few minutes' preparation time.

Throughout the country, a few school districts have clung to baking—even hamburger rolls. The breads they produce look and smell great to adults, but frankly, even the adults have to admit the hamburger made with a school-made roll tastes different from what McDonald's serves. The cost of the roll may be twice that of a purchased roll, and food waste may be staggering on the day served because students eat the patty and leave the unfamiliar bun. Many school districts fail to check the cost of producing from raw ingredients because they have convinced themselves that such foods are always better and less expensive.

Some important questions to consider are what the customer prefers, is it more nutritious, whether the cost is affordable, and whether the item is priced correctly when sold a la carte.

Preparation Goals

Whether the food and nutrition services program is using raw ingredients or convenience foods, the primary functions of food preparation are to:

- Improve the digestibility of the food
- Conserve the food's nutritive value
- Improve flavor and appearance
- Provide the quality food the customer wants
- Make the food safe for consumption

Preparation starts with good-quality ingredients and achieves all of these goals.

Creativity and skill are required to make food attractive, appetizing, and interesting. Probably the area that school food and nutrition services programs need to improve the most is in food presentation—how it looks and smells to the customer. Many smaller children will smell food before they eat it—and if the aroma penetrating the building before lunch is that of ground turkey, ground beef, reconstituted onions, broccoli, or cabbage cooking, they may be turned off before they get to the cafeteria. Contrast that to the appetizing smells of apples with cinnamon baking, pizza, chocolate chip cookies, or cinnamon rolls permeating the halls. These smells attract students and school staff alike. Unfortunately, some of the most nutritious foods do not smell so appetizing when cooking.

Standardized Recipes

A quantity recipe is not necessarily a standardized recipe. Even convenience foods and components that are combined need recipes or directions—even if it is just heating and assembling. School food and nutrition services cannot afford to prepare food without following directions and prescribed portions, which can be done best with standardized recipes.

> **Definition:**
>
> *STANDARDIZED RECIPE*—Recipe that has been tested for consistency and yield.

A standardized recipe is like a blueprint to a builder—exact and tested for yield. Using standardized recipes and standard weights and measures:

- Ensures uniform quality and eliminates "trial and error"
- Helps obtain desired yields and prevent waste
- Saves time and money
- Facilitates more accurate precosting of menus
- Simplifies the job for employees
- Helps determine what to order and how much
- Helps ensure compliance with meal requirements
- Helps maintain customer confidence

The recipe should be selected or developed before an item is put on the menu. Every item on the menu needs a recipe. Numerous published sources of standardized recipes are available. The standardized school foodservice recipes published by the USDA in *Quantity Recipes for School Food Services (PA-1371)* were updated with Hazard Analysis & Critical Control Point (HACCP) and the addition of directions for 50 servings, as well as 100 servings. The advantage to using these recipes is nutritional analysis and the contribution to the school lunch and breakfast meal requirements information.

> *USDA Quantity Recipes for School Food Services (2012, rev).*
> (See Online Resources at end of this chapter.)

When using recipes from other sources, it is necessary to use the U.S. Department of Agriculture *Food Buying Guide for Child Nutrition Programs* (1984, rev. 2012) to determine the contribution the recipe makes toward the menu. When no standardized recipe is available or when the recipe used is not standardized, one needs to be established. Recipes may be the cook's own, but when used in the nutrition programs they need to be standardized.

<u>Abbreviations Commonly Used in Recipes:</u>

tsp	= teaspoon	No.	= number
Tbsp	= tablespoon	cyl	= cylinder
c	= cup	ml	= milliliter
pt	= pint	g	= gram
qt	= quart	kg	= kilogram
gal	= gallon	wt	= weight
oz	= ounce	°F	= degrees Fahrenheit
lb	= pound	°C	= degrees Celsius
fl oz	= fluid ounce	AP	= as purchased
pkg	= package	EP	= edible portion
		CCP	= critical control point

Periods may or may not be needed after abbreviations for clarity—but when abbreviations are used, it is important to be consistent.

Each school district should have a set of recipes to accompany menus—the set may be made up of recipes from several sources. The recipes should provide some basic information regardless of the source. Exhibit 7-2 gives a list of the essential parts and desirable additional information. Good examples can be adapted from *On the Road to Professional Food Preparation,* 2nd edition (NFSMI, 2007). It is recommended that the recipes be typed using a large-size print (12–14 size font), with the original recipe laminated. See Online Resources at the end of this chapter for additional information.

Exhibit 7-2 Standardized Recipe Information Suggested

1. Name of Recipe
2. Category
3. Quantity for 25 or 50 and 100 Portions
4. Serving Size
5. Ingredients
6. Weights and Measures
7. Directions or Procedures
   a. Temperature and Cooking Time (if applicable)
   b. Cooking Method
   c. Pan or Container Size
8. Nutritional Information and Contributions
9. Critical Control Points (in Hazard Analysis Critical Control Points)
10. Additional Information

Descriptions of the parts of a standardized recipe are as follows:

1. **Name of Recipe.** Use chief food in name of recipe or a name that is readily understood. Simple, descriptive terms such as "Fruited Gelatin," "Grilled Cheese Sandwich," and "Deli Sandwich" are examples of good recipe names.
2. **Category.** Some of the categories are main dish, vegetable, salad, dessert, sauce, and bread.

3. **Quantity in Number of Portions.** Adjusting a recipe is extremely easy if the original recipe yields 100 portions. It might be helpful to list if the quantity of ingredients for 25 or 50 portions, as well as 100 portions. Cooks may prefer the yield filling certain size pans. Add this information to the recipe for future reference.
4. **Serving Size.** Give serving sizes in common measures (e.g., ½ cup), numbers (e.g., 5 chicken nuggets), or weight units (e.g., 1½ ounce portion) and indicate the total number of servings the recipe will yield (e.g., 100 ½-cup servings).
5. **Ingredients.** List ingredients in the order they are used in preparing the recipe. Use a descriptive term after the ingredient name to indicate the type or style to be purchased or the cooking needed before the ingredient is used (e.g., "tomatoes, canned," "rice, cooked," "broccoli, florets," "apple, fresh, slices").
6. **Weights and Measures.** Give weights and measures when practical. Use weight alone when the item is not easily measured. Use measure alone for liquids, such as water, broth, and milk, and for small quantities too small to weigh accurately. "Part One: General Information" on USDA website, *Food for Fifty,* 13th ed. (Molt, 2010), and *On the Road to Professional Food Preparation,* 2nd ed. (NFSMI, 2010) are useful when developing recipes.
7. **Directions or Procedures.** Make sure recipe directions or procedures are simply written and easy to understand and follow. Eliminate or combine as many steps as possible to reduce the time required to prepare the recipe. Use as few words as possible in describing procedures. The directions or procedures should appear in the same order as the ingredients are listed. The number and size of pans should be indicated along with

the cooking method, baking temperature, and time required. When a recipe does not have all this information, add it to the recipe to make preparation easier the next time the recipe is used.

8. **Nutritional Information and Contributions.** Provide the nutritional content for the size portion or the nutrients required in the nutrient analysis of the menus. List the recipe's contribution to the menu (e.g., one slice of pizza may contribute 1½ grain/bread, 2 ounces meat alternate, and ⅛ cup vegetable).
9. **Critical Control Point (CCP).** This safety issue is described in more detail in Chapter 8, "Food Safety." USDA recipes have been updated with CCP information. Any recipes from other sources will need the CCP added to the directions.
10. **Additional Information**. Include other information that is helpful in preparation, menu planning, serving, and ordering. For example, variations can be obtained by changing:
    - An ingredient
    - The method of cooking
    - The method of combining ingredients

Adjusting Recipes

When increasing or decreasing a recipe, the conversion factor method or conversion chart can be used. It is explained in detail in the information section of the USDA *Quantity Recipes for School Food Services*. The factor method simply stated is to first divide the number of servings needed by the base yield of the recipe (using decimals). This calculation will determine the conversion factor. The quantity of each ingredient is multiplied by the conversion factor. The factor will be greater than 1.0 when increasing the number of servings and less than 1.0 when decreasing the base yield. For example: If 475 portions are needed, follow the three steps below:

1. Divide 475 by the yield of the recipe (50 portions); 475 ÷ 50 = 9.5 factor, or if the recipe is for 100 portions, the factor is 4.75.
2. Convert measures to weights (Molt's *Food for Fifty*, 13th edition [2010], or the USDA *Food Buying Guide* [1984, rev. 2012] for conversion tables).
3. Multiply the weight of each ingredient by the factor to obtain the amount to be used for the number of servings desired (see Exhibit 7-3). The formula is:

$$\frac{\text{New Yield}}{\text{Base Yield}} = \text{Conversion Factor}$$

4. Convert to easy to measure or weigh quantities.

Exhibit 7-3 Adjusting a Recipe for Grilled Cheese Sandwich

Ingredients	Base Yield 100 Portions Weights Measures	For 475 × Conversion Factor =	New Yield 475 Portions Weights Measures
Cheese, Sliced Low-fat, 1 oz	6 lb 4 oz (6.25 lb)	× 4.75 =	29 lb 11 oz (29.7 lb)
Margarine, Light, Melted OR Butter, Melted	8 oz (0.5 lb)	× 4.75 =	2 lb 6 oz (2.4 lb)
Bread, Sliced (20/loaf)	200 slices or 10 loaves	× 4.75 =	950 slices or 48 loaves

Computer software, such as Heartland's NUTRIKIDS and Horizon's BOSS, manage recipes. These programs provide for pre-costing recipes/menus, increasing yield of recipes, and determining nutrients provided. The advantages of the computer calculation are:

- Accurate extensions of quantities
- Convenience of determining exact quantities (the number of portions)
- Quick conversions
- Conversion of quantities to the largest measurable units

Leftovers are costly and are being "made" every day by not correctly adjusting recipes when the need changes. The attitude of the cook may be, "I've always made this recipe for 350" (they serve 275) thus creating 75 servings of leftovers.

Quality Control

Quality control starts with the quality of the ingredients that make up the product. To maintain the quality takes careful handling during:

- The delivery process
- Preparation
- Storage and holding on site up to the point of service
- Storage and reuse of leftovers

Using a standardized recipe, using standardized measures, and following the directions in the recipe or on the package are necessary to obtain a good-quality safe product. Regrettably, the quality of a product is often damaged after cooking or heating, while it is being kept hot. Food is ready too long before serving because:

- A fear the food will not be ready on time.
- The employees want to eat together before serving lunch, rather than eating in shifts.
- Too much slack time before breakfast is served and between breakfast and lunch. Better scheduling of when employees come to work can resolve this problem.

A quality assurance program is needed for checking food receiving procedures, food-handling practices, and serving techniques at the school level. Quality assurance is also important for determining whether the customer is satisfied with the quality of food served. Large operations (with four or more employees) may find it saves time and quantity of food ingredients to have one person weighing and measuring and setting up the work center for the other employees. This "quality and quantity control" process is a modified ingredient room approach to controlling quality and quantity.

MANAGING PRODUCTION

Managing or supervising production of food is an important role, and in most small to average-size schools it is the role of the manager. Many managers are in their offices doing paperwork when their supervision is needed in the kitchen. Many good sources of information are available from USDA and the foodservice industry on the details of producing food. It is important for the manager or the person supervising to know what defines a good-quality product; otherwise, the lasagna may not look like lasagna or the spaghetti and meat sauce may be unfit to eat. Recipes may be standardized and seem complete with enough detail in directions and still not communicate to the person preparing the recipe how the product should look—and certainly not how it should taste. Graphic illustrations or photos of the steps and finished products are helpful.

Production Records

The production records, which are required by USDA (federal regulations), should demonstrate how meal requirements have been met. In addition, production records are a good management tool that documents the use of inventory. The records should provide:

- An audit trail to determine whether enough food was planned and prepared to serve the appropriate portion size.
- Information to guide the one in charge of production as to how much to prepare the next time the menu is served.

With the introduction of "offer versus serve" into the school lunch and breakfast programs, it is more difficult, indeed nearly impossible, to determine by auditing production records alone, if enough food is available so each student can be served the required meal pattern.

The information on a completed production record shows how the federal meal requirements are met. The information on the record should conform to what the state agency requires. Some tips to make the job easier are:

- Plan a short menu cycle.
- Use standardized recipes for each item on the menu. If a recipe is not available, develop one. Secret ingredients need to be put on the recipe.

- Make the production record a part of the menu-planning process.
- Complete part of the record in the centralized food and nutrition services office (e.g., recipe numbers, portion size).
- Do forecasting before placing orders.
- One or more employees can record quantity produced.
- Record quantity of leftovers and plan use immediately after service of the meal.

Production Board

A production board is different from production records, though both show how much to prepare. In a large kitchen, the board can help each department (main dish, salad, sandwich) know what to prepare and how many to prepare. Many school districts have purchased a form of chalkboards or the white wipe-off boards (40" × 60") where special pens are used in various colors. This board sits in a visible spot in the production area.

A production board controls production, and should be easy for employees to see and follow.

If short menu cycles are used, this production board is easier to maintain than if a long menu cycle is used. Exhibit 7-4 illustrates the use of the production board. The manager or production supervisor may use it to:

- Record the number of portions to prepare.
- Assign the persons responsible.

The person assigned to take care of leftovers can record the number served, which then becomes the forecasted number for the next week when a one-week cycle menu is used. The one-week cycle menus work only when several choices are made available.

Exhibit 7-4 Example of a Production Board

Menu Item	Monday	Tuesday	Wednesday	Thursday	Friday
LUNCH Mama's Kitchen	Crispy Chicken 50 BBQ Ribs 35	Hot Wings/ Roll 45 Hot Ham 'n' Cheese 40	Chicken Nuggets 75 Roast Beef 25	Baked Potato 50 Local Special 35	Country Fried Steak 75 Macaroni Ham & Cheese 25
Fiesta Fare	Beefy Burrito 40 Taco Basket 35	Enchiladas 45 Red Beans & Rice 40	Chicken Fajita 50 Nachos and Cheese 100	Beefy Bean Burrito 50 Frito Pie 50	Crunchy Tacos with Meat 50 Jumbo Tostado 50
Pizzeria COMBO I	Double Cheese Pizza 325	Cheese/Saus Pizza 300	Cheese/ Pepperoni Pizza 325	Double Cheese Pizza 325	Cheese/ Pepperoni Pizza 350
COMBO II	Chicken Parmesan/ Roll 50	Spaghetti/ Meat Sauce/ French Bread 100	Cheese Ravioli/ French Bread 50	Lasagna/ French Bread 75	Macaroni Ham 'n' Cheese 50
Grille Works COMBO I COMBO II	Hamburger 50 Cheese-Burger 250 Hot Dog 50	Hamburger 50 Cheese-burger 250 BBQ Ribs 60	Hamburger 50 Cheese-burger 250 Chicken Fillet 60	Hamburger 40 Cheese-burger 230 Steak Sub100	Hamburger 50 Cheese-burger 250 Fishburger 50
Sub Shop COMBO I	Tuna Salad 50	Italian Sub 30	Roast Beef Sub 40	Ham & Cheese 50	Chicken Salad Sub 30
COMBO II	Sliced Turkey 30	Ham & Cheese 50	Italian Deli 40	Grilled Chicken 35	Sliced Turkey & Cheese 50
Chef Salads	Turkey 25	Ham & Cheese 25	Egg & Cheese 23	Ham & Cheese 25	Sliced Turkey 25

Source: Pannell-Martin and Applebaum, 2005.

Note: This example does not reflect the complete and current menu requirements. It is an example of production board for directing employees of assignments.

Scheduling Just-in-Time or Batch Cooking

Scheduling just-in-time cooking to match what is needed for service is a skill that has to be learned. Unfortunately, not many school foodservice cooks practice just-in-time or batch cooking. The advantages of using these techniques are:

- Helps maintain quality
- Helps keep hot food hot and cold food cold
- Reduces waste

Hot foods in particular need to be cooked by batch (in quantities needed for a short period of time), as close to serving time as possible. Most student complaints about quality will be due to cooking too far ahead, not about the quality of the ingredients that go into the product.

To schedule cooking close to service, the cook needs to know how long it will take for the product to cook and the amount of time to prepare for service. Regrettably, only a few time studies have been conducted, and many recipes do not provide information on preparation time. A number of variables need to be considered; therefore, it may be necessary for standards to be set locally or within the state. (An example of a time study is shown in Exhibit 7-5.) All recipes should indicate how many minutes preparation will take. If work scheduling is prepared by computer software, the time required for each recipe must be calculated.

Work schedules will help direct employees as to when the cooking/preparation should take place. Chapter 5, "Personnel and Staffing," has an example of a work schedule.

Portion Control

Portion control means giving a specific quantity of food for a definite price and obtaining the number of servings planned from

Exhibit 7-5 Example of a Time Study on How Long Different Jobs Take (in Minutes)

Cut watermelon into portions (100 6 oz portions)	20 minutes
Butter toast for browning in oven. Use four 18" × 26" pans with 24 portions in with each, 96 portions	3 minutes
Prepare cinnamon toast for browning in oven. Use 4 18" × 26" pans with 24 portions in each, 96 portions	5 minutes
Fill and roll 96 burritos	6½ minutes
Assemble 100 hamburgers in buns	10 minutes
Make 100 mini ham and cheese submarine sandwiches (using hot dog–size rolls, 2 oz of ham, and ½ oz of cheese)	17 minutes
Make and cut 100 peanut butter and jelly sandwiches (applying peanut butter and jelly separately)	25 minutes
Fill tortillas and roll into 120 quesadillas	18 minutes
Fill and roll 120 tacos with meat and cheese	20 minutes
Assemble 96 grilled (toasted) cheese sandwiches	8 minutes
Ice (frost) and cut an 18" × 26" cake into 50 pieces	1 minute
Pan cookies for baking – 96 portions	7½ minutes
Portion 96 lettuce and tomato cups (servings)	12 minutes
Pack 100 bag lunches with fruit, vegetable, cookies, sandwich, napkin, and straw	20 minutes

Source: Major, 1996.

a given recipe. Portion control plays an important part in cost control and meeting the dietary guidelines. For example, if a roll recipe for 100 portions yields only 90 rolls, the cost per roll goes up. When food cost is high, one of the reasons may be the lack of portion control—serving portions that are too large are frequently the case.

Some of the essential tools needed to achieve portion control are slicers, scales, scoops (spoodles or dishers), ladles, and other measurers. Scoops and ladles come in different sizes. Menu planners usually determine portion sizes, and should make certain the tools are available. Charts like the ones in Exhibits 7-6, 7-7, and 7-8

Exhibit 7-6 Common Abbreviations, Equivalents, and Scoop (Dipper) Equivalent Chart

COMMON WEIGHTS AND EQUIVALENTS:			PORTIONING TOOLS AND EQUIVALENTS:		
1 ounce	=	2 Tbsp = ⅛ cup	**Scoop/Spoodle Size**		**Measure**
8 ounces	=	1 cup	No. 6	=	⅔ cup
1 pound	=	1 pint = 16 ounces	No. 8	=	½ cup
COMMON MEASUREMENTS AND EQUIVALENTS:			No. 10	=	⅜ cup
3 teaspoons	=	1 Tbsp	No. 12	=	⅓ cup
4 tablespoons	=	¼ cup	No. 16	=	¼ cup
8 tablespoons	=	½ cup	No. 24	=	2 ⅔ Tbsp
16 tablespoons	=	1 cup	No. 30	=	2 ⅕ Tbsp
1 cup	=	½ pint	**Ladle Size**		**Measure**
2 cups	=	1 pint	1 ounce	=	⅛ cup
2 pints	=	1 quart	2 ounce	=	¼ cup
4 quarts	=	1 gallon	4 ounce	=	½ cup
1 gallon	=	16 1-cup servings	8 ounce	=	1 cup
	=	32 ½-cup servings			
	=	40 ⅜-cup servings			
	=	48 ⅓-cup servings			
	=	64 ¼-cup servings			
1 quart	=	4 1-cup servings			
	=	8 ½-cup servings			
	=	10 ⅜-cup servings			
	=	12 ⅓-cup servings			
	=	16 ¼-cup servings			

can be posted near the serving line. These charts will save time and can mean the difference in whether the correct portion size is served.

Establishing the number of servings that should be obtained before the portioning begins will help in obtaining the proper yield.

Exhibit 7-7 Pan Capacity and Portion Chart*

Serving Pan Size (1)	Capacity (2)	Cup Measure (3)	Scoop Number (4)	Portions Per Pan (5)
Full Size 12" × 20" × 2¼"	7½ quarts or 30 cups	¼ ⅓ ⅜ ½	16 12 10 8	120 90 80 60
Full Size 12" × 20" × 4"	13 quarts or 52 cups	¼ ⅓ ⅜ ½	16 12 10 8	208 156 138 104
Full Size 12" × 20" × 6"	19½ quarts or 78 cups	¼ ⅓ ⅜ ½ 1	16 12 10 8 8 oz ladle	312 234 208 156 78
Half Size 12" × 10" × 2½"	3¾ quarts or 15 cups	¼ ⅓ ⅜ ½	16 12 10 8	60 45 40 30
Half Size 12" × 10" × 4"	6½ quarts or 26 cups	¼ ⅓ ⅜ ½	16 12 10 8	104 78 69 52
Half Size 12" × 10" × 6"	9¾ quarts or 39 cups	¼ ⅓ ⅜ ½ 1	16 12 10 8 8 oz ladle	156 117 104 78 39
Third Size 12" × 6 ⅞" × 2½"	2⅖ quarts or 9 cups + 9 tablespoons	⅛ ¼ ⅓ ⅜	30 16 12 10	76 38 28 25
Third Size 12" × 6 ⅞" × 4"	3⅞ quarts or 15½ cups	⅛ ¼ ⅓ ⅜	30 16 12 10	124 62 46 41

*These are approximate numbers, depending on how full the pans are. See "Basics at a Glance," National Food Service Management Institute, 2004 for additional information.

This information should be written on the recipe, and if the recipe does not yield the number of portions planned, it needs to be noted on the recipe.

A precosted recipe will need to be changed to reflect the actual number of portions obtained from the recipe. Many foods are purchased today by portion, making it easier to control yield. Pre-portioning items like chilled fruit cups, tossed salad, and sliced meats before service can also help with speeding service and reducing number of employees during serving time, and help control portions. The portioning/weighing out of meats ahead is a good "downtime" job (when workers have free time). An inexperienced employee can be taught to do this job quite well.

Exhibit 7-8 Example of Scoop Equivalent Chart

Scoop Size	Measure	Weight
#6	= ⅔ cup	5 ounce
Example: Tuna, Chicken, and Turkey Salad for Sub		
#8	= ½ cup	4 ounce
Example: Fruit, Mashed Potatoes, Hot Green Vegetables, Tuna, Chicken, and Turkey Salad; Meat Sauce for Spaghetti		
#10	= 6 tablespoons	3 ounce
#12	= ⅓ cup	2½ ounce
Example: Chili for Nachos		
#16	= ¼ cup	2 ounce
Example: Cheese Sauce for Nachos		
#20	= 3 tablespoons	½ ounce
#24	= 2⅔ tablespoons	1⅓ ounce
#30	= 2 tablespoons	1 ounce
Example: Cream Cheese or Peanut Butter for Bagel		
#40	= 1⅗ tablespoons	⅘ ounce

Food Presentation and Garnishing

The preparation of good food is an important step to customer satisfaction, but how the food is presented and garnished can make a difference to the overall customer satisfaction. Food may be of excellent quality but be dull and uninteresting in appearance, so the customer won't try it because of how it looks. Does the food have that "cafeteria look" or does it look so good that customers can't resist it? A high school boy's comment about the school cafeteria food was, "I wish it showed you cared." Garnishing refers to the serving and decorating of food in such a way as to make the food more appealing. People tend to select food based on its appearance, and students notice the difference. A meal of excellent quality may be perceived as dull and uninteresting because of presentation—or it can be mouth-watering and interesting-looking.

Eye appeal is influenced by the color and shape of food, dishes/containers in which the food is served, portion size, neatness, and expectations caused by the food's appearance. Garnishing is the finishing touch that makes food look better and increases its eye appeal. A garnish can be as simple as a sprinkle of paprika or as elaborate as a radish rose. Garnishes should be:

- Cost effective
- Not time consuming
- Simple for the employees to create (not everyone is an artist)
- Seasonal and appropriate
- Natural
- Simple and colorful (e.g., add color to fruit dishes, salads, etc., with red apples, leave the peel on for texture, color, and freshness)
- Varied in shapes (e.g., raw carrots chopped, grated, or cut into sticks or circles)

- Contrasting in color (e.g., small amount of fresh spinach in iceberg lettuce salad; green, white, or red onions chopped or in rings or strips; beets cut in julienne strips)
- Contrasting in texture (e.g., red, green, or white cabbage, grated or shredded)

A pastry bag (with decorative tips) is a useful garnishing tool. Whipped topping available in disposable bags, for example, dispenses topping much more attractively and efficiently than when dropped by the spoonful. A twig of parsley or a mint leaf can add the fresh look desired. The addition of red and green bell peppers to corn can create a colorful Mexican-type dish. Cutting French bread on an angle makes it look like a larger piece. The extra touch is what food presentation and effective garnishing are all about. Garnishes should become a standard part of the recipe and, in turn, the food order.

Garnishes have to be planned because they will not "just" happen. Each week's produce order should contain some materials for garnishing. In addition to planning the garnishes, how the food will be presented, the container or dish, and what condiments go with it, need to be planned. Disposable products allow more flexibility in container, but the cost must be considered.

MANAGING SERVICE

Generally, food in schools is served cafeteria style. Today very few colleges, universities, and commercial foodservices display the food cafeteria style in the traditional pans—it is becoming an outdated style of service. Self-service for vegetables, as well as salad/deli bars, are popular in schools, but hard to control. Family style is used in few instances in schools. Setting up the serving area/line or the self-service bar correctly is essential to efficient service and needs to be planned. California and Texas have probably led the way in schools with food courts and window-type service, particularly in high schools.

A diagram of where food will be placed on the line or on a cart can reduce the possibility of leaving something off or placing it in an inappropriate area. When time is important, the setup has to consider every movement of the server/cashier in order to reduce wasted motion and increase speed of service.

Time Required to Serve

The principal usually schedules elementary students to eat by class at a specific time. These schedules can work well by encouraging just-in-time or batch cooking. But, ordinarily, middle and high school students go in larger groups and have fewer lunch periods (e.g., 11:30 a.m.–12:00 noon, 12:00 noon–12:30 p.m.). Secondary school students are not willing to stand in line more than 10 minutes. If the rate of service is 10–12 meals per minute, then a line of more than 100 students will cause discontent.

Running out of food slows a serving line. Not having the advertised menu items and having to make students wait while more food is prepared delays a line and makes for unhappy customers. Students may be forgiving the first time (usually), but not after repeated occurrences.

In recent years, block scheduling in some high schools has meant one lunch period and an entire student body. The story in Chapter 4, "Foodservice Management Systems and Facilities," shows how San Benito (TX) district's staff adjusted to one lunch period. Additional serving areas and people, pre-portioning, and packaging food, will speed service. All the students are served during the same lunch period. The San Diego (CA) Unified School District, as do many other school districts, employs students to serve/sell food during meal service. San Diego has been quite successful using students with the window-type service. The students are paid and trained—the result is an efficient operation.

Temperature of Food

Hot food should be served hot (not cold), and cold food served cold (not warm). The serving temperature should be appropriate to each food. Hot food should be served hot–135° F. Chapter 8, "Food Safety," discusses the importance of temperature. Little is written on "how" best to hold cooked foods at the appropriate temperature; however, more damage occurs to quality during the holding period, after the food is cooked, than at any other stage of the process. The newer temperature and humidity-controlled heated holding cabinets help maintain a high-quality product, but they do not take the place of just-in-time cooking.

Just-in-time, or cooking in batches according to need, should be encouraged when feasible to prevent food from having to be held for long periods of time (discussed earlier). Hot- and cold-holding equipment placed near the serving line can help provide the proper temperatures necessary for safe and good-quality food.

How Food Is Served

How food is served, as well as the type of container used to serve the food, makes a difference in appearance. For example, serving hamburgers and other sandwiches in wraps as used by fast-food restaurants has been found to increase customer satisfaction and keep the sandwiches warm longer. However, the cost has to be considered. Can the cost of the serving container be justified? For example, serving fresh fruit wedges or vegetable sticks in clear sandwich bags makes portion control easier and keeps the freshness longer. Students feel content because all serving are the same size. Using a serving style similar to popular restaurants and making the portions look much the same may be desirable.

Novel ways of serving food will spark interest. For example, some districts prepare peanut butter and jelly sandwiches, cut into quarters, and call them "lunchables" or "biteables." Another idea is to package for "doing it yourself." This is done by putting the ingredients for a peanut butter and jelly sandwich (No. 30 scoop of peanut butter, No. 30 scoop of jelly, and two slices of bread cut in half with a disposable small knife) in a disposable tray (like a nacho tray). This idea of making your own sandwich can be fun for elementary children and often increases the popularity of this menu item.

Attitude of Employees

The attitude of employees toward their jobs and the customers makes a lot of difference in how customers feel about the school's food. Too often, when students are questioned about their school cafeteria, they complain that those serving the food are "mean," "always grumpy," or "always yelling." It is important to be friendly, patient, and nurturing to the first graders and kindergarten children, who at the first of the school year may be frightened and uncertain. Those students will be the customers for the next six years.

The people on the serving lines and at the cashier stands can make the difference in school foodservices. It doesn't matter if the student paid for the meal or it is free; the student deserves to be treated as a customer. Restaurants and retail stores have learned (or are learning) that the people who come in contact with the customers are instrumental to the success of the establishment.

The attitude of the foodservice employee toward the students, the school staff, and the job influences the number of meals served. Many famous people thank their school lunch employees for their successes in life. It is important for the foodservice employee to be customer focused. The customer may be having a terrible day in class, but the cafeteria is the one positive place to go and have a good breakfast or lunch.

USING LEFTOVERS

A key to controlling or reducing food costs is to forecast, order, and prepare **just enough** food for the number of customers served. It is impossible to always meet this goal because of unexpected events that may occur. "That's all we've got" is an undesirable reply. The customer may be so disappointed and turn away. On the other hand, excessive leftovers can be expensive.

Restaurants that stay in business and school foodservices that have low food costs usually are the ones that (among other good practices) utilize their leftovers. Planning the use of leftovers is a job that should be assigned to someone. Leftovers should be documented on the production record when left over and on the production record on the day they will be used. With the new menu planning requirements, managers must work leftovers into the menus carefully as choices with like items.

USDA has sponsored a "National Summit on Food Recovery and Gleaning," with the purpose of encouraging school foodservices to utilize food leftovers to serve people in need. While helping the hungry is commendable, the goal of the foodservice manager should be to plan well so not enough food is left over on a typical day to make it worth picking up for distribution elsewhere.

SUMMARY

All the regulations and management skills come together when the food is prepared and served to the customers. If the manager and staff prepare nutritious, top-quality meals within the budget, and make the customers (students and school staff) feel good about the experience, the goals have been met.

QUESTIONS AND ANSWERS

1. Forecasting accurately food and supply needs influences the food cost.
   a. True
   b. False
2. A manager needs the following to order just enough just in time:
   a. Financial report from prior month
   b. Last month's order, recipes, and line setup
   c. Menus, recipes, and production records
   d. A lot of experience and time
3. Convenience foods are always more expensive than fresh foods.
   a. True
   b. False
4. The purpose of food preparation is to:
   a. Make foods more digestible and safer to eat
   b. Conserve nutritive value and keep quality
   c. Improve flavor and appearance
   d. All of the above
5. A standardized recipe is:
   a. Developed in a laboratory
   b. Tested for consistency and yield
   c. Requires a specialist
   d. Less expensive than nonstandardized recipes

ANSWERS: 1.a., 2.c., 3.b., 4.d., 5.b.

REFERENCES

Boettger, J. & Story, C. 2013. "To Chop Or Not To Chop," presentation at SNA Annual Conference.

Major, Y. 1996. *Work methods: Work smarter not harder.* San Diego, CA: San Diego Unified School District, Food Services Department.

Molt, M. 2010. *Food for fifty,* 13th ed. New York: Prentice Hall.

Morgan, E. 2010. *On the road to professional food preparation,* 2nd ed. NFSMI ET5-03. University, MS: The National Food Service Management Institute.

National Food Service Management Institute. 2004. *Basics at a glance.* University, MS: Author.

National Food Service Management Institute. 2008. *No time to train.* University, MS: Author.

Ninemeier, J. 2010. *Management of food and beverage operations,* 5th ed. East Lansing, MI: The Educational Institute of the American Hotel and Motel Association.

Pannell-Martin, D. & Applebaum, G. 2005. *inTEAM Food System manager's manual.* Santa Monica, CA: inTEAM Associates, Inc.

Theis, M. & Payne-Palacio, J. 2008. *West and Wood's introduction to foodservice,* 13th ed. Upper Saddle River, NJ: Prentice-Hall, Inc.

U.S. Department of Agriculture. 2013. *Food buying guide for child nutrition.* Retrieved September 25, 2013, from http://www.fns.usda.gov/tn/resources/foodbuying guide.

ONLINE RESOURCES

NFSMI's Recipes for Schools
http://www.nfsmi.org/Templates/TemplateDefault.aspx?gs=cEIEPTEwMG==

Now We're Cooking: A Collection of Simple Scratch Recipes Served in Minnesota Schools
http://healthymeals.nal.usda.gov/hsmrs/Minnesota/now-were-cooking.pdf

School Day Just Got Healthier: Showcase of Chef Recipe Book
http://healthymeals.nal.usda.gov/hsmrs/Michigan/showcaseofchefs.pdf

USDA Recipes for Schools (Standardized Recipes)
http://teamnutrition.usda.gov/Resources/usda_recipes.html

Whole Grain Recipes for School Foodservice 2012 Edition (Whole Grains Council)
http://wholegrainscouncil.org/files/WGFoodserviceRecipes2012.pdf

Chapter 8

Food Safety

STUDY QUESTIONS

1. What regulations address food safety in school nutrition programs?
2. What are the primary components of a food safety plan based on HACCP principles?
3. What does *food tracking* mean, and what relevance does it have in school nutrition programs?
4. List two common foodborne illnesses.
5. What should be checked regularly and recorded in logs?
6. What is the difference between food safety and food defense?
7. How can a recalled product be identified?
8. What steps are necessary to prepare for food-related incidents?

Chapter 8

"Allergen Cross-Contamination"

by Mary Swift, BS, RD, LD, SNS

Executive Director of Food and Nutrition Services, Albuquerque Public Schools (NM)

We received USDA commodity walnuts and decided to make candied spiced nuts as a treat for students. All students with documented tree nut allergies sat at their nut-free tables and did not receive the walnuts. Later that afternoon, a teacher with a tree nut allergy had a reaction requiring an EpiPen® (epinephrine). After interviewing the teacher it was determined that, she did not eat the walnuts or any other food containing tree nuts.

After an investigation, it was discovered students went into the computer lab after lunch. The allergen was traced to a keyboard in the computer lab. A student who had eaten the walnuts had also used the keyboard. The teacher then used the same keyboard after the student.

Although this incident was linked to the computer keyboard, the incident could have been caused by any number of contact surfaces such as a student touching a doorknob or turning on a water faucet. Students with severe allergies are not completely protected unless all sources of cross-contamination are identified and processes put in place to eliminate potential contamination.

This incident could have been prevented by requiring all students and staff to wash their hands after meals. It is not always possible to eliminate all sources of an allergen within a school. Implementing procedures that eliminate allergens from all food-contact surfaces, including customers' hands, provides an added layer of protection.

School nutrition policies have been changing to enable schools to comply with new laws and to shift the approach of food safety from considering risks within the operator's organization to thinking about risks along the entire school nutrition supply chain.

INTRODUCTION TO FOOD SAFETY

Signed into law in 2011, the Food Safety Modernization Act addresses the prevention of foodborne illness as well as minimizing the impact of food-related incidents by improving the ability to track foods from "farm to fork."

Ensuring that school food and nutrition service management purchase products produced, manufactured, and transported safely is as important as keeping products safe once the food arrives on the dock. When food-related problems do arise, every entity that handled the product must quickly obtain information about where the product was received, sold, or served. These modifications require school food and nutrition service management to stay abreast of changes in regulations, adopt new practices, and enhance record keeping in order to verify compliance.

REGULATIONS

Federal, state, and sometimes local agencies regulate food safety in school food and nutrition service programs, which can be confusing to a new manager since regulations between agencies may conflict. A good place to begin is with the state agency responsible for school nutrition programs administration. The state agency representatives know the federal regulations related to school nutrition and are familiar with the state public health laws as well. In some locations, a county or city may also maintain a health department that inspects local foodservice operations such as restaurants, hospitals, and schools. The Department of Public Health determines the *Food Code* in use by the state.

Because most food companies sell and transport products between states, three federal agencies regulate products purchased by schools.

Federal Agencies Responsible for Regulating Food Production and Manufacturing

USDA, Food Safety and Inspection Service: Meat, poultry, and whole shell eggs

U.S. Department of Commerce, National Marine Fisheries Service: Seafood

U.S. Department of Health and Human Services, Food and Drug Administration: All foods other than seafood, meat, poultry, and whole shell eggs

In order for schools to serve food that is safe to eat, the whole supply chain of production, processing, and delivery must ensure safe conditions. Food safety audit programs assist buyers in determining food is safe. These programs include:

- Good Agricultural Practices for fruit and vegetable growers
- Good Handling Practices for produce packers
- Qualified Through Verification for fresh-cut produce
- Good Manufacturing Practices for food processors and manufacturers

These programs ensure compliance with basics such as clean water and soil, employee hygiene, equipment sanitation, and other food safety processes. Accurate records of food temperatures, inspections, and training must be maintained and accessible in the event of a food-related incident. Organizations across the supply chain must track every food ingredient used "one step back and one step forward." In other words, the ingredient is tracked from the source of the product to the buyer. This requirement is a critical piece in solving the cause of foodborne illness or contamination incidents.

One important element of audit programs is verification of the effectiveness of the organizations' Hazard Analysis & Critical Control Points (HACCP) food safety program. HACCP is a food safety management program that examines biological, allergenic, physical, and chemical hazards from the point of procurement through consumption by the end user. Since 2006, schools have been required to develop and implement a food safety plan based on HACCP principles.

Food Safety Plan

To ensure the safety of all food items served in schools, Section 302 9(h) (5) of the Richard B. Russell National School Lunch Act requires schools to develop and implement a food safety plan based on HACCP principles. The plan must cover any facility or part of a facility where food is stored, prepared, or served, including hallways, classrooms, vending machines, buses, and outside locations such as courtyards (USDA, 2013).

The food safety program must include a written plan for each facility that stores, prepares, or serves food. The schools plans must address:

> **Standard Operating Procedure (SOP)**
>
> A standard operating procedure, commonly referred to as SOP, is a set of detailed written instructions to provide consistency in the performance of a task.

- Cleanliness and sanitation of employees, food contact surfaces, utensils, and equipment
- Temperature control during storage, preparation, holding, and service of food

- SOPs for addressing sanitation and cleanliness
- Staff training to properly implement SOPs
- Process for monitoring compliance with SOPs at least once a month
- Corrective action when SOPs are not followed
- Recordkeeping to provide proof that all provisions of the plan are met
- Evaluation procedures to review and update the plan on an ongoing or annual basis

The National Food Service Management Institute (NFSMI) has an excellent template to assist schools in developing a food safety plan. The "Online Resources" section of this chapter provides a link to the template.

Inspections

Schools are required to have a minimum of two health inspections each year. The *Food Code* adopted by the state and local public health jurisdiction, governs the inspections. Typically, inspectors conduct risk-based inspections and note the areas of deficiency as critical or noncritical.

Risk-based inspections target establishments that have a history of critical deficiencies, prepare several menu items the day before service, serve a large number of people, serve a vulnerable population, or have a history of complaints or foodborne illnesses. These criteria rank establishments on a scale of 1 to 4, with 1 being the least risky. Because of the population they serve, schools are generally ranked as 3 and preschools are ranked 4.

Critical violations are issues that may lead to a health hazard. Critical violations fall within five broad areas recognized as foodborne illness risk factors:

1. Food from unsafe sources
2. Inadequate cooking
3. Improper holding temperatures
4. Contaminated equipment
5. Poor personal hygiene

Noncritical violations usually do not lead directly to a foodborne illness. Examples include general cleanliness and equipment maintenance. Time frames for correcting critical violations are usually short and require a follow-up visit. Noncritical violations must be addressed by the next scheduled inspection.

Each school is required to post the most recent health inspection report in a location that is visible to the public. School districts are also required to provide a copy of the report to anyone requesting it. Many schools post the report on their websites.

Food Code

Every four years the Food and Drug Administration (FDA) publishes the *Food Code* for more than 3,000 state and local agencies to use as a model on which to base their own food safety rules. Although it is not law or a regulation, the *Food Code* is based on current scientific research and legal regulations covering management and personnel; food; equipment and utensils; water, plumbing and waste; facilities; poisonous or toxic materials; and compliance and enforcement.

Many states adopted FDA's 2009 *Food Code* and aligned state and local regulations with this version. Supplements are published between versions when new food safety–related science or regulations indicate a change is necessary. A link to the newly released 2013 *Food Code* is under "Online Resources" at the end of this chapter. A Spanish version of the *Food Code* and previous versions of the *Food Code* can be found on the FDA's webpage.

HAZARD ANALYSIS AND CRITICAL CONTROL POINTS

Some school districts have been utilizing HACCP principles for many years. When Congress passed legislation requiring schools to develop written food safety plans, USDA decided to use HACCP as a basis for the plan but did not require schools to implement HACCP in its entirety. The effectiveness of HACCP is based on having established prerequisite programs addressing issues such as the following:

- Basic sanitation and cleanliness procedures
- Vendor certification programs
- Employee training programs
- Allergen management
- Recipe/process instructions
- First in, first out procedures for storage
- Other SOPs

Once prerequisite programs are in place, the food and nutrition service director is to implement HACCP's seven principles.

HACCP Principles

Principle 1: Conduct a hazard analysis.

Principle 2: Determine the critical control points.

Principle 3: Establish critical limits.

Principle 4: Establish monitoring procedures.

Principle 5: Establish corrective actions.

Principle 6: Establish verification procedures.

Principle 7: Establish record keeping and documentation procedures.

Process Approach

A process approach to HACCP takes a proactive effort in eliminating hazards at each step of the food production process.

Temperature control is critical to preventing foodborne illnesses. Each time a food passes through the temperature danger zone (41° F to 135° F), the risk of a food safety problem increases. To identify the potential hazard, menu items are classified by how many times they pass through the temperature danger zone. Exhibit 8-1 indicates these occurrences by the lightly shaded process steps.

Exhibit 8-1 Steps in Food Production Process

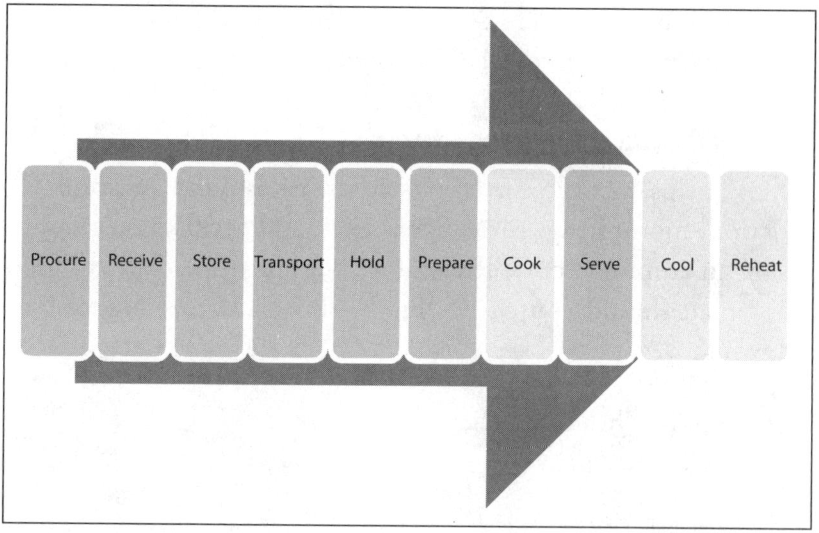

Hazard Analysis and Control Measures

Menu items prepared or served at each facility, fall in one of these three following categories:

1. No cook – refers to foods that do not pass through the temperature danger zone (e.g., ready to eat foods).
2. Same day – refers to foods that pass through the temperature danger zone once (e.g., foods heated and discarded if not consumed).

3. Complex – refers to foods that pass through the temperature danger zone more than once (e.g., foods heated and later cooled).

It is possible within the same school district to classify the same menu items differently. For example, spaghetti prepared at a central kitchen and chilled before transporting to a satellite school would be classified as a "complex" item. At the satellite facility, spaghetti may be classified as "same day" if it is heated and leftovers discarded.

Control measures are established to prevent or reduce hazards. Control measures include SOPs and identification of critical control points essential to preventing foodborne illnesses.

Standard Operating Procedures

A SOP helps to train an employee on a task and contains instruction, monitoring, corrective action, and verification steps to ensure an employee completes the task correctly. A district's food safety plan should contain SOPs (Exhibit 8-2) that address the following:

- Employee health policies
- Personal hygiene
- Cleaning and sanitizing
- All steps in the food production process for foods that are time- and temperature-controlled for safety
- Use and calibration of thermometers
- Use and storage of chemicals

Monitoring

The monitoring component of a SOP ensures compliance and provides corrective actions when the outcome of a task is not what was

Exhibit 8-2 Sample Standard Operating Procedure

CONTROLLING TIME AND TEMPERATURE DURING PREPARATION

PURPOSE: To prevent foodborne illness by limiting the amount of time that potentially hazardous foods are held in the temperature danger zone during preparation.

INSTRUCTIONS:

1. Wash hands prior to preparing foods. Refer to the Washing Hands SOP.
2. Use clean and sanitized equipment and utensils while preparing food.
3. Separate raw foods from ready-to-eat foods by keeping them in separate containers until ready to use and by using separate dispensing utensils.
4. Prechill ingredients for cold foods, such as sandwiches, salads, and cut melons, to 41° F or below before combining with other ingredients.
5. Prepare foods in small batches as close to serving times as the menu will allow.
6. Limit the time for preparation of any batches of food so that ingredients are not at room temperature for more than 30 minutes before cooking, serving, or being returned to the refrigerator.
7. If potentially hazardous foods are not cooked or served immediately after preparation, quickly chill.

MONITORING:

1. Use a clean, sanitized, and calibrated probe thermometer.
2. Take at least two internal temperatures from each pan of food at various stages of preparation.
3. Monitor the amount of time that food is in the temperature danger zone. It should not exceed 4 hours.

CORRECTIVE ACTIONS:

1. Retrain any foodservice employee found not following the procedures in this SOP.

(*Continued*)

Exhibit 8-2 *(Continued)*

2. Begin the cooking process immediately after preparation is complete for any foods that will be served hot.
3. Rapidly cool ready-to-eat foods or foods that will be cooked at a later time.
4. Immediately return ingredients to the refrigerator if the anticipated preparation completion time is expected to exceed 30 minutes.
5. Discard food held in the temperature danger zone for more than 4 hours.

VERIFICATION AND RECORD KEEPING:

Foodservice employees will record the date, product name, start and end times of production, the two temperature measurements taken, any corrective actions taken, and the amount of food prepared on the Production Log. The foodservice manager will verify that foodservice employees are taking the required temperatures and following the proper preparation procedure by visually monitoring foodservice employees during the shift and reviewing, initialing, and dating the Production Log daily. The foodservice manager will complete the Food Safety Checklist daily. Keep the Food Safety Checklist on file for a minimum of 1 year.

DATE IMPLEMENTED: ________________ **BY:** ________________

DATE REVIEWED: ________________ **BY:** ________________

DATE REVISED: ________________ **BY:** ________________

Source: NFSMI, 2005.

expected. The SOP should indicate who is monitoring the outcome of the task.

A food safety checklist assists the process and allows monitoring of several SOPs at one time. A manager or assigned employee completes the checklist. When a task is not completed correctly, the corrective action should be indicated on the checklist. Once completed, the checklist serves as verification the tasks included were completed correctly.

Record Keeping

In addition to a checklist, a food safety plan may also include other types of record keeping such as logs. Several different types of logs are recommended for school food and nutrition programs, including the following:

- Cooking temperatures
- Cooling temperatures and time
- Reheating temperatures
- Refrigeration/freezer temperatures
- Thermometer calibration
- Receiving temperatures
- Damaged or discarded product
- Dish washing machine final rinse temperature
- Food safety training

Logs are maintained manually on paper or computerized. A variety of thermometers available on the market produce a printout of temperatures and sound an alarm indicating when temperatures are out of compliance. These monitors are becoming more common, especially for refrigeration and dish washing machines. When an automated temperature monitoring system is used, it is important to train staff to check reports frequently and to record corrective action when needed.

SOP and Standardized Recipes

A properly written recipe is an SOP for preparing a menu item. It should contain:

- Process classification (no cook, same day, complex)
- Critical control points
- Critical limits
- Record of temperatures and time intervals (e.g., production record, temperature log)

The verification or monitoring section of an SOP clarifies to management and agencies reviewing school food and nutrition programs whether the completion of the various tasks was done correctly. From a health department's point of view, unless a written record of compliance for food safety tasks is provided, the assumption is that the task was not completed.

Training

Food safety plans are not effective if they sit on a shelf and gather dust. Employee training is essential and *required* as part of an effective food safety plan. SOPs help train employees. Trainers can use monitoring tools for checking the effectiveness of training. It is important to keep a training agenda and roster of those trained with other school nutrition records for program accountability reviews.

FOOD TRACKING

When food-related incidents occur (e.g., recalls), school food and nutrition management must be able to accurately track food products involved. Tracking is the ability to identify the path a specific food product has taken throughout the entire food chain. Traceability requires that each entity in the supply chain do the following:

- Adopt a common manner of identifying each product.
- Know the source of a specific product.
- Know to whom a product was sold.
- Keep accurate records about the handling of products in the facility.

Food manufacturers adopted Global Trade Identification Numbers (GTINs) to standardize product identification. GTINs contain, at a minimum, GS1 company prefix, and Universal Product Code. GTINs are encoded in bar codes but also are human readable. Because barcode readers scan GTINs, product information stores easily in a database for quick retrieval.

In addition to the GTINs, information such as the date, time, and line of food production or harvested field further identifies the product. Sometimes, the GTIN includes the lot number.

> **What is GS1?**
>
> GS1 is a not-for-profit organization that assists businesses implement GS1 product identification standards for improving product safety and supply chain efficiency.

The Bioterrorism Act of 2002 requires any company that manufactures, processes, distributes, receives, holds, or imports food products to keep records on the source of food and the recipients of food from their company. Referred to as "one step back, one step forward," the company goes one link back in the supply chain and one link forward.

Although not covered under this Act, it is important for schools to know when a particular food was served and the source of the product. If prepared at a central facility, records must track each food ingredient. Records are used to determine critical tracking events and should include:

- Date of delivery
- What company delivered the food
- Date the food was used in a menu item

FOOD-RELATED INCIDENTS

Food safety policies and practices aim at preventing illnesses from food. Even when good policies are well-implemented, things can go wrong. Planning for emergencies can reduce the stress of the situation and may even create a better outcome. To prepare for emergencies, have a written plan that includes:

- SOP for each type of emergency
- Response team with clearly defined responsibilities
- List of resources to call for assistance
- Communication plan for before, during, and after the event
- Contact names and numbers for staff members

Practice emergency procedures yearly to ensure that the plan is current and complete. Schools should be prepared to deal with recalls, foodborne illness, allergy-related incidents, and natural disasters. *Food defense* is a term that means reducing or preventing hazards intentionally introduced into food. A comprehensive emergency plan also addresses incidents from intentional food contamination.

Recalls

According to a USDA study (2011), the average school district purchases more than 700 food products. Although the food supply in the United States is safe, situations occur that require recall of products. A recall is an action taken by a manufacturer to remove a product from the marketplace due to a potential health hazard. The three classifications of recall indicate the probability of a health-related problem. Exhibit 8-3 discusses the classes of recalls that occur.

When a recalled food is an ingredient used in other products, the recall process expands and becomes quite lengthy. An example was a recent recall of peanut butter used in products produced by several different manufacturers.

Exhibit 8-3 Classes of Recall

Class	Definition	Example
Class I	A health-hazard situation with a moderate probability that eating the food will cause adverse health consequences or death	Undeclared allergen or bacterial contaminate
Class 2	A health-hazard situation with a remote probability of adverse health consequences from eating the food	Foreign object found in food (e.g., plastic part from a machine)
Class 3	A situation in which eating the food will not cause adverse health consequences	Undeclared ingredient that is not an allergen

Source: NFSMI, 2013.

For schools, the recall process is different depending on whether the food is a USDA Food, a commercial product, or commercial product containing a USDA Food. When the offending food product was purchased commercially, regardless of whether it contains a USDA Food, the manufacturer is responsible for notifying all of its customers (e.g., distributors) about the recall and providing instructions about how to handle it. In most cases, schools would receive information about recalls from the distributor that sold them the product.

If the product is a USDA Food, notice of the recall, specific product information, and instructions for disposing of the product come from the state agency administering the food distribution program. USDA's Food and Nutrition Services utilizes the Rapid Alert System in the Web-Based Supply Chain Management System and the USDA State Emergency Notification System to notify state agencies so that they can track product to the recipient agencies, including school districts.

Schools must immediately isolate and label the recalled product so that it is not used. The school district must conduct an inventory and determine the amount of the product used and stored. It is crucial to determine and report the following:

- The amount served to students
- Storage of product at schools, warehouses, and with distributors
- Potential product with other program participants (e.g., day care programs)
- Product waiting to be processed by manufacturers

Within 48 hours, this information must go to the state agency. The state agency then sends the information to USDA's Food and Nutrition Services. USDA recommends school food and nutrition programs conduct mock recalls to test the effectiveness of their recall process (NFSMI, 2013).

Information Needed to Identify Recalled Products

- Company name
- Brand name
- Case markings
- Establishment number for meat, poultry, and eggs
- Can codes, lot numbers, and product dates

The food and nutrition service director may sign up to receive recall information by email from USDA. A link to the website is located in the "Online Resources" section at the end of this chapter.

Foodborne Illness

A foodborne illness is a disease transmitted to people through food. A foodborne illness becomes an outbreak when two or more people have the same symptoms from eating the same food. When these illnesses happen, the state and local regulatory authorities conduct an investigation, and laboratory analysis confirms the outbreak.

Interviewing customers to find out what they ate, when they ate, and specific symptoms can help determine whether food served at school was a possible cause of illness. In the case of suspicion of a foodborne illness, the following actions should be carried out

- Write down the name and contact information of the customer reporting the illness, what was eaten, when the food was eaten, and the symptoms.
- Secure a sample of the suspected food.
- Report the incident to the appropriate school administrator.
- Call the health department to investigate.
- Communicate relevant information to the public if the problem is widespread.

An outbreak of a foodborne illness is the nightmare of every foodservice operator. Luckily, most gastrointestinal illnesses in schools are not caused by food; however, it is important to know the organisms that cause illness, the foods typically implicated, and the time of onset. Exhibit 8-4 provides a chart of common illnesses comprising 91 percent of all foodborne illness in 2011.

Allergic Reactions

According to the Food Allergy Research and Education website, one in 13 children in the United States suffer from a food allergy. Studies have shown that 16–18 percent of students with allergies experience a reaction at school. In 25 percent of the allergy reactions at school, the student has not been diagnosed with an allergy. Clearly, these studies indicate that school personnel should know

Exhibit 8-4 Top Five Foodborne Illnesses in 2011

Disease	%	Food Implicated	Incubation	Symptoms
Norovirus	58%	Any food especially ready-to-eat foods, leafy greens, fresh fruit, shellfish	24–48 hours	Abdominal pain, nausea, vomiting, diarrhea
Salmonella	11%	Poultry, eggs, meat, and recently tomatoes, sprouts, and peanut butter	12–72 hours	Abdominal pain, fever, diarrhea
Clostridium perfringens	10%	Meat, poultry	8–12 hours	Abdominal pain, diarrhea
Campylobacter	9%	Undercooked poultry, water, unpasteurized dairy, or cross-contamination from these products	2–5 days	Diarrhea, which may be bloody, fever, nausea
Staphylococcus	3%	Ready-to-eat foods, deli meats, puddings, pastries	1–6 hours	Nausea, cramps, vomiting, dehydration

Source: CDC, 2011.

the symptoms of an allergic reaction and be prepared to respond to the emergency. Allergy-related online resources are available at end of this chapter.

Eight foods account for 90 percent of all allergic reactions. A severe and potentially fatal allergic reaction is "anaphylaxis." Although any allergens could trigger a severe reaction, the most common are peanuts, tree nuts, fish, and shellfish.

Eight Most Common Food Allergens

Milk	Soy
Peanuts	Tree nuts
Egg	Wheat
Fish	Shellfish

Children who experience anaphylaxis when exposed to certain foods should always have an epinephrine auto-injector available at school. Always call 911 if a child is experiencing anaphylaxis, administer the epinephrine auto-injector, and take the child to the emergency room.

A written plan is crucial for how the school will handle students with severe allergies. The plan should encompass:

- School meal programs, including after school snacks
- Field trips
- Classroom parties

The school food and nutrition program is responsible for obtaining a physician's statement with a diagnosis and list of foods to eliminate from the student's diet. Most school districts now use point-of-sale programs that can alert the cashier to a student's allergies so that student gets no foods containing the allergens.

Food Defense

After the 9/11 attack, federal agencies began to look at the security of our food system and determined that various vulnerabilities needed to be addressed.

> ***Food Safety or Food Defense?***
>
> *FOOD SAFETY*—Protection of food from unintentional contaminants and controlling biological contaminant growth with time/temperature control.
>
> *FOOD DEFENSE*—Protecting food from intentional contamination with intent of harm or death.

School food and nutrition programs are encouraged to create a plan to assess, minimize, and respond to product tampering or intentional product contamination. Although many of the elements considered for food safety also apply to food defense, a plan should include additional precautions as follows:

- Use tamper-proof packaging for food products.
- Require advance-shipping notices for all deliveries and log deliveries.
- Secure receiving areas and delivery vehicles except when vehicle is being loaded or unloaded.
- Check identification for all delivery personnel
- Train personnel to look for signs of tampering and procedures for rejecting products or reporting suspicious changes to shipping documents.
- Secure all food and chemical products and maintain a list of those with access.

A comprehensive biosecurity checklist for use in assessing a school nutrition operation's risk is in the "Online Resources" section of this chapter.

CHEMICALS

The U.S. Department of Labor Occupational Safety and Health Administration (OSHA) developed a Hazard Communication Standard for use on chemical product labels and Safety Data Sheets. Exhibit 8-5 offers two examples of OSHA labels. Training of all current and future employees ensures employees have information about hazards in order to protect themselves. Training must include instructions on how to read and understand the product label and the Safety Data Sheets. These include:

- Product identification
- Signal word either "danger" or "warning" for a less severe hazard

Exhibit 8-5 Sample Pictograms

Exclamation Mark
- Irritant (skin or eyes)
- Respiratory tract irritant

Health Hazard
- Carcinogen
- Target organ toxicity

Source: OSHA, 2012.

- Pictograms and their meaning
- Hazard statement about the potential harm
- Precautionary statements (e.g., prevention, treatment)

Training on the use of Safety Data Sheets should include where to locate specific information used by the employee (e.g., Section Eight: Exposure Controls/Personal Protection contains use of personal protective equipment). Employers are required to provide information in the language and manner that their employees can understand.

Employers are required to label any container used to store chemicals with all information provided on the original label. All chemicals, including cleaning products, must be stored away from food to prevent accidental contamination.

SUMMARY

Several agencies govern food safety in school food and nutrition services programs. School food and nutrition services program regulations require a minimum of two health inspections per year and a written food safety plan based on HACCP principles. In addition, schools are required to follow state and local health codes.

Food safety plans contain an assessment of personnel, facilities, and menu items to determine the level of food safety risk. Identifying critical control points and establishing critical limits minimizes risks. The plan must also contain SOPs to train employees, monitoring and corrective action plans, and a record keeping system to provide verification of the plan's implementation.

The ability to track food used in schools from the producer to students is important to food safety. When a food safety risk occurs, the school food and nutrition service staff needs a method to identify the specific food involved and the ability to track it back to the supplier to forward to the customers who may have consumed it. A key component of tracking is keeping records to identify each unique product and know whether it has been received and whether it is stored or has been served.

A plan for responding to food-related emergencies reduces the chaos that can occur and provides the opportunity for a better outcome.

QUESTIONS AND ANSWERS

1. How many health inspections are required for school nutrition programs each year?
   a. One
   b. Two
   c. Three
   d. Four
2. Which of the following is an example of a HACCP process?
   a. Cooked
   b. Overcooked
   c. No cook
   d. Control point
3. The ability to track a product across a supply chain is called:
   a. Track-enabled
   b. Traceability
   c. One step-forward
   d. One step-back
4. Effectively responding to a food-related incident requires:
   a. Accurate record keeping
   b. A media specialist
   c. Providing detailed information to the press
   d. None of the above
5. A severe allergic reaction is called:
   a. Anaphylaxis
   b. Dermatitis
   c. Eczema
   d. Rhinitis
6. Food recalls can be voluntarily issued by manufacturers for:
   a. A biological health hazard
   b. A physical health hazard
   c. An undeclared allergen
   d. All of the above

ANSWERS: 1.b., 2.c., 3.b., 4.a., 5.a., 6.d.

REFERENCES

CDC estimates of foodborne illness in the United States. 2011. Retrieved from *http://www.cdc.gov/foodborneburden/2011-foodborne-estimates.html#illness.*

Cross, E. & Lofton, K. 2012. *Identifying emergency preparedness and readiness to respond to issues faced by school nutrition professionals.* University, MS: NFSMI.

GS1. 2009. *GS1 standards document: Business process and systems requirements for full chain traceability (1.1.0).* Retrieved from *http://barcodes.gs1us.org/dnn_bcec/Documents/tabid/136/DMXModule/731/Command/Core_View-Collection/Default.aspx.*

National Restaurant Association Foundation. 2012. *ServSafe for managers,* 6th ed. Chicago: Author.

NSFMI. 2013. *Conducting a mock recall of produce in a school nutrition program operation.* University, MS: Author.

NFSMI. 2005. *Guidance for school food authorities: Developing a school food safety program based on the process approach to HACCP Principles.* University, MS: Author.

NFSMI. 2010. *Health inspections in schools: Supporting food safety programs.* University, MS: Author.

NFSMI. 2011. *Meeting children's special food and nutrition needs in child nutrition programs,* rev. ed. University, MS: Author.

NFSMI. 2012. *Responding to a food recall: Procedures for recalls of USDA Foods.* University, MS: Author.

Occupational Safety and Health Administration. 2012. OSHA quick card: Hazard communication standard pictograms. Retrieved from *https://www.osha.gov/Publications/HazComm_QuickCard_Pictogram.html.*

Stretch, T. 2008. *Managing child nutrition programs.* J. Martin & C. Oakley (Eds.). Sudbury, MA: Jones & Bartlett.

USDA. 2013. Policy memo SP 37-2013: Enhancing the school food safety program frequently asked questions (FAQ).

ONLINE RESOURCES

Biosecurity Checklist for School Foodservice Programs
http://nfsmi-web01.nfsmi.olemiss.edu/ResourceOverview.aspx?ID=332

Center of Excellence in Food Safety Research for Child Nutrition Programs
http://cnsafefood.k-state.edu/

Developing a School Food Safety Program
http://www.nfsmi.org/ResourceOverview.aspx?ID=57

Emergency Preparedness Resource Guide for School Nutrition Professionals
http://www.nfsmi.org/documentlibraryfiles/PDF/20130522093042.pdf

FDA Food Code
http://www.fda.gov/Food/GuidanceRegulation/RetailFoodProtection/FoodCode/default.htm

FDA Food Safety Modernization Act
http://www.gpo.gov/fdsys/pkg/PLAW-111publ353/pdf/PLAW-111publ353.pdf
or
http://www.fda.gov/Food/GuidanceRegulation/FSMA/default.htm

FDA Protecting Safety and Security of Food and Drug Supply
http://www.fda.gov/RegulatoryInformation/Legislation/ucm155769.htm

Food Allergy Resources
http://www.nfsmi.org/ResourceOverview.aspx?ID=428

Foodservice GS1 U.S. Standards Initiative
http://www.gs1us.org/industries/foodservice/foodservice-initiative

Health Inspections in Schools: Supporting Food Safety
http://www.nfsmi.org/ResourceOverview.aspx?ID=264

Inventory Management and Tracking
http://www.nfsmi.org/ResourceOverview.aspx?ID=431

National Coalition for Food-Safe Schools Action Guide
http://www.foodsafeschools.org/

NEA Health Information: The Stomach Bug Book
http://www.neahin.org/educator-resources/stomach-bug-book-english.html

Norovirus Resources
http://www.nfsmi.org/ResourceOverview.aspx?ID=399

Produce Safety Resources
http://www.nfsmi.org/ResourceOverview.aspx?ID=394

Responding to a Food Recall
http://www.nfsmi.org/ResourceOverview.aspx?ID=444

Serving It Safe
http://www.nfsmi.org/ResourceOverview.aspx?ID=327

Thermometer Information Resources
http://www.nfsmi.org/ResourceOverview.aspx?ID=113

USDA, Food and Nutrition Services, Food Safety
http://www.fns.usda.gov/food-safety/

Wash Your Hands: Educating the School Community
http://www.nfsmi.org/ResourceOverview.aspx?ID=118

CHAPTER 9

TECHNOLOGY

STUDY QUESTIONS

1. What are the basic considerations when selecting a technology product?
2. Which school food and nutrition functions can benefit from automation?
3. What key factors are important to consider when evaluating a technology purchase?
4. What are the components of an effective technology implementation plan?
5. What are the considerations in determining the "real cost" of a computerized product?
6. Why is a software company's technical support important to the school district?
7. Describe support services offered with a software product.
8. What is the difference between proprietary and open source hardware standards?
9. What benefits may result from standardizing a food and nutrition process prior to computerizing the process?
10. How can computerized reports improve decision making?

Chapter 9

"Maximizing Online Applications" by Angela Haney, BS, SNS

Director, Student Nutrition, Los Lunas Public Schools (NM)

Los Lunas School District has a student enrollment of 8,500, and 74 percent of the students qualify for free or reduced-price meals. Los Lunas began scanning meal applications in 2005. We mailed the application to each family and included a stamped return envelope; however, we received about 25 percent of the letters back due to incorrect addresses. Each year it took me and a person from my office the entire weekend before school opened to process all the applications. Because it was more efficient than processing applications manually, we decided to add an option to submit applications online in 2010.

We opened up the application program to parents the first week of July. We mailed postcards to market the program to each family. We made computers available for parents to use for submitting applications at registration and in the school libraries. We also encouraged parents to ask their employers to let them use computers at work. Parents were also encouraged to use computers at the community library.

Although all families, except those directly certified, are notified of the availability of free and reduced-priced meals, paper applications are given out only when parents request them. This year, only 550 students out of 8,500 had not submitted applications by the first day of school. We have seen several benefits to the online applications:

- Applications are readable and have complete information when we receive them.
- The space required to store applications has shrunk from eight file drawers to one file folder.
- One person without working overtime handles all applications.
- Nearly 98 percent of all applications are submitted online.
- During the first year, in schools where the principals were onboard with online applications, the percentage of those approved for free and reduced-price meals increased by 4 percentage points.
- The time to process an application has decreased from 30 seconds when scanning to 10 seconds when submitted online because information was easier to validate.

After the first year, we realized that we needed to increase the number of computers in our office in order to make online submission more accessible to parents. Our automated calling system notifies parents when the program is ready for them to use. We also use the automated call system to notify parents of the student's meal status once the application is processed, which allows the student to receive meals before the notification letter arrives, increasing our meal count.

School food and nutrition leaders have long recognized the value technology investments can add to food and nutrition programs. As early as the mid-1980s, point-of-sale (POS) systems were solving accountability problems with federally subsidized school meal counts and cash collection procedures. In the past two decades, the use of technology has expanded into every aspect of school food and nutrition services, helping staff to be more effective and efficient.

INTRODUCTION

School food and nutrition customers understand technology and expect to interact with meal program personnel through personal technology devices such as smart phones and tablets. A savvy operator realizes the importance of utilizing technology in revenue-generating functions (sales and marketing) as well as cost-control functions (inventory management).

Recently, focus has shifted from simply collecting information more efficiently toward using information to make better program decisions. Often referred to as "data-driven decision making," the use of technology to analyze key measurements helps program managers answer questions such as which schools, what menu items, or which customers make the school food and nutrition program a success.

Determining the needs of a school food and nutrition service program to collect, share, or analyze information efficiently is the starting point in deciding on the needed technologies. This chapter provides information to help school food and nutrition personnel with the following:

- Identify needs.
- Make sound technology purchasing decisions.
- Plan smooth implementations.
- Evaluate value from technology investments.

NEEDS ANALYSIS

As in all purchasing decisions, the first step in adopting a new technology is determining the needs of the program. Starting with solutions without first identifying the problems can lead to a wasted technology investment.

Prioritize Needs

The director can make a list and then prioritize needs. Management may need to focus on high-priority items and consider limitations such as:

- Technology infrastructure of the district (e.g., Novell®, interoperability)
- Skill set of employees
- Standardization of food and nutrition department processes
- Size of the school district program
- Budget

Technology Infrastructure

School food and nutrition programs are rarely self-contained when it comes to technology. Even programs that can afford to hire technology personnel depend on the school district's Internet connections. The district may have requirements that all new technology must conform to system platforms already in place. It can be an expensive mistake to select a product using a Microsoft database (e.g., SQL Server®) if the rest of the district strictly uses Oracle®.

Software systems within a district often collect the same data. It may require an interface system in order for school food and nutrition programs to take advantage of data collected by other departments in the school district (e.g., student information system). This interface may eliminate data entry, thereby saving money in labor and preventing potential errors. Interfaces can be time consuming and difficult to support when new product versions are released. In order to eliminate proprietary connections between multiple programs, the Schools Interoperability Framework (SIF) Association created a standard set of rules and data definitions to enable data sharing. Software products conforming to these standards are SIF-certified. The "Online Resources" section at the end of this chapter offers a link to check software products with SIF certification.

Staff Technology Skills

Any technology acquisition will have a learning curve. Selecting a program that requires a technically well-informed operator may slow implementation due to employees needing to learn prerequisite technology skills (e.g., keyboarding versus touch screens). Many districts find it necessary to add technology skills and experience into job descriptions.

Standardization of Food and Nutrition Service Processes

Evaluation of the process to computerize is critical. Most software programs enforce standardization. For example, when implementing a POS program, the software setup must include a list of items and prices to ensure that cashiers across the school district ring up items at the same price. If the district does not want this degree of standardization, it is important to look for software that has the ability to customize prices (e.g., based on grade groups).

Size of the School District

The enrollment or number of schools in the district determines performance of the computer programs containing a database or requiring an Internet connection. If a large number of users or transactions occur at the same time (e.g., transactions during lunch, prepayments when schools begin to open in the fall), the users may find transaction times at slow to unacceptable levels or to "time out" before completion.

Budget

The director needs to plan a budget before actively searching for products. Prospective vendors will provide estimated cost information to assist with planning a budget.

Cost Considerations for Technology

- Hardware
- Implementation
- Annual technical support fees

Other school district directors using the same product can be helpful to validate pricing and confirm any expected revenue enhancement or cost savings. A realistic budget helps to eliminate purchasing products that are unaffordable.

Increased Efficiency

Often the driving factor for a technology purchase is increased efficiency. Reducing time spent coding, issuing, and accounting for meal tickets helped advance the sale of early point-of-sale systems. By reviewing work schedules, one can identify tasks that add time to the day without adding value to the services offered.

Student payments result in many labor hours collecting prepayments, entering data into software, and preparing bank deposits. Implementing online prepayments eliminates this labor as well as providing a benefit to parents desiring to pay for meals using a credit card. Adding "cashless lines" at the point of sale further reduces cash-handling labor as well as lowers risk due to theft. South Madison Community Schools (IN) phased in cashless lines by first depositing all change (leftover monies from a payment) in student accounts. Rich Township High Schools (IL) implemented a cashless policy the first day of the school year. Both directors of these two school districts promoted the new policy in advance. The results in line speed and improvement with cash control pleased the directors.

Temperature monitoring systems for refrigeration equipment may improve efficiency by eliminating the need for employees to complete paper temperature logs. Temperature control systems continuously record temperatures that operators can review to see whether temperatures remained at safe temperatures during power outages. Alerts sent to security or maintenance departments when temperatures rise or fall outside of preset thresholds protect against food loss.

Before automating a task, collect information about the amount of time the task currently requires. The time saved by automating the task is used to calculate a "return on investment." For example, the information can help with the following:

- Deciding how much to spend on the product
- Convincing upper management that the purchase is worthwhile
- Evaluating the product effectiveness after implementation

Decision makers benefit from case histories written by other product users. Collecting information before and after implementation and sharing results helps make products better and implementation smoother by allowing users of technology to learn from the experience of others.

Data-Driven Decision Making

Early technology products simply processed transactions faster and performed tabulation. The needs of today's school districts are more sophisticated. Directors and managers also want software to analyze transactions, providing information for decision making. For example, why did the school district spend 42 percent of revenue on food even though the goal was to keep food cost at 40 percent or below? On the surface, it may seem that planned menus cost more. If analysis software was utilized it may reveal that only high schools had high food costs or that a la carte items sales resulted in a 50 percent food cost. Having this information allows management to take the right corrective action.

Some school districts and state agencies are investing in data warehouses that store large volumes of historical data. Such warehousing allows the user to create reports on trends and analyze data generated from more than one program (e.g., test scores for students who eat breakfast at school). School food and nutrition software vendors are beginning to collect data across their customer base to enable customers to compare their food and nutrition program to similar programs or peers within the state or even across the country. Exhibit 9-1 shows an example of a report in which Elementary School 1 has higher labor costs (54.5%) than nine peer schools (37.4%); however, the other costs (12.1%) are considerably better than the peers (26.4%).

It is wise for district personnel to prepare for discussion of requirements by doing an analysis of information requirements and desires of the food and nutrition program. Before putting out a request for proposal (RFP), it helps if the food and nutrition services personnel collect reports and spreadsheets to identify information currently collected. What other information would be useful but is not available? The information needs review in order to clarify the following:

- Information useful in making decisions related to program operations and goals

Exhibit 9-1 Sample of District Cost to Revenue Report With Peer Comparison

District/ Building/ (peers)	Revenue		Cost	Cost % of Revenue		Peer Cost % of Revenue
Presentation Demo District	$1,545,304		**$ 1,503,856**	**97.3%**		
		Food	$ 694,723	45.0%		
		Labor	$ 530,167	34.3%		
		Other	$ 208,996	13.5%		
		Admin	$ 69,910	4.5%		
Elementary 1	**$ 62,460**		**$ 70,329**	**112.6%**		**115.2%**
Peers: {9}		Food	$ 26,201	41.9%		42.6%
		Labor	$ 34,018	54.5%	↓	37.4%
		Other	$ 7,575	12.1%	↑	26.4%
		Admin	$ 2,534	4.1%		8.8%
Elementary 10	**$ 48,390**		**$ 49,602**	**102.5%**	↑	**112.6%**
Peers: {5}		Food	$ 22,445	46.4%		41.6%
		Labor	$ 17,047	35.2%		35.3%
		Other	$ 7,575	15.7%	↑	26.5%
		Admin	$ 2,534	5.2%		8.9%
Elementary 11	**$ 54,681**		**$ 45,760**	**83.7%**	↓	**75.5%**
Peers: {5}		Food	$ 21,296	38.9%		36.2%
		Labor	$ 14,356	26.3%		25.9%
		Other	$ 7,575	13.9%	↓	7.3%
		Admin	$ 2,534	4.6%		6.1%
Elementary 12	**$ 33,593**		**$ 34,536**	**102.8%**	↑	**115.2%**
Peers: {9}		Food	$ 13,660	40.7%		42.6%
		Labor	$ 10,767	32.1%	↑	37.4%
		Other	$ 7,575	22.5%		26.4%
		Admin	$ 2,534	7.5%		8.8%

Source: DST software report used with permission from inTEAM Associates, Inc.

- Historical information needed to make predictions about the future (e.g., participation after the last price increase)
- Filters (e.g., filtering participation information by meal status) and sort orders that provide more specific information
- Frequency information needed in order to be useful (e.g., daily, weekly, or monthly)
- Display of information to make it easier to understand (e.g., trend line, bar graphs)

Once this information is collected, a school district can issue an RFP. A director can expect an astute vendor to conduct research and come prepared with standard reporting applicable to meet the district needs.

FUNCTIONS TO AUTOMATE

Technology is changing at a rapid pace. Whereas point-of-sale and financial accounting were the only systems used a few years ago, nearly every aspect of school food and nutrition operations includes technology solutions today. A recent study on technology use in the Southwestern region found that nearly all school food and nutrition directors used office applications and point-of-sale (Pratt et al., 2012). The majority also used menu-planning systems (78.4%).

Online purchasing, application processing, prepayment systems, and training programs are currently in more than 50 percent of school food and nutrition programs. School food and nutrition directors with greater computer skills, more education, and larger programs tend to use technology the most to help manage their program. Exhibit 9-2 provides a list of newer technology solutions used in school food and nutrition programs. Indeed today, knowledge and experience in use of technology are essential skills for all levels of foodservice personnel.

Exhibit 9-2 Technology Solutions Found in School Food and Nutrition Programs

Function	Interesting Technology Solutions
Customer contact and marketing	Online, smart phone applications, and kiosks used to: • Submit meal benefit applications • Pay for meals and other school fees • Access menus and preorder meals • Order catered meals and snacks Embed Quick Response Code in menus and other correspondence. Automated call systems contacting parents with: • Customer account balances • Announcements Contact management software Social media (e.g., Facebook, Twitter, LinkedIn) Website design and hosting Digital menu boards Virtual café or meal tray for nutrition and allergy information Online survey tools (example is in Chapter 10, "Marketing.")
Front of the house (e.g., point-of-sale)	Touch screens Handheld (e.g., tablets) for mobile carts Vending machines with access to customer accounts Bar coding products on the line for faster cashiering
Document management and automated payment	Online state applications and reimbursement claim submission Scan invoices, meal benefit applications, employee files Tablets for capturing checklists and forms (e.g., On-site Review) Electronic fund transfer to pay vendors, receive government reimbursement checks, and reconcile bank deposits
Back of the house (e.g., menu planning, ordering, inventory, and distribution)	Scanning received orders and inventory (e.g., Global Trade Identification Number bar code) GPS tracking on delivery trucks Delivery route scheduling software Develop product specifications and evaluate bids Nutrient analysis of planned menus and individual customer transactions Allergen tracking Recipe management Online product databases

(*Continued*)

Exhibit 9-2 *(Continued)*

Function	Interesting Technology Solutions
Safety and security	Temperature monitoring Web-enabled kitchen and service area monitoring Tracking trends in accidents and worker's compensation claims Keyless entry to secure areas
Equipment and maintenance	Ovens with scanners for recipes and product directions Work order and repair tracking Asset management Online energy management calculators
Human resources	Online employee applications Tracking professional development activities Online meetings and learning activities (e.g., webinars) Develop training content (e.g., YouTube, courseware) Work scheduling
User identification	Bar code scanners Magnetic stripe scanners Personal Identification Numbers (PIN) Contactless smart cards Biometrics (e.g., finger or palm scan)

School breakfast and lunch menus are required to conform to targets for certain nutrients such as calories and saturated fat. School districts using software to analyze menus are required to use software approved by USDA for this purpose. Exhibit 9-3 provides a list of software approved for the SY2014. It is best to check the software brands and approved versions on USDA's website before purchasing a new program. A link to the latest approved software is under "Online Resources" at the end of this chapter.

The hottest technology trends in schools are the use of social media, technology to empower parents and students, and reports that provide program analysis and identify trends. Today's parents and students have grown up with computers. They expect to engage school services, including food and nutrition programs, using mobile technology. Even low-income families have access to

Exhibit 9-3 USDA Approved Menu Planning Software

Brands	Manufacturer
CookenPro Commercial	Barrington Software, Inc. www.cooken.com
Eatec Solutions	Agilysys, Inc. www.agilysys.com
eTrition	Harris School Solutions www.harrisschoolsolutions.com
KidServe, OneSource, and Visual B.O.S.S.	Horizon Software International www.horizonsoftware.com
Meal Magic	Meal Magic Corporation www.mealmagic.com
Meals Plus Menus	Education Management Systems, Inc. www.mealsplus.com
MSchoolTools	MCS Software, LLC www.mcssoftware.com
NUTRIKIDS and WebSMARTT 3	Heartland School Solutions www.heartlandpaymentsystems.com
PrimeroEdge	Cybersoft Technologies, Inc. www.cybersoft.net
TrakNOW	PCS Revenue Control Systems, Inc. www.pcsrcs.com

Source: USDA, 2013.

computers through libraries and government service offices. School City of Hammond (IN) collected 90 percent of meal benefit applications through online submissions in the first year of this service.

Digital photography creatively improves program management. In San Benito (TX) Consolidated Independent School District, the director has school foodservice managers take photos of the serving lines before lunch and email them to the director so that she can see whether all menu items are offered and food is well merchandised. Providing digital cameras to schools can enhance marketing efforts, document conditions related to an employee accident, provide visual documentation of a damaged product delivery, or communicate a description of a part needing replacement. The possibilities are endless.

PURCHASING DECISIONS

Some major points to consider in making the technology purchase are: the cost, the support available, hardware and peripherals required, and how bid will be evaluated and awarded.

Total Cost of Ownership

Evaluating the cost of technology involves more than looking at the purchase price. It is important to consider all costs of the components. The product that is lowest in price may actually cost the most. Because technology products all have natural life cycles, costs are over a period of multiple years, which is the "total cost of ownership."

Technology Useful Life Expectancy

Computer, desktop: 4–5 years

Computer, laptop: 3–5 years

Software: 5 years with annual updates

Keypad: 3–5 years

Printers: 2–5 years, depending on number of pages printed

Although computer hardware and software can physically last many years, the speed of technology development makes products obsolete before most products physically wear out. Software manufacturers may stop supporting software versions after five years or not provide updates for hardware versions. This situation can be frustrating to operators who have not planned for technology upgrades. When selecting a system, the calculation of costs is generally made over a five-year period:

- Software (including database and operating system software)
- Computers (including servers)
- Peripherals (e.g., printers, scanners, keyboards)
- Supplies (e.g., printer cartridges)
- Extended warranties (e.g., terminal maintenance)
- Installation, training, and other start-up support
- Internal training and support
- Technical support and maintenance

Many software companies include the cost of yearly upgrades in technical support costs. Some companies have the ability to connect to school district computers remotely to perform installations and upgrades. This capability can save school districts many dollars and reduce wait time. Training costs decrease with online courses and tutorials.

Support Considerations

Support costs are a necessary part of software acquisition and generally worth the expense. Most software has many features that can benefit a program. Retraining helps staff members utilize features not introduced during initial training. Access to a technical support network cannot only resolve problems when they occur but also help operators implement additional software functions (e.g., matching direct certification files to enrolled students).

Technical support subscriptions that include program updates help ensure the software addresses new program regulations. In the last few years, software companies have been busy addressing changes in federal menu planning, verification, direct certification, and application processing. It is costly to purchase new software each time a new regulation goes into effect.

Technical support fees can include many different types of service, such as the use of an 800 number for support calls. It is important that the technical support call center is available during the district's workday. Good technical support should include access to a website that allows authorized users to do the following:

- Report a problem online
- Download program updates, drivers, and reports
- Access knowledge (problem/solution) database
- Connect and chat with a technician
- Access user message boards
- Upload files
- Register for and watch tutorials and online courses
- Access call tracking records
- Download documentation and help files

Support may also include annual end-of-school-year maintenance. This service is beneficial to ensure safe, clean, and stored data for audits. For additional fees, technology companies can provide many other services such as:

- Customize reports or software
- Review district data for errors
- Develop file imports
- Develop integration interfaces with other software programs (e.g., district financial systems)

The school food and nutrition director should select a technology company that provides tools for customers to resolve problems on their own. A responsive and knowledgeable technical support staff is as important as the software itself. Call current customers of any considered software product and ask how the software company handles problems. What is the response time? How well do the technicians to communicate with district staff? Excellent support and customer service can make basic software a great investment whereas poor service can greatly limit the value of even well-designed software.

Hardware and Peripherals

Another important consideration when selecting software is the type of hardware required in order for software to operate properly. Hardware is used to store data, run software, allow user input, and/or produce data output. In addition to the computer processor, monitor, keyboard, mouse, and printer, school food and nutrition software may also include hardware for POS and other specialty peripherals. The most important consideration for hardware options is using those developed with proprietary or open standards.

> Hardware Standards
>
> *PROPRIETARY*—Hardware designed to work exclusively with a specific software product.
>
> *OPEN SOURCE*—Hardware designed with software that is available to any developer in order for the product to work with a wide range of software products.

Most school food and nutrition software now supports open source hardware components. Often, the cost of POS hardware is less through computer hardware companies compared to software companies. It is important to obtain hardware specifications (e.g., ports, supported versions) from the software vendor to ensure that components are compatible. On the other hand, directors with little technical support within the district may find it worth the extra expense to purchase hardware and software from the same vendor to ensure that all work together smoothly. It is also important to note that when problems occur, it may be difficult to diagnose and resolve when the hardware brand is unfamiliar to the software technical support team.

In the past, hardware decisions were limited to whether to use pin pads or bar code scanners. Today options seem limitless with creative new products released frequently including:

- Tablet, smart phones, and other mobile devices
- Scales
- Change makers and receipt printers
- Thermometers
- Kiosks
- Digital menu displays
- Biometric input devices (e.g., finger and palm)
- Bar code, magnetic strip, and radio frequency identification readers
- Scanners (e.g., meal applications)
- Vending machines

After so many years of school districts using so little automation/technology of equipment, this practice is changing. For example, a trend is developing to automate more production equipment. Hobart makes a combi-oven with scanners that read bar codes on packages and recipes that will automatically set thermostat, steam, and timer on the oven to the correct temperature and time so that products cook perfectly. The North American Foodservice Equipment Manufacturers Association has developed standard data protocol for equipment manufacturers to use so that equipment pieces can share information easily. A link to the standards is in the "Online Resources" section at the end of this chapter.

Bid Evaluation and Award Criteria

Writing RFP documents for technology products can be challenging. Often technology manufacturers bid through third-party purchasing organizations and cooperatives in order to make products easily attainable. If technical resources within the district are unavailable to assist with RFP development, purchasing through a cooperative may be the best option. The purchasing process does not differ if purchasing food or technology. An invitation for bid may be the process to use when buying a specific brand and model of hardware. When purchasing software, a RFP allows evaluation of a vendor's capability, as well as technical aspects of the software. Both of these are important to consider in addition to price. Stating the factors used in evaluating the RFPs is essential in order to have a fair and open process. Generally, four different criteria should be included:

1. Mandatory requirements (e.g., network capability)
2. Technical capability and solution approach (e.g., how the software solves the business problem)
3. Organization and staff capability (e.g., years in business, experience in supporting product)
4. Cost proposal

Usually, the cost proposal goes directly to the school district purchasing office in a separate sealed envelope and is opened after assessment of the other criteria. If a product does not meet the mandatory requirements, it is eliminated before all else is considered. Generally, assigning a weighting to the capability factors and cost is helpful; 60/40 is a typical split with cost accounting for 40 percent of the decision factor and 60 percent depending on the bidder's solution and technical and staff capability.

A team of people should evaluate products and vendors' staff capabilities. The team should include one or more representatives from technology versed in database management, networks, software, and/or hardware support. Also, the team should include employees who will be entering information into the system (e.g., cashier, meal application processor) and those who will receive information from the program (e.g., supervisor, accountant). A school district should schedule product demonstrations by the finalists to ensure that functionality works as expected. Demonstrations can help to identify usability and technical issues in the procurement process, which will reduce problems during implementation and training.

IMPLEMENTATION

Most technology vendors offer installation services. Even when a district purchases a "turnkey" system, staff members will need to be involved in implementation and training. Installers will need access to networks, ports, and data. After the installation, it is necessary for a transition period to occur so district staff is ready to maintain the system.

Components of an effective implementation include:

- Implementation team with the right skills
- Effective team leader
- Comprehensive written project plan

The implementation team should have members with operational and technology skills. There should be one point of contact identified through which the technology company can communicate. It is essential the team identify who has decision-making authority. One person may handle a small project. A large implementation (e.g., a district-wide project) requires a team consisting of several people from multiple departments. In either case, to ensure the project is on time, a written plan with tasks assigned to specific personnel and deadlines is crucial.

In technology implementation, dependent tasks dictate the order of task completion. Exceeding budgeted costs and timelines are often the result of not identifying the relationship between tasks and ensuring that personnel know when their assigned tasks are due.

The person in charge of implementation needs to create a checklist of all deliverables prior to installation, which translates into accountability for acceptance testing of the product. Before installers leave, the end users should run through items on the checklist to make sure that all functionality is set up and usable to the extent agreed upon in advance.

It is also useful and interesting to collect operational data both before and after implementation. If information such as participation or sales data differ significantly after implementation, it may be a sign of either a problem or a great success story. In either case, the information collected will be important to the outcome of the implementation.

EVALUATION

After technology is operational, evaluation occurs to review the outcome. The evaluation results allow further improvements in processes or identify user problems. Positive feedback from users and benefits associated with adding the technology supports the purchasing decision.

Online survey tools gather user feedback. Information from the system compared to prior periods ensures the achievement of expected outcomes. If technology purchases do not enhance the program in some measureable way, money, personnel, and time are wasted. Consider how results can be measured before the project begins so that information is gathered at the right moments.

SUMMARY

Identifying goals the school food and nutrition program wants to achieve is a basic consideration when selecting a technology product. The goal may be to resolve a problem, make a process more efficient, or to collect and report data needed for decision making. In addition, the director needs to consider the technology infrastructure of the district, skills of the employees, standardization of the food and nutrition processes, size of the school district, and the budget.

School food and nutrition programs can improve many operational functions with technology. Technology solutions are available for nearly every function, including sales and marketing, production, human resources, safety, and procurement. Web applications make transactions more convenient for parents.

When evaluating a technology purchase, district directors must consider the total cost of the product over the span of five years. In addition to the purchase price of the technology, the cost of hardware, technical support, peripherals, warranties, installation, training, and supplies are part of the cost.

Putting together a team representing end users as well as technology personnel is an important component of an effective technology implementation. Choosing a leader with the ability and authority to make decisions is critical. Having a written project plan that identifies each task, when the task is to be completed, and who is responsible helps to ensure a smooth implementation that is on time. The implementation is not complete until acceptance testing ensures that all functionality included in the specification is working as expected.

QUESTIONS AND ANSWERS

1. Which of the following is a step in determining the technology needs for a school food and nutrition program?
   a. Hire a technology expert to introduce the latest technology
   b. Gather a list of needs from staff members
   c. Find out what technology other directors are using
   d. Set a technology budget
2. In school food and nutrition point-of-sale systems, customers are recognized using:
   a. Bar-coded cards
   b. Personal identification numbers
   c. Fingerprints
   d. Any of the above
3. Total cost of ownership means:
   a. Cost to purchase, run, staff, and maintain the product
   b. The cost to lease a product versus buying it
   c. The annual support cost
   d. The return on investment
4. What is the one critical step in implementing a technology project?
   a. Determining a budget
   b. Acceptance testing
   c. Determining the information needs
   d. Negotiating a price
5. Hardware that is designed to work with many different software programs is called:
   a. Proprietary
   b. Stationary
   c. Open source
   d. Closed source

ANSWERS: 1.b., 2.d., 3.a., 4.b., 5.c.

REFERENCES

Nettles, M. & Conklin, M. 1996. Using computer simulation to solve school foodservice problems. *NFSMI Insight*, 5. Retrieved from *http://www.nfsmi.org/documentlibraryfiles/PDF/20080313011445.pdf.*

Nettles, M. & Rushing, K. 2012. *Data-driven decision making: Guide for school nutrition programs.* University, MS: National Food Service Management Institute.

Pratt, P., Bednar, C., & Kwon, J. 2012. School nutrition director's perceptions of technology use in school nutrition programs. *Journal of Child Nutrition and Management*, 36 (2). Retrieved from *http://ww.schoolnutrition.org/Content.aspx?id=18047.*

USDA. 2013. Nutrient analysis software approved for use in the National School Lunch Program and School Breakfast Program. Retrieved from *http://healthymeals.nal.usda.gov/menu-planning/nutrient-analysis-software-approved-usda/nutrient-analysis-software-approved-use.*

White, P. 2013. Positive identification. *School Foodservice & Nutrition*, 61 (1), 18–23. Retrieved from *http://www.schoolnutrition.org/Content.aspx?id-1678.*

ONLINE RESOURCES

Hospitality Technology
http://hospitalitytechnology.edgl.com/home

NAFEM Data Protocol
https://www.nafem.org/information-resources/whatisndp.aspx

SIF Association
https://www.sifassociation.org

USDA Nutrient Analysis Software Approved for Use in the National School Lunch Program and School Breakfast Program
http://healthymeals.nal.usda.gov/menu-planning/nutrient-analysis-software-approved-usda/nutrient-analysis-software-approved-use

Chapter 10

Marketing

STUDY QUESTIONS

1. Why is marketing important for a school food and nutrition service program?
2. Who are some of the players to sell on school food and nutrition service program?
3. What is traditional marketing
4. How can social media be used in marketing?
5. What social media options are available?
6. Why should a website be updated frequently?
7. How can Twitter be used to promote school food and nutrition services?
8. How can branding be used?
9. What type of promotions work?
10. What is the value of publicity?

Chapter 10

"Engaging, Educating, and Empowering"

by Brent Craig, MS, RD, SNS
Director of Nutrition Services, Douglas County (CO) School District

I learned five years ago, and have followed ever since, the basic principle of marketing in this age. It really works. When I became the director of Douglas County Schools District, I spent the first six weeks listening to parents complain about how bad the lunches were. It became obvious to me that these parents were mostly drawing from their own experience from when they were in school. In other words, we were doing a lousy job marketing our healthy meals. Well, I set off after that in the direction of using the basic principles of marketing: engaging, educating, and empowering our students and parents. It really makes a difference. Now we spend the first six weeks focused on our business, and most of the communication from parents is to praise us for what a great job we are doing.

We live in a world of short attention spans. With the Internet and eyes that prefer digital communications, information is at the snap of a finger, which has dramatically changed the way everyone does business. School nutrition is no different. Gone are the days when posters and stickers are effective marketing tools. We now embrace a world of mobile apps, digital screens, and technologies, which are intuitive and part of the DNA of this growing generation.

When we evaluated our secondary audiences, we recognized that they were engaged with mobile devices in their hands. It is their "second language." We thought, "We should engage these secondary students on their level, speaking their language." So, we built out a mobile texting platform. Each day, during lunch, we ask fun questions from nutrition education to pop culture. Kids text in, and we do daily and weekly prizes for participation.

Once engaged, we need to educate our audiences and ensure they are aware of the value we provide in every meal. The old adage remains true, "In the absence of information, people assume the worst." Continuing with the texting example, when they text into our system, we get to send them a message back. Our messages are filled with encouragement to make healthy choices.

Finally, we need to be empowering. It is not enough to push information. We want our customers to actually do something with it! This is my favorite part of marketing: When we've done our job, our customers actually are empowered to act and make smart, healthy decisions.

Marketing school food and nutrition services is important to maintaining program participation and is critical to a program's success. By 2010, the way to market products and services took on a completely new approach. Social media has flourished and is one of the most popular and effective ways to market to today's students, teachers, and parents.

MARKETING SCHOOL FOOD AND NUTRITION SERVICES

In September 2012, the changes in the Child Nutrition Program regulations regarding food offered at school had negative effects on participation. The number of free meals increased because of the economy, but the number of paying customers decreased. Because of the decreases, some of the federal regulations were relaxed. "Better-for-you" food advocates learned you could not force students to eat "healthier" foods.

Marketing is more necessary now than ever. It has become obvious that serving good food at low prices or even free is not enough. When students do not want to eat school lunches, they will not—the elementary students will bring their lunches from home and high school students will find another place to eat or just not eat. The challenges and opportunities to market and promote are great in school food and nutrition services.

Why can't a large high school create its own food court with "imitation" fast-food chains and still meet the federal meal requirements?

Other segments of the foodservice industry have similar problems (e.g., military bases as far back as early 1980s). At that time, foodservice management began treating the troops as customers, "marketing" to them and using "branding" of popular foods. One popular way to meet that market is to have a food court of popular foods. Today, because obesity is a concern, the military base foodservices are concentrating on leaner, healthier armed forces.

High schools are successfully offering healthier foods using the food court concept. Even though the school's staff prepares all the food, students feel more like customers when they are in charge of the decision where and what to eat.

Experts in marketing have discovered how challenging the school food and nutrition services programs are to market. In Exhibit 10-1, the audiences are well defined. It shows how many segments one has to consider when marketing a school lunch.

Exhibit 10-1 Segments to Consider When Marketing a School Lunch

- **Kids** – Our "customer." While mom and dad may provide money, ultimately the child chooses to buy or not.
- **School Board** – The management company is under contract with them, they are our client. Keeping all the other groups happy keeps the board happy. Saving money makes them even happier.
- **School Principal** – The boss of the school. They have to manage complaints from kids, parents, and teachers. They report to the School Board.
- **Cafeteria Team** (i.e., "lunch ladies") – The front-line workers. They make it all happen. Although the school district employed them, the management company hired, let go, trained, managed, and recognized their good work.
- **Parents** – If the parents are uncomfortable with the food quality and/or get complaints from their child, we are doing something wrong.
- **Teachers** – Teachers themselves get tired of the same lunchroom food. Yet another customer.
- **U.S. Government** – Constant oversight and reporting to/from the government ensures quality for the kids.
- **Local Media** – A slow news week often leads to a cafeteria pop-in visit to report, "What they are *actually* serving our town's youth."
- **Community** – Unless you have kids of your own and join them once in a while in the lunchroom, you probably assume what is served today is exactly what was served when you were in school. As does the rest of the community.
- **My Employer** (management company) – Keep the boss happy and manage with the resources provided by the company.

Source: Williams, 2009.

The customer has changed over the years. Whether referencing restaurant food or school food, today's customers want information when they ask for it. The school food and nutrition service customers have to be sold food in the way they want to be sold.

In high school in particular, lunchtime maybe the one free time of day students are able to socialize so they want food to be "fun." Today's students have grown up with thousands of commercials telling them what they ought to eat in order to be big, strong, popular, or part of the "in" crowd. Because fast foods are a central part of their lives, to them the perfect lunch may be a Big Mac, fries, and a Coke—not cafeteria sliced turkey on a whole wheat roll, green vegetable, fresh fruit, and milk. As a result, many school managers are beginning to look at students as "customers," and "marketing" school meals and the other food items for sale. If this does not occur, a school foodservice program can lose out to neighborhood fast-food restaurants, local coffee shops, and convenience stores at lunchtime. Today's children may even be using their cell phone and credit card to order pizza or other foods for delivery to the school. This option may be a problem in the future, with tighter federal regulations restricting the availability of food at school from outside sources.

What Is Marketing?

Marketing is the process of promoting, advertising, merchandising, and selling. It includes:

1. Defining what the customer wants and needs
2. Providing products or services that meet those wants and needs
3. Informing the customer of the availability of the services or products
4. Describing the benefits that can be gained
5. Selling products at prices the customer considers fair

Most restaurants understand the importance of marketing. The commercial industry spent more than $6 billion in 2011 to market their products (Business Insider, 2012). McDonald's spent nearly $1 billion in 2011 on advertising their products.

When comparing what successful commercial foodservices have in common with successful school food and nutrition service programs, researchers found the following:

- Products (foods) are promoted. Menu is the single most important variable.
- Popular foods are served.
- Food is consistently of good quality.
- Atmosphere is pleasant.
- Personnel are friendly. Attitudes of the foodservice employees are upbeat and happy.
- Prices fit students' budgets. Prices charged students are no longer the single most important variable.
- Service is fast.

In school food and nutrition programs, other factors influence students of today:

- Students qualifying for free meals participate at a much higher rate.
- Students image of the program is important—particularly with high school students.
- Parents place value on nutrition and have a perception of how nutritious the meals are at school.
- Ages of students affects participation—older students participate in school lunch programs less frequently than younger ones.

- Sex of students also affects participation—male students participate more frequently than females.
- Location, urban or city, makes a difference—students from rural areas participate more often than students from urban areas.

Every school food and nutrition service program has an image. The image may be negative in a community because of adverse publicity or lack of publicity. A foodservice's image is intangible thoughts and impressions. All the senses influence the image and can be changed. In order to make change, the foodservice program needs to determine what the current image is and what the desired image should be.

> *"Dull cafeteria food is an image to avoid and one that profoundly affects the financial bottom line."*
> *(Boehrer, 1993).*

A dull, institutional-type school cafeteria can be made a fun place to eat. Just simple things can create the image and a "fun place to eat." These include:

- Presenting food in a more contemporary way (e.g., wraps)
- Painting the serving line and dining room areas brighter colors
- Having employees smile and be positive while serving students and school staff

The Federal Child Nutrition Program requirements have changed rapidly, perhaps more quickly than the students changed.

Pushing a program (e.g., breakfast) will work when it meets the needs of the students. The breakfast may need to be served in a bag on the school bus or in the classroom.

Today's students want food when they want it—convenient and easy to eat.

Before selecting a marketing approach, food and nutrition service personnel should examine the factors associated with nonparticipation. A study of one major school district's lunch participation showed that:

- The lowest interest in school food and nutrition is at the 9th grade level, or at about age 15.
- Food variety was more of a concern among senior high students.
- Different ethnic groups showed substantial differences in food preferences.
- Some ethnic groups of students were more embarrassed by association with free/reduced-price programs than other ethnic groups.
- Breaks in the morning reduced the number who ate lunch.

To increase the participation of female students or others concerned with losing weight, a salad bar opened and promoted with a sign saying, "Make it your way" or "You decide how many calories you eat."

To prepare a marketing approach, a school food and nutrition service manager or supervisor needs to identify and study the competition. It is usually one or more of the following: fast-food establishments nearby, convenience stores, lunches brought from home, going home for lunch, vending machines (if available), or not eating at all. Stay-at-home parents in some communities take turns bringing food to school for their children and friends.

The marketing approach should be planned and executed in big segments or all at one time—not gradually; the gradual approach does not get attention. Students will not see the marketing approach as anything new. The theme and image to be marketed should be enhanced by the presentation of food, the type of services offered, the appearance of the serving and dining areas, the uniforms the employees wear, and the attitudes the employees display. It may be helpful to do a "kickoff" event or big opening with balloons and banners to show off the changes.

Projects to increase participation and student satisfaction in the Palm Beach (FL) Schools have gotten good media press and accomplished their goals. The result in September 2012 was a 25 percent increase in two high schools' lunch participation. The school food service department changed not only the way the dining/serving areas looked, but also how the students were served. The department produced two videos highlighting their "reengineered" high schools. Training for the employees was the emphasis in one of the videos, "Employee-Geared Expectations." The other video is a "Student-Geared Teaser." The two videos can be viewed online.

MANAGING SOCIAL MEDIA

The School Nutrition Association (SNA) introduced many directors to social media when they introduced TrayTalk (www.traytalk.org). A promotional campaign launched by SNA in mid-2010, it quickly became a popular website. It targets parents and highlights school nutrition success stories from coast to coast. Managers can get many new ideas for promoting food at school from this forum. Many school foodservice programs website have links, including TrayTalk.

The Facebook page, "School Meals That Rock," shares and celebrates what is RIGHT with school food and nutrition services in America today. The upbeat, beautifully done website has as one of its goals to convince parents that a lot has changed about food at school since they were students.

> *Social media, which has become popular fast, is about getting the message out quickly and expecting quick reactions.*

The Internet provides many avenues for school food and nutrition service programs to get the message out. Parents may be using this avenue more than students. Marketing is more personal with use of technology that connects point-of-sale with the email address.

When using any social media, a big challenge is keeping the account updated and responding to questions quickly. It is time consuming and requires quick response by a knowledgeable person.

Today social media is not limited to creating a website or Facebook page. In addition, one should use more interactive means with Twitter and blogs. As social media continues to evolve, it is important to keep current with technology. The adult who asks any teen what they are reading on their phone will find he/she is a step behind.

Facebook

The district website or Facebook page is probably where parents and students start when they are searching for information regarding the school district. School food and nutrition service departments need to get involved with setting up the district or school's website. From a district or school website, a link to Facebook, and other social media, should be available. Here, the latest information should be current and relevant. Comments and questions may be posted and should be answered quickly. Care should be taken to remove anything not appropriate. It may be popular to offer trivia, games, and photos.

SNA has provided two excellent introductions to the use of social media: *Social School Lunch: A How-To Guide on Social Media for School Nutrition Programs* (2010) and *Marketing 101*, an online course.

Definitions:

FACEBOOK—A popular free social networking website that allows registered users to create profiles.

HASHTAGS—Key words or phrases with the prefix "#" in front of the text used with Twitter (e.g., #nutrition nuggets).

BLOG—Allows a school district to provide longer descriptions or more detail.

YOUTUBE—Large video-sharing site on the Internet.

LINKEDIN—Social media that allows users to network with other people or businesses; may be good for reaching parents.

TWITTER—A popular instant-messaging system that lets a person send brief text messages of up to 140 characters through social networking.

Exhibit 10-2 features some websites as good examples of how they can be used.

Exhibit 10-2 Websites as Examples of Uses

Team up with local business

Framingham Public Schools, MA

www.framingham.k12.ma.us/foodservice.cfm

This site highlights the scholarship offered to provide meals for a year for families with hardship.

Small can make a big statement

Okemos Public Schools, MI

http://www.okemosschools.net/education/components/scrapbook/default.php?sectiondetailid=710&linkid=nav-menu-container-1-44203

Even smaller districts can offer extensive information and a "web store" for payments.

Website companies offer service

Colonial School District, DE

http://www.colonial.k12.de.us/parents-students/lunch-menus-and-nutrition

Websites can be set up and managed for a school program by outside firms.

Interactive fun

San Antonio Independent School District, TX

http://www.saisd.net/dept/foodnutrition/

A Kids Corner with nutrition games students can play.

Professional look

Fairfax County Public Schools, VA

http://www.fcps.edu/fs/food/

(*Continued*)

Fairfax offers near instant language translation for over 60 languages that match the extensive demographics of this metropolitan area.

Visual and full of action

Wayzata Schools, MN

http://www.wayzata.k12.mn.us/domain/434

Use of pictures and videos make this an interesting site.

State guidance made easy

Oregon Department of Education

http://www.ode.state.or.us/search/results/?id=207

This is a well-organized website with easy to find information. It takes only a single click.

School districts often have rules and regulations regarding the district's use of social media. The quality of districts' websites varies greatly. Two of the most interactive, informative websites are Dallas (TX) Independent School District and Fairfax County (VA) Public Schools.

Twitter

Twitter is a popular and free media tool. Many school districts use it to promote school meals and increase participation. Twitter is an effective platform for marketing to the local community. Some of the ways to use it are:

- Marketing the school food and nutrition service program
- Creating a positive image
- Broadcasting and advertising
- Posting daily breakfast and lunch menus

- Sharing nutrition information
- Offering nutrition tips
- Providing kid-friendly recipes
- Promoting new products or menu items
- Introducing new foods and major events
- Answering questions, even creating the questions
- Surveying the customers, parents, and administration
- Obtaining feedback and complaints
- Offering a sounding board when price increases are necessary
- Running specials
- Highlighting emphasis (e.g., eating more fresh fruits and vegetables)
- Featuring an employee of the month
- Featuring a guest student of the month

> *The goals of Twitter are to:*
> - *Grab attention.*
> - *Create a positive image.*
> - *Get the message out.*

Following Twitter requires creative and timely responses. When complaints are received, the answers should be kind and apologizing, but stick with what has to be done while offering solutions.

Twitter provides an excellent platform for communicating with teenagers, students, parents, coaches, teachers, and group organizations. Some of the challenges for directors are learning how to "tweet" and create hashtags, staying legal, and coming up with creative ideas. Searching online will help with these new terms.

The food and nutrition services office can start by creating a catchy "hashtag," such as Glendale (CA) Unified School District Food and Nutrition's Health-e Living website. To get a "following," management needs to involve key individuals at the schools, such as star athletes, cheerleaders, and winning coaches, because all these contacts bring with them a following. In larger school districts that have a nutrition education specialist on the staff, the job is often extended to include marketing.

To obtain a following, the tweets must be interesting, original, not too self-serving, but showing concerns for students. They must be informative, friendly, sound like a real person, and provide reputable information. Offer live tweeting with a class, give out assignments, and offer prizes (e.g., pizza party for a class or club with the most participation). At the party, serve the larger pizzas, fresh vegetable sticks, and fresh fruits that make up a healthy lunch and meet the meal requirement. Invite groups to join your discussion on Twitter.

> **Website Wellness Messages:**
> "Keep Your Balance"
> "Aim for Healthy Weight"
> "Ask a Dietitian"
> "All Foods Fit"
> "Harvest Time"
> "Food Myths"
> "Get Moving!"
>
> Source: Health-e Living Website

If the school board or policy allows advertising, the food and nutrition service program can involve companies (vendors) to provide promotions. Use branded products in the district's menus and as specials. Some companies will provide discount pricing, prizes, and perks for the company name/logo to appear in your social media. Students like giveaways and competition. For the companies it is a way to advertise their brand name.

YouTube

YouTube videos can be posted on the Internet to promote signing up or actually completing application for free and reduced meals, summer lunch programs, and special activities. Much of what is available on YouTube regarding school food and nutrition services includes news clips, vendor information, and training videos. This may be an untapped opportunity to promote school meals and provide exposure for the program and making healthier choices.

Email and Texting

Using email for promotions can be as quick as the click of the fingers. For example, Chili's targets their "senior citizens" market by offering a Tuesday night special of a "Classic Hamburger." They send coupons on their slowest day of the week via emails for popular free items, such as sweet potato fries or yummy chocolate desserts. Many of the restaurants target customers, by sending personalized emails and coupons for events such as birthdays and anniversaries. School food and nutrition services that are serious about increasing participation, whether free or paid, can use the same marketing techniques. It may require some programming, but targeted emails and texts can be used for school lunch programs.

MANAGING TRADITIONAL MARKETING

> *Positive articles in newspapers are often available online and can be passed on to customers/parents via Facebook.*

Traditional media—television, radio, and local newspaper—have been used quite effectively in the past. Even today, a local morning television or radio program is still a popular way of publicizing menus for the day, along with the weather. Parents may be watching and listening to determine what the child should wear. Students can also choose school lunch for that day. It is not as personal as social media, but currently is still a means of communicating.

Branding

School Foodservice & Nutrition (February 1997) defines branding as "relying on name recognition in developing menus, as well as for advertising and promotional strategies." In the late 1990s, nearly

40 percent of all public school districts used "branding" to draw customers (USDA, *School Food Purchase Study*, 1998). Branding was initially used in the 1980s, and it is still around today. However, it is on the decline, down to 25.9 percent according to SNA (2011). It has decreased as the federal regulations have become tighter and the emphasis on good nutrition has become more forceful. Some of the other reasons school districts have been reluctant to increase use of branding include:

- Fear of paying a higher price
- Resistance to sharing the revenue with a company (franchise fee)
- Perception of poor nutrition quality
- Concern that the "branded food" will take money that otherwise would go to the regular lunch
- Resistance to change

The question is, "Why would a school district want to use branding?" It costs more for the "name." Is it worth it? Undoubtedly a lot of colleges, universities, and military bases think so, which is where branding has really flourished. The answers to the question about why schools should use branding are name recognition, perceived value, quality assurance from the company, marketing support, and often increased revenue.

Three types of branding:

1. "Quick-serve" restaurants
2. Manufacturers' brand name products
3. In-house brand or signature items

Quick-Serve Restaurants

Quick-serve types of food establishments are popular restaurants well known by students, such as Pizza Hut, Domino's, Taco Bell, Subway, and McDonald's. Many have tested the school food and nutrition services market, but pulled back because of federal regulations, not enough business, or too little profits. Domino's and Subway have made adjustments and are still in the market.

The San Juan Capistrano (CA) School District was one of the first to open a fast-food court in 1992 with Pizza Hut, Taco Bell, and Kentucky Fried Chicken (all PepsiCo Food Service) franchises. In the early 2000s, they started in-house branding and developing a more nutritious approach to school food and nutrition services. In the 1990s, Minneapolis (MN) School District offered a "Taco Bell Express" in one of its high schools. Now they are promoting "grown locally foods." The Henrico County (VA) School District has had a Subway franchise since 1993. The Subway turkey sub is available every day, and students can add their favorite vegetables toppings

Manufacturers' Brands

Manufacturers' brands that are sometimes "advertised" in the school menus or on the signage at the school are Otis Spunkmeyer cookies, Big Daddy Pizza, Red Baron pizza, Minute Maid juices, Jamba Juice, Kellogg's cereal, and many others. Many companies provide display equipment and marketing materials when their products are used and promoted. Some school districts view this as inappropriate advertising and won't permit it.

In-House Brands

School districts have developed logos and used them on their websites, menus, even on sandwich wraps, cups, napkins, lunch bags, lunch boxes, and placemats.

School brands have done fairly well for the Hillsborough County (FL) Public Schools with specialty dishes. Glendale (CA) Schools begin switching over to school brands on most items in 1998 and now have emphasis on "Health-e Living." Their website explains.

Indianapolis (IN) Public Schools Food and Nutrition Service staff made the decision not to use ready-to-serve brands, such as Pizza Hut, Subway, and Kentucky Fried Chicken, but instead they borrowed concepts from popular brands and developed in-house brands (self-branding).

Food Courts

Though food courts are really a style of service, they are a break from the norm in a rather traditional program. Atmosphere and food presentation make a difference. Participation increases when a school district makes a change from the traditional to a more contemporary approach.

When designing a new food court arrangement, flexibility is key. What is popular today may change tomorrow. Five broad approaches are:

1. Local favorites (traditional)
2. Grill or sandwich bar
3. Pizza
4. International
5. Salad—make your own or grab and go

Reimaging the Dining Area

Many of the school cafeterias look today as they did in 1980, but the students see a much different environment when they go out to eat. Many school districts are changing how the cafeteria looks through renovations referred to by some as reimaging, reengineering, or makeovers.

Greenwich (CT) High School has had a total makeover or "reimaging," and the results in participation have been significant. They averaged another $100 per day more in a la carte sales and a 15 percent increase in participation immediately. Their revenue averages $6,000 per day.

The neon lights, convenience stores, computerized point-of-sale, and many food court ideas help keep students happy and eating on campus. School districts can spend a lot or a little to bring about change and create food court arrangements.

It takes imagination and determination to bring a change about. The best and most creative ideas for changing the look of serving and dining areas can be obtained from professional journals like *FoodService Director,* or from a trip to shopping mall food courts and university campus foodservices. The John C. Stalker Institute of Food and Nutrition at Framingham State University (MA) provides excellent information, seminars, templates, and many ideas to market and promote school foodservices.

The concept of creating interesting dining areas should not be limited to high schools Certainly the high schools are challenging and probably should be the first to reimage. However, the middle and elementary school cafeterias need changes too.

Promotions

Promotion, or public relations, can be described as the "act of promoting goodwill" as related to school food and nutrition service. It should result in the public's having a positive image of the operation. Public relation is an attitude of management, which places public interest as the first priority when making management decisions.

Promoting goodwill can mean something as simple as giving a straw to a child who brings a drink from home. Though "freebies" have to be controlled, the public relations benefits of giving the straw must be considered by management in making the decision to do so. Goodwill can also include customer service gestures such as replacing a student's food because the student did not like what he or she chose.

Students like getting something free as well—for example, a frequent diner card can be successful. A free dessert with six punches or a lunch free for ten punches may work. The main use of "promotions" in school food and nutrition services can be to keep students interested in eating at the same place each day throughout the school year. The Sodexho Corporation Food Services Division calls promotions "monotony breakers." Looking at the commercial industry can provide ideas for school foodservice promotions.

A promotion can have positive results (e.g., recognizing students' birthdays). It is an excellent way to encourage students to try something new and buy more than just a lunch (if the customers have the money). Promotions generate enthusiasm for the program.

Advertising and Publicity

For many years, schools opened their doors to advertising in a big way with Coca-Cola, PepsiCo, Papa John's, and other companies, but drew strong criticism. Some school districts have a policy banning advertising inside the classroom or anywhere on the school grounds. Others use the business partners effectively on their menus, websites, and in promoting the program. Federal regulations have changed many things since 2010. School food and nutrition services must work within the restraints of the federal regulations, the school board policy and of what is acceptable to the district and the community.

The objectives of publicity and advertising are to create and reinforce an image. Publicity is usually free, while advertising is usually purchased. Both are techniques used to inform and persuade the public or the customers. Both can be used to call attention to, tell about, or praise someone or something. The fact that publicity is free does not guarantee that positive publicity will happen. School food and nutrition service management should be assertive and imaginative in obtaining "free publicity." It can be accomplished by preparing feature stories and making them available to small newspapers that have lean budgets—they may be used as fillers, but the school district tells the story they want the community to hear.

One sure way to obtain positive publicity, though usually not free, is through paid advertising. However, paid advertising is rarely used by school food and nutrition services. Why not purchase an ad in the school newspaper? Why not run a 50¢ off coupon in the drama club's program? The cents-off coupon is one of the most popular and effective sales promotions used in the retail food market. School districts in the Phoenix area have been able to purchase time on television and radio by forming a corporation through which companies contribute funds for advertising school food and nutrition services in relationship to products purchased from the companies

Advertising of school foodservice activities and offerings usually qualifies for "free time" or "free space" in the media. Menus are often published in local newspapers. However, social media is a more likely source of information.

Merchandising

Merchandising is so much a part of food production that it should be written on the standardized recipe as a step. This topic is discussed in Chapter 7, "Managing Ordering, Production, and Service." Effective merchandising can increase participation in a school food and nutrition services program, and it can particularly increase satisfaction. In narrow terms, merchandising refers to making the customer want to buy a product because of the product itself.

In a school food and nutrition service, it involves offering good food that looks attractive at a price the customer considers fair, in a courteous manner, and in a pleasant environment.

One of the greatest downfalls of school food and nutrition services has been the lack of merchandising. This may be due to the volume of food being produced, a tight budget, time limits, or the lack of competition and knowledge on how to merchandise. Below are some elements of merchandising.

Five key elements of food presentation are:

1. Color—natural to the food, bright, fresh, crisp
2. Flavor—never too strong or contrasting, clean and crisp
3. Contrast in texture, crisp foods with soft foods
4. Shape—varying (e.g., not all mounds or strips)
5. Natural—appropriate, edible garnishes

Selling

Selling (like advertising) is a new word to some school foodservice managers. Certainly the schools are no place for high-pressure selling, but using suggestive selling and good business sense in displaying food is appropriate in most school food and nutrition services. Making a la carte food items accessible—easy to see—will make a difference in sales of these items. Self-service may not work in some schools because of theft. How foods are priced will have an effect on sales. For example, if the price of lunch is $3.25, having a 75¢ item (e.g., water) will increase the revenue.

To make the nutritious food more popular, increase participation, and serve in less time, are the goals. It means the manager needs to know what the customer wants. Preferences can be determined through surveys, listening, questioning, and staying in touch with the customer.

A friendly, simple survey for evaluating the school cafeteria atmosphere and the lunches served is provided in Exhibit 10-3. The "bottom-line" to successfully managing school food and nutrition services in the twenty-first century is keeping the customers happy with nutritious meals at a price their parents are willing to pay.

Exhibit 10-3 Sample Form for Evaluating School Lunches

School Name ______________________________ **Date** ______________

Please place an "X" by your answers.

1. **How often do you eat the school lunch?**
   - o Never
   - o Sometimes
   - o Always
2. **If never, why?**
   - o Food does not taste good
   - o Food does not look good
   - o Too expensive
   - o Lines are too long
   - o My friends don't eat there
3. **If always, why?**
   - o Food tastes good
   - o Food looks good
   - o Inexpensive
   - o Like menu choices
   - o My friends eat there
   - o I have no choice
4. **What do you prefer for lunch?**
   - o Hot dinner-type lunch
   - o Soup and sandwiches
   - o Fast-food-type lunch
   - o Box or bag lunch

(*Continued*)

- o Salad bar
- o Yogurt
- o Snack items
- o Other

5. List five foods that you would like to see served for school lunch.

1. ______________________________
2. ______________________________
3. ______________________________
4. ______________________________
5. ______________________________

MEETING THE PRESS

Not all publicity will be positive. It helps to develop a cooperative working relationship with the press. A good relationship becomes especially useful in handling unpleasant situations that may arise. For example, reports of food poisoning, or high levels of some undesired nutrient or chemical in school lunches, can cause very negative publicity. Most reporters will be fair. One must remember, "Nothing is off the record."

The food and nutrition service director should have a written "crisis communications" policy. In the case of crisis, it is usually wise to take the initiative in disseminating information. Facts can stop rumors and gossip while providing reassurance to the public. The best public relations results come from an "act," not a "reaction." The public can usually be won over with frank, candid responses and a sincere concern for the welfare of the customers.

Many school districts have a media director and all communication to the press must go through the media office. Anyone who speaks to the press on behalf of the food and nutrition services or school district should be a skilled communicator and have the primary objective of getting the right message to the right audience in a believable way.

COMMUNICATING WITH CUSTOMERS

How can a director or manager know what the students like or dislike? Certainly, production records indicate preferences. However, it is important for the manager to have a way to get feedback that is more definite. The following are some techniques for communicating with customers—students and adults—regarding their likes and dislikes:

- Formal questionnaires and surveys (Exhibit 10-3)
- Informal interviewing of students and adults
- Small-group discussions
- Suggestion boxes
- Asking for immediate feedback (Exhibit 10-4)
- Tasting parties or sampling

Social media is an excellent way of communicating with students (Exhibit 10-4). Students and parents want their opinion heard.

Small-group discussions with students, teachers, and parents can be beneficial. It may be a matter of explaining the federal regulations. Student leaders can be the best advertisement for healthy choices and the new federal regulations. For example, in the South students may want to know why they cannot have sweet tea as a beverage. High school students may not want the "cafeteria telling them" what they can or cannot have to eat and drink. An editorial in the student newspaper can be a positive way of communicating with students.

Ideas from a group of students may be rewarding. Asking for suggestions may result in ways to improve the program, along with help in carrying out the changes.

Exhibit 10-4 Text for Feedback

Source: Craig, 2013.

By circulating throughout the dining area during lunch time, a manager or designated person can effectively solicit customers' opinions and give them a chance to ask questions. This practice should be a regular occurrence. In addition, employees on the serving line and in the dish room window can obtain useful feedback and identify happy and unhappy customers. This information should be communicated to the manager.

Tasting parties help in determining whether a new product will be accepted. They can be formal or informal, small or large, and can involve students, parents, faculty, and/or foodservice supervisors or managers. New recipes can be tested in this format. The National Dairy Council has excellent materials.

The Youth Advisory Council (YAC) and Nutrition Advisory Council are organizations made up of students interested in school food and nutrition service. Federal regulations for many years required that schools participating in the National School Lunch Program have student and parent involvement. Corpus Christi (TX) Independent School District has an active youth advisory team that provides excellent feedback to the food and nutrition service program. Orange County (FL) Public Schools has a food show for parents and students that is popular. Like many school districts, the Chapel Hill Carrboro City Schools (NC) has an advisory council that parents are encouraged to join.

The problem with involving students and parents in the menu-planning process today is that it has become so complicated. It is nearly impossible to make it a meaningful, fun experience. After all, the customer does not really care what the federal regulations are when it comes to planning menus.

Marketing is important to customer satisfaction even when most or all of the students qualify for free meals. Some schools serve 90–95 percent of their students at lunch time.

SUMMARY

Marketing has changed drastically in the last 10 years with the growth in the use of social media. School food and nutrition service management needs to involve students in the marketing program. Changes in technology are occurring fast, and the student is one of best ways of keeping up with how to market the meals.

QUESTIONS AND ANSWERS

1. Offering lunches free ensures participation.
   a. True
   b. False
2. The school lunch needs marketing to these consumers:
   a. Students and parents
   b. Teachers, principals, and cafeteria staff
   c. The community, including local media
   d. All of the above
3. In marketing, which needs to be considered?
   a. School district policy
   b. Creating a positive image
   c. Promoting the foodservice programs
   d. All of the above
4. Male and female students participate in school nutrition programs equally.
   a. True
   b. False
5. Which social media involves "tweeting" and a "following"?
   a. Facebook
   b. Twitter
   c. LinkedIn
   d. YouTube
6. Branding is useful but a current fad.
   a. True
   b. False
7. An example of branding may include offering:
   a. Coupons to go to a local fast food
   b. Turkey sub from Subway
   c. Fruit for free
   d. Games to name the food

ANSWERS: 1.b., 2.d., 3.d, 4.b., 5.b., 6.b., 7.b.

REFERENCES

Boehrer, J. 1993. Managing to meet the bottom line. *School Business Affairs*, 57 (11), 3–8.

Castillo, A. & Nettles, M. 2012. Exploring trends and barriers to implementation of branding and marketing concepts in school nutrition setting. *Journal of Child Nutrition and Management,* 36 (2). Retrieved from *http://www.schoolnutrition.org/Content.aspx?id=18049.*

Hayes, D. 2008. *Six features of an awesome website.* Nutrition Link, 33 (1).

McKinsey & Company, Inc. 2010. *Foodservice 2010: America's appetite matures.* Falls Church, VA: Foodservice Distributors International—NAWGA/IFDA, Inc.

Nettles, M. 2013. *Why calories count: From science to politics.* NY: John Wiley, Inc.

School Nutrition Association. 2010. *Social school lunch: A how-to guide on social media for school nutrition programs.* National Harbor, MD: Author.

School Nutrition Association. n.d. *Marketing 101.* National Harbor, MD: Author. Retrieved from *http://www.schoolnutrition.org/Content.aspx?id=13627.*

Simon, M. 2006. *Appetite for profit: How the food industry undermines our health and how to fight back.* New York: Nation Book.

USDA Food and Nutrition Services. 1998. *School food purchase study: Final report.* Washington, DC: Author.

U.S. Department of Education and the Kentucky Department of Education. 2002. *Marketing and merchandising concepts for school food services.* Frankfort, KY: Author.

ONLINE RESOURCES

Broward County (FL) Public Schools Food and Nutrition Services
www.broward.k12.fl.us/foodservice

FoodService Director
http://www.foodservicedirector.com/

Marketing lessons from School Lunch
http://www.idea-sandbox.com/blog/2009/08/marketing-lessons-from-school-lunch/

National Dairy Council Menu Marketing Tools Fun Facts
http://www.nationaldairycouncil.org/ChildNutrition/Pages/MenuMarketingToolsFunFacts.aspx

Ohio Farm Bureau Guide to Social Media
http://ofbf.org/uploads/social-media-guide.pdf

Palm Beach (FL) Schools—Two Videos

- *http://vodcast.palmbeachschools.org/player/5O6UO*
- *http://vodcast.palmbeachschools.org/player/VY6NC*

School Meals that Rock Facebook Page
https://www.facebook.com/SchoolMealsThatRock

School Nutrition Association Marketing 101
http://www.schoolnutrition.org/Content.aspx?id=13627

School Nutrition Association Promoting Your Program
http://www.schoolnutrition.org/Content.aspx?id=54

School Nutrition Association Social School Lunch: How-To Guide on Social Media for School Nutrition Programs
http://www.schoolnutrition.org/uploadedFiles/School_Nutrition/101_News/NewsArchives/SNA_News_Articles/Social%20Media%20Guide%20for%20SNA%20Members.pdf

School Nutrition Association TrayTalk
http://www.traytalk.org/

The John C. Stalker Institute of Food and Nutrition at Framingham State University
http://www.johnstalkerinstitute.org/

CHAPTER 11

RESOLVING FINANCIAL PROBLEMS

STUDY QUESTIONS

1. Why are monthly or more frequent financial statements important?
2. List three steps to resolving financial problems
3. What is the recommended percentage of revenue for food and labor costs?
4. Who is responsible for financial losses in food and nutrition services?
5. Describe the difference in cash-based accounting and accrual accounting.
6. What are some benchmarks to use when evaluating financial reports?
7. List five ways of reducing labor costs.
8. How can training of employees help with reducing costs?
9. List five ways of reducing food cost.
10. Why is it important to know the break-even point before adding new services?

Chapter 11

"Successful Turnaround" by Lora Gilbert, MS, RD, SNS

Executive Director, Food and Nutrition Services, Orange County Public Schools (FL)

By 2001, the Orange County Public Schools foodservice program had a substantial deficit. The administration realized that drastic decisions and changes needed to be made. Instead of outsourcing the program to a food management company, the district hired consultants Dot Martin and Gertrude Applebaum.

The analysis showed the kitchens were managed by the school-based principals. They were not held accountable for food costs, which were averaging 47 percent of total revenue. All of the managers planned their own menus and ordered from salespeople, who came to their schools. Every school's manager had a specialty day on Friday for adults.

In 2002, a new director was hired and the work began. A district menu with choices was planned and food bids awarded. Changing to a district-wide menu was a culture shock. Many principals complained that menu choices would cause long lines, and said students could not make up their mind what they wanted. The principals still had the authority over foodservices at their schools. However, they were expected to keep food costs to 40 percent (of revenue) or lower.

By then the focus had changed from selling a la carte items (48.1% of revenue) to reimbursable meals. A la carte meals were a large portion of business in secondary schools and most schools did not serve breakfast. Outside organizations were allowed to sell doughnuts, pizza, breakfast sandwiches, and other items at breakfast and lunch and throughout the day. The administration supported the decision to take all outside vendors out of the lunch program in 2003.

Reimbursable meals at lunch grew by 22 percent over the next two years.

Principals did not always have the time to run their foodservice program. In FY2005, area superintendents asked for the foodservice central office to take over the administration of the program. It was the beginning of real centralization of the programs, focus on using more commodities, a strong wellness policy, and on good nutrition for all students. Breakfast programs were extended to every school and participation increased by serving in hallways, at entrances, by the bus loop, or wherever students gathered before school.

By 2013, the number of meals served to students and total federal reimbursements doubled. The current budget has a healthy fund balance of three months of expenditures and has plans to build a central production kitchen.

Financial problems may be caused by failure to operate using financial data. School districts that had no financial problems in the past began to experience financial difficulties after 2010. The obvious problem today is that revenue is not keeping pace with expenditures. Unlike the late 1990s, when the labor cost was the main problem, the cost of food has become a challenge, too.

OVERVIEW OF RESOLVING FINANCIAL PROBLEMS

The school food and nutrition service operation has become more complex and is changing at a faster pace than ever before. Many school district administrators find their food and nutrition service programs have turned into three-meal-a-day operations. The menus are featuring more fresh foods and resulting in more cooking from raw ingredients. Unlike earlier days, the employees of today may not know how to cook when they come to work.

By federal law, the foodservice program must not end a school year with a deficit. A fund balance from prior years can be used to offset the deficit. If no fund balance is available, the school district's general fund has to cover the deficit. Depending on the administration and school board's philosophy, a deficit may not be a desired option. When a deficit for the year does occur, it is time to begin planning ways of resolving the problem.

The three main steps to resolving financial problems are:

1. Determine what is causing the financial problem.
2. Take action to reduce cost.
3. Increase revenue to offset the increased expenses.

Following these steps will require analyzing financial reports. More detail is available in Chapter 2, "Financial Management."

This chapter will provide numerous ways for reducing cost and increasing revenue. Directors and managers need to decide what will work for their school district. It is wise to check with the state agency before making major changes. States may differ in their requirements.

Consider the following when reducing cost of labor and food and increasing revenue:

- Politics of the school community
- Economy of the area
- Customer and parent acceptance of change

To resolve financial problems successfully, it is necessary to sell the changes for reducing cost and increasing revenue. Who needs to be "sold" or "informed" on the proposed changes before going forward? Success often depends on people being informed.

A school foodservice budget may have little room for error. The budget is complex and based on estimates of numbers served, which determines revenue and much of the variable cost. In many cases, the central office cannot control costs. It may require help from the bottom up, with managers and staff at each cost center (school) focused on the goals. Moreover, it may require some major changes in the production system.

ANALYZING FINANCIAL REPORTS

With technology today, resolving financial problems should be data driven. The following basic questions need answers:

- Is an accurate, timely financial report of revenue and expenses available?
- Are the financial data used?
- Does management understand the financial reports?

- What are the benchmarks? Budget, national norms, and/or former year's data may be used.
- Is the budget a useful, meaningful report?
- Is the accounting system cash-based accounting, accrual-based accounting, or modified accrual–based accounting?

Definitions:

CASH-BASED ACCOUNTING—A system of accounting recording revenues when received and expenses in the period they are paid.

ACCRUAL-BASED ACCOUNTING—A system of accounting in which revenues are recorded in the period earned and expenses are recorded in the period they occur.

MODIFIED ACCRUAL-BASED ACCOUNTING—A system that recognizes revenue when collected, and expenditures as liabilities when they occur.

Analyzing the statement of revenue and expenditures (net gain/loss statement) will help determine what is causing a financial problem. This report is a profit and loss statement in the commercial foodservice industry. This report becomes more meaningful when comparing percentage of the revenue used for labor, food, and supplies.

Goals for percentage of revenue are:

- 35–40% for labor and benefits
- 35–40% for food (including value of USDA Foods)
- 3–5% for supplies
- 15% for other costs

For example, to determine labor costs' percentage of revenue:

Labor and benefits are $7,000 and revenue is $20,000
$7,000 is divided by $20,000
$7,000 ÷ $20,000 = 35%

According to a federal study (2008) of several school districts, the average food cost was 46 percent of the expenses, labor 45 percent, and supplies 9 percent. When those percentages are added together, the costs are 100 percent. Does that mean the school district broke even? The percentages in this study are of expenses. Since the study does not address how much revenue was available, the percentages are meaningless for analyzing financial situations. For example, if the total expenses are $50,000, but the total revenue is only $45,000, the loss would be $5,000.

The accounting system used in financial reporting (and the accuracy and timeliness of the reports) are important for management to control finances. Chapter 2, "Financial Management," offers more details. The National Food Service Management Institute (NFSMI) has excellent courses, seminars, and videos on school food and nutrition services financial management.

Cash Accounting or Accrual Accounting

With a cash-based accounting system, revenues include what has been received at that time, and expenses are recorded when paid. This system does not give a federally subsidized school food and nutrition service program an accurate picture of the financial situation. The federal reimbursements are based on the number of meals/snacks served. The reimbursement is received after the end of the claiming period (end of month). With cash-based accounting, it may be the end of the budget year before all revenues and expenses show up on the report. Exhibit 11-1 provides a comparison of a statement of revenue and expenditures using accrual-based accounting and cash-based accounting systems.

Exhibit 11-1 Cash-Based Accounting and Accrual-Based Accounting Monthly Financial Statements at End of First Month

Category or Source	Cash Accounting	Accrual Accounting
Revenues for Month		
Cash Student Sales for Month	All	All
Cash Adult Sales for Month	All	All
Cash Extra Food Sales for Month	All	All
Federal Cash Reimbursements for Month[1]	-0-	All
State Cash Reimbursements for Month[1]	-0-	All
Catering & Contracted Services Payable[1]	-0-	All
USDA Foods Value	-0-	All
Total Revenue	**Cash Received**	**Earned**
Expenses for Month		
Cost of Food	Paid	
Beginning Food Inventory		All
Food (purchased & USDA Foods)		
+ (plus) Purchased Foods		All
+ (plus) USDA Foods Received Value		All
– (minus) Ending Inventory = (equals)		All Used
Cost of Food Used	-0-	All
Cost of Supplies and Paper Items	Paid	
Beginning Supplies Inventory		All
+ (plus) Purchased Supplies		All
– (minus) Ending Inventory = (equals)		All Used
Cost of Supplies		
Labor and Benefits	Paid	
Payroll/Salaries	Paid	All
Benefits	Partial	All
Total Cost Labor & Benefits for Month	Paid	All
Operating Expenses	Partial	All
Total Expenses		All
Net Profit (or Loss)	**Cash Received/ Expenses Paid**	**Actual Gain (Profit) or Loss (Deficit)**

[1]Federal and state reimbursements will be after the end of the month.

The difference in cash-based and accrual-based accounting is *timing*. With true cash-based accounting, the financial report will not show how a fund is doing until the end of the accounting cycle—generally the end of school year, which is too late to take corrective action.

Inventory value of food and supplies (e.g., paper goods, detergents) are assets. Purchased food and USDA Foods inventories do not have to be separate according to federal law. Regardless of whether the inventories are together or separate, the value in inventory of USDA Foods and purchased foods are revenue. When used, USDA Foods and purchased foods are expenses.

School food and nutrition service management should receive a statement of revenue and expenditures with accruals on a weekly basis (at latest, monthly basis). This report should show revenue earned (including federal and state reimbursements) and expenses when incurred (including bills to be paid and payroll owed). These reports should consider the value of USDA Foods as revenue. The expenditures should determine purchased foods, USDA Foods, and supplies used by showing beginning and ending inventory. If management has accurate, timely reports that show how the program is doing financially, then management should be held responsible.

Many school district accounting departments focus on meeting budgets. School food and nutrition service programs are generally dependent on federal and state revenues earned according to the number of meals/snacks served. The program should be treated as an enterprise account (business), not a budgetary account. The revenue is to be compared to the expenses for the same period to determine financial status. Chapter 2, "Financial Management," offers additional information.

Definitions as related to Child Nutrition Programs:

ENTERPRISE FUND—Revenue is generated by the number of meals/snacks served; if more meals/snacks are served, the revenue will be more than budgeted, and expenses (particularly variable cost) will be more than estimated in budget.

BUDGETARY FUND—The revenues and expenses are preset. The customer count and revenue does not vary from day to day as it might with customer count in a school foodservice operation.

The Denver (CO) Public School district has established several departments as enterprise accounts. Food and Nutrition Service Department is under the Enterprise Management Division in the school district and operates like a business.

Corrective action needs to be taken early in a school year. Accrual-based accounting shows receivables and payables posted when revenues are earned and expenses are incurred. This approach gives a clearer picture of whether the program is making or losing money. With computerization, it is possible to produce financial data on timely bases, which enables management to take corrective action quickly.

A director needs to know whether the program's financial report includes receivables and payables. In Exhibit 11-1, the two systems and the differences between the two methods of accounting are compared. The accrual accounting column shows revenue and expenses for the same period. If expenses exceed revenues, there is a loss, which will grow and become a financial problem.

Determining Problem Areas

To determine what is causing a deficit requires comparing the *expenses to revenue* in percentages with goals or norms.

The key performance indicators to use in determining problem areas are:

- Budget, which will be more meaningful when percentage of expenses are compared with estimated revenue
- Goals or norms for expenses (percentage of revenue)
- Meals per labor hour (MPLH)
- Previous year's performance
- Other school districts of similar size

After the reasons for the financial problem have been determined, it is time for action. With the emphasis on financial management in the 21st century, the director of the program needs to understand the concepts involved. This understanding will become more important to management in controlling costs when it exceeds revenue. Today, the food and nutrition service program is changing rapidly and costs are growing fast. Even the experienced financial manager/director will be challenged.

REDUCING TOTAL LABOR COST

When labor costs exceed 40–45 percent of the revenue, steps must occur to reduce these costs. Personnel are an area most administrators do not want to touch because community politics may be involved. Making changes to personnel may be necessary for the financial success of the program and for job security reasons.

Today the labor costs in some school districts exceed 50–60 percent of the revenue. One or a combination of factors causes high labor costs:

- Pay scales are too high.
- Benefits are too high.
- Productivity is low.
- Schools are overstaffed.
- Overtime and substitute use are out of control.
- Revenues are not high enough.

Exhibit 11-2 illustrates how low productivity effects labor costs using equal revenue and hourly labor cost to illustrate. (Chapter 5, "Personnel and Staffing," has more information on MPLH.)

Exhibit 11-2 Comparison of Productivity Effect on Cost of a Lunch

Category	District A	District B	District C	District D
Average Revenue per Lunch	$3.00	$3.00	$3.00	$3.00
Average Meal per Labor Hour (MPLH)	12	14	16	18
Average Cost of a Labor Hour (including manager salaries and benefits)	$20.00	$20.00	$20.00	$20.00
Average Cost Labor/Lunch Percentage of Revenue	$1.67 56%	$1.43 48%	$1.25 42%	$1.11 37%

If nine-month employees receive pay over twelve-month period, the actual monthly cost of labor may not be showing up until paid. Some directors have misinterpreted this to mean that the summer school labor is very high. The labor needs to be accrued when earned (not paid).

Reducing the Cost of a Labor Hour

In the preceding comparison of labor information, corrective action may not be popular with the employees. Grandfathering current staff and changing the pay scale may be an option when it becomes necessary to reduce costs. The following suggestions are ways to reduce labor costs:

- Replace pay scale. Conduct salary study, reclassify employees, and realign pay scale to more closely resemble commercial foodservices pay scales.
- Reduce number of step raises and tie raises to performance.
- Place restrictions on benefits (e.g., staff employees are not eligible for the retirement program or eligible after one or more years of employment, or only managers are eligible for health insurance and retirement).
- Pay less of the costs of health insurance (e.g., less on part-time than for full-time employees). Legislatures in some states set benefits, such as retirement and health insurance.
- Replace full-time positions with part-time employees, who do not qualify for many of the expensive benefits.

When a school district begins reducing wages and benefits for employees, the results may be higher turnover, lower morale, and loss of dedicated, motivated, and qualified staff. This can mean negative changes in the quality of the food and/or service. However, many of the commercial foodservices function successfully with high turnover and employees with no pervious foodservice experience. Their secrets may be a short menu cycle, standardized recipes and procedures, and a good training program. Chapter 3, "Nutrition and Menu Planning," offers suggested menu changes that can aid in standardizing the school food and nutrition service, reducing cost, and increasing revenue.

Reducing Total Labor Cost

After reducing the cost of a labor hour, the labor cost may still be too high. If labor costs are over 40 percent of the revenue, the question is WHY? The answer could be overstaffed, too many in management roles, and inefficiency. Below are some ways to reduce labor cost:

- Staffing the school properly (Chapter 5, "Personnel and Staffing," provides guidelines.)
- Staffing with fewer hours than suggested and fewer full-time employees
- Scheduling work effectively; scheduling employees when needed because idle time is expensive time
- Increasing the span of control of management; establishing dual-management roles (assigning one manager responsibility for two or more schools)
- Paying for performance because incentive to be more productive
- Employing and paying student labor for just the time needed (e.g., 30 minutes during lunch service)
- Increasing productivity (Exhibit 11-2 shows the effects of improving productivity on cost of producing a lunch.)

Increasing Productivity

One of the main reasons for high labor costs, as mentioned earlier, may be low productivity. According to the U.S. Department of Labor, productivity in the foodservice industry was at a standstill in 2012. To determine whether the productivity rates in a school district (or school) are high or low—determine the number of MPLH.

Increasing productivity means improving output per labor hour. It means producing more meals with the present number of labor hours or producing the same with fewer labor hours. The motto is "working smarter not harder."

Management can increase productivity by:

- Training in time and motion economy and improving job efficiency (Details on ways of training for improved job efficiency appear later in this chapter.)
- Applying work simplification methods
- Arranging the kitchen for an efficient flow of work
- Establishing the time a job should take
- Utilizing automation
- Eliminating the need for some positions (e.g., dish machine operator by changing to disposables)
- Planning the workday for each employee in 15-minute intervals (Chapter 5, "Personnel and Staffing," has an example of work scheduling.)
- Scheduling employees to eat on their own time.
- Monitoring use of substitutes and eliminating use when overstaffed
- Pay only for required breaks (e.g., allow one 15- minute break in a 5-hour day)
- Reducing the number of hours full-time employees work from 7–8 hours to 5½ hours

It is important to check with the state agency for state laws and with local union contracts before making change in breaks and hours worked. When reducing staff or labor hours, training is necessary to improve productivity. Training and making changes in the work site are usually important to accomplishing the scheduled workload.

Using more convenience foods and disposable supplies to reduce the number of labor hours should be analyzed carefully. The cost of the convenience food should be compared with the total cost of making the menu items from raw ingredients.

A study of three school districts in the South showed the breakfast menus contain 70–80 percent convenience foods, which meant two labor hours could handle 100 breakfast meals. In these school districts, several employees were coming to work by 6:30 a.m. to serve breakfast at 7:45 a.m., because they had always come to work at that time. Too much labor with nothing to do often results in lunch being ready to serve by the time breakfast was ready, or shortly thereafter.

It is important that the addition of convenience foods and disposable dishes be matched by a cutback in staff or hours. Otherwise, according to Parkinson's Law—*"Work expands so as to fill the time available"*—the staff will simply slow down and adjust to the lighter workload.

Training to Improve Job Efficiency

The school food and nutrition service manager should be trained in the basic principles of motion economy, to improve productivity. The manager can illustrate the principles of motion economy during training and when motivating employees to increase productivity. When the manager demonstrates the basic steps of motion economy in on-the-job training, kitchen employees view the principles as a way to improve their jobs.

Using the principles of motion economy in school food and nutrition services lead to increased productivity.

Three principles of motion economy will make a real difference in the results:

1. Hand and body motions
2. Work process or sequence
3. Design of tools, equipment, and workplace

Observation is one of the main ways of determining jobs to improve. Training in principles of motion economy will increase productivity and in turn enable the program to reduce labor cost. Details on the principles of motion economy along with examples follow.

Principles of Motion Economy and Examples

1. Hand and Body Motions
    - Use both hands at the same time to do useful work whenever possible. *Examples:*
        - Pan cookies, biscuits, rolls, etc.; pick up one or more items in each hand and put onto the pan.
        - Rack dishes: pick up a plate, a bowl, etc., in each hand to put in the dishwashing racks. Use both hands to take dishes out of the racks and stack.
        - Serve food: pick up a plate with one hand and bring midway to meet the food that has been dipped or picked up by the other hand.

- Perform work in a rhythmic way. *Examples:*
  - Use a French knife: place the knifepoint on the cuttin board and with other hand move the food under the knife; rock the knife up and down, cutting the food and developing a rhythm.
- Develop a natural rhythm: practice with motions such as stirring, racking dishes, rolling, or cutting rolls and biscuits. Use smooth, continuous, curved motions when possible rather than straight-line motions with sharp changes in direction. (This can increase productivity by 25%.) *Examples*:
  - Wipe tables: Use wide archlike motion rather than straight-line motions.
  - Spread sandwich filling on bread: Spread with circular motion without lifting the tool.
- Use the fewest, shortest, and simplest motions. *Examples:*
  - Brush and spread: use a 2-, 3-, or 4-inch pastry brush instead of a 1-inch brush for greasing pans, or a spatula for spreading mayonnaise and butter on bread; reduce strokes by using the largest brush feasible.
  - Measure: use the largest measure practical, not multiples of a smaller one (e.g., 1 cup measure instead of 16 table-spoons, a 2-ounce ladle to obtain a 2-ounce quantity) and add the measurement information to the recipe for sugar, salt, and other spices.
  - Use short menu cycles and standardize all procedures.
- Combine operations and eliminate all unnecessary parts of the job. *Examples:*
  - Cook in serving pans.
  - Add dry milk to dry ingredients, and then add water—eliminating reconstitution of milk.

  - Use the serving dish or portion cup to congeal gelatin.
  - Combine peanut butter and jelly before spreading on bread.
- Standardize jobs. *Examples:*
  - Put the same number of items (hamburger patties, cookies, etc.) on a pan each time.
  - Time jobs and establish a reasonable amount of time for doing each job. Example: How long should it take an employee to portion 250 fruit cups and tossed salads?
  - Use short menu cycles and standardize all procedures.
- Eliminate unnecessary walking, reaching, stretching, and bending. *Examples:*
  - Use a cart to carry supplies needed from the storeroom.

2. <u>Work Process or Sequence</u>
   - Arrange the kitchen layout to accomplish the best flow of work.
   - Divide kitchen into work centers (e.g., salad preparation, baking).
   - Schedule employees to come and leave work to fit the job.

3. <u>Design of Tools, Equipment, and Workplace</u>
   - Use ergonomics (e.g., adjust work surface to the height of the employee).
   - Color code work centers and tools for ease of returning after cleaning.
   - Use well designed tools.
   - Color code refrigerator doors to designate work centers (e.g., salad department in a large school has a specific refrigerator).

- Use automation and technology (e.g., vending machines to dispense lunches).
- Reduce number of serving lines when meal count does not justify them.
- Arrange storeroom with most frequently used items closer to the entrance and in the most convenient location.
- Design inventory form in the same order as storeroom layout.
- Place equipment needed in more than one work center on wheels or have duplicate pieces of equipment in each work center.
- Replace dishwasher position with disposable supplies, if more cost effective.

San Benito (TX) Food and Nutrition Services has an average of 23 MPLH with on-site production. They accomplished this productivity rate by changing processes, planning a short menu cycle, improving equipment design, and standardizing procedures.

Steps to Resolving Low Productivity

When tasks take more time than they should, use the following steps to improve productivity.

1. Select the job to be improved and define the situation.
2. Break down the job into parts by using a flow chart.
3. Question each step and each process to determine:
   a. Is there a better way?
   b. Can steps be eliminated?
   c. Can steps be simplified?

4. Arrive at a new method.
5. Put new method into action.
6. Follow up and evaluate.

Example of a situation and job:
Making 1,000 peanut butter and jelly sandwiches for bag lunches is taking eight employee hours.

- Four employees are working at the same table as they talk.
- One employee starts process by spreading peanut butter on a piece of bread; second employee adds jelly; third employee places top pieces of bread on sandwich and cuts; and fourth employee wraps sandwich and puts into lunch bag.

Productivity is not as great when employees are talking and waiting for each other to complete tasks. Each task does not take the same amount of time. If this job is to be improved and productivity increased, consider setting up two sandwich assembly stations with one person in each (Exhibit 11-3).

Exhibit 11-3 Sandwich Assembly

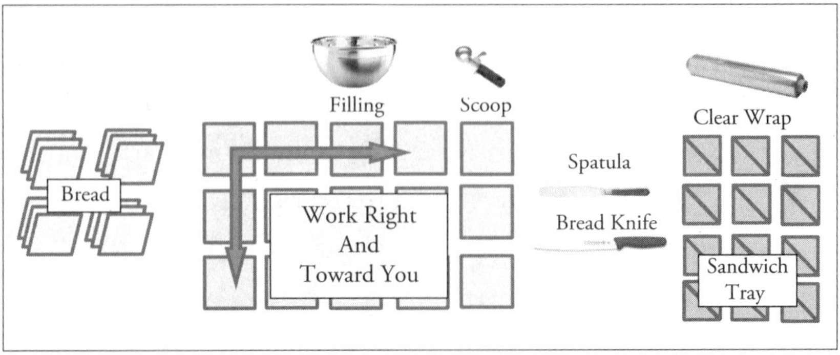

<u>Steps to sandwich assembly:</u>

1. Collect all ingredients and supplies ready for assembly. Use cart.
2. Set up work center with all ingredients, pans, utensils, and supplies needed. Supplies should include:
   a. Cutting board
   b. Sharp knife
   c. Scoop for filling
   d. Spatulas for spreading
   e. Combined peanut butter and jelly
   f. Selected wrap or baggie
   g. Pans or containers to hold finished sandwiches (put in lunch bag when all items are ready for assembly line).
3. Place all ingredients and supplies within easy reach of the assembler.
4. Work in sequence; avoid backtracking; finish process of first two layers of sandwiches before starting others.
   a. Have opened loaves of bread to left.
   b. Cover cutting board with one layer of bread.
   c. Put filling on bread using scoop of appropriate size.
   d. Use spatula and circular motion to spread filling to edges of bread.
   e. Place two slices of bread on top, begin the process for second layer.
   f. Cut through two layers of sandwiches.
5. Wrap the two halves to best merchandise the sandwich.
6. Place in serving pan or container of choice.

REDUCING FOOD COST

What is a high food cost? According to *Foodservice Director's* 2012 School Census Report the average cost for food (excluding USDA

Foods) was $1.62. The range extended from a low of 85¢ to a high of $3.45. When the cost of food exceeds labor cost in school districts it often results in s deficits.

A number of ways can be used to reduce food costs, including the following:

- Planning less expensive menus
- Obtaining more competitive food prices
- Reducing waste—in preparation, on students' plates, and from overcooking
- Utilizing leftovers, following Hazard Analysis & Critical Control Point rules
- Purchasing a less-expensive product
- Reducing portion sizes
- Carrying out "offer versus serve"
- Utilizing USDA Foods better
- Ordering only what is needed
- Checking in orders and storing properly
- Eliminating theft by employees, distributors, and students/customers

Another consideration is to treat the cost of employees' lunches as a benefit. Some school districts charge employees for their lunches. If a meal cost $3.25 to prepare and serve, the cost to the district is more than $500 annually per employee to provide a free lunch.

Planning Less-Expensive Menus

By precosting menus, the planner is able to tell whether planned menus need less-expensive items. For example, if the average revenue for lunch is $2.87 and the goal is to keep food cost at 40 percent of the revenue, the planner needs to determine how much money is available for food.

$2.87	Total Revenue for Meal
x .40	(40% for Food)
$1.15	Amount for Food

The menus should be planned to meet basic federal requirements. Any additional foods may consist of the condiments served with the foods. However, extras may be limited or eliminated from the menu in order to reduce waste and costs. Examples of additional foods are second portions and some desserts. Sold as a la carte, these are for those who need or want the additional calories. Providing more items on the menu than are needed is nice, if the district can afford the extra cost.

Some menu items may no longer be affordable or must be sold a la carte or as part of a higher lunch price. If 75–80 percent of the students pay for lunches (25% or less free and reduced-price), two differently priced lunches may be a solution.

For Example: Combo 1 $2.50 Combo 2 $2.75

This approach works particularly well in high schools, where the appetites of students are widely different—from athletes to weight-conscious girls. The higher-priced lunch menu can include more expensive items, like a chicken tender, or customized service (e.g., Subway-style sandwich). The students who are eligible for free and reduced-price lunches must have the option of the higher-priced lunch if the lunch is to be claimed for federal reimbursement.

Obtaining Better Food Prices

Some smaller school food and nutrition service programs are having problems obtaining competitive food prices. The lack of competition among distributors and a dairy monopoly (only one dairy bidding on the school business) has resulted in higher food costs. Some school districts are keeping prices lower by awarding food bids to a prime vendor (with one or two distributors providing most of the purchased foods and supplies).

Hospitals and colleges have done excellent jobs of forming cooperatives, and it may be possible for the school district to join a cooperative or start one. Mississippi, Montana, and Texas, for example, have state school foodservice cooperatives handled by the states' departments of education. Reducing the number of deliveries per week can help make dairies more interested in the business. Some schools have added more milk coolers to store two days of milk and accept/expect every-other-day milk deliveries. Reducing the varieties of products (e.g., several different types of potatoes and a la carte items offered will increase the volume and may reduce the price paid). Chapter 6, "Procurement and Inventory Control," provides more information.

It may be necessary for a school district to reduce the vendors' costs of doing business with their schools in the future to obtain better prices. Many school districts have established warehouses, which may or may not achieve a savings. The expenses of storing and distributing may be costing the school district more than is saved.

Purchasing the grade of product actually needed is the goal. For example, using Grade A fruits and vegetables may not be necessary. For instance, fruit cobbler does not need Grade A sliced peaches. It is desirable to use seasonal foods when possible and plan menus accordingly. Purchasing beef products that contain soybean products will reduce the cost per pound. Using a different piece of chicken or cut of meat may reduce costs.

Using a less-expensive ingredient that will do the job is desirable. Using refried beans and kidney beans in Mexican-type dishes will reduce the costs of many of these popular lunches. Salad dressing, for example, may be satisfactory substitute for mayonnaise and may cost less. Consider other imitation or substitutes, such as imitation whipped topping and sour cream.

Reducing Food Waste

Food waste creates an unnecessary cost that can be reduced. In reducing food waste and controlling production, consider the following:

- Producing just what is needed by better forecasting
- Instituting "offer versus serve" at all grade levels
- Putting someone in charge of planning the use of leftovers
- Practicing just-in-time cooking, reducing holding time and loss
- Practicing portion control
- Pre-portioning food for service when possible
- Providing close supervision during preparation and service

Offer versus serve is the regulation that allows food and nutrition service to offer a complete meal and the students the option of taking less. Though "offer versus serve" is required by regulation at the high school level, the local school district can decide whether it will be carried out at other grade levels.

By auditing or observing trash at end of lunch periods, management will realize when to make changes in menu. "Offer versus serve" and offering choices are ways of reducing plate waste. Instituting offer versus serve will reduce costs by 30¢ to 40¢ per meal.

If the plate waste is heavy, why?

- Is it because the students do not like the food?
- Is it because the portions are too large?
- Is it because recess is after lunch and students' attention is focused on play rather than eating?

It may be a combination of these factors causing heavy waste.

Correct portion sizes are critical to meeting the menu planning guidelines. Serving too large a portion is often a problem and increases food cost. Managers should always be aware that portion control needs supervision. Pre-portioning can help ensure a standard portion.

The saying is that "the more one has in inventory the more one uses." Managers fear running out of food and often over order to ensure it does not happen. Over ordering can result in waste, particularly with produce. Well-stocked storerooms may encourage theft. It takes careful planning to order just enough for delivery at the right time. Aramark, a management company, requires schools to take an inventory weekly before placing their orders and has strict guidelines that limit the number of days of inventory a school can have.

Determine Number of Days in Inventory and Number of Turnovers

1. Divide food cost for month by number of days served equals average daily cost of food (e.g., $20,400 cost of food used ÷ 18 days served = $1,133 average daily food cost).
2. Divide the end of month inventory dollars by the average daily food cost per day equals number of days in inventory (e.g., $8,100 inventory ÷ $1,133 average daily food cost = 7.1 days of inventory; 30 days in month ÷ 7.1 = 4 turnovers).

Over production of food is common, particularly in schools that offer choices. The answer to this problem is not discontinuing food choices, but instead cooking just-in-time and using the production records for better forecasting. It is important for the menu planner to check the numbers served on previous menus before ordering. Over production results in leftovers, which often become food waste. Some leftovers can be frozen and used the next time the items are on the menu. Fresh fruits can be offered the following day as an additional choice.

No food, including leftovers, should go home with employees. Do not allow employees to take leftovers home, because this practice encourages over production.

Utilizing USDA Foods Better

Considering USDA Foods (formerly called commodities) at their purchased value rather than as "freebies" is important to the attitude toward the use of USDA Foods. The fact that a food is "donated" does not justify giving very large portions or serving the food simply to "use it up." This philosophy was taught in the early days of USDA Foods. Today, the USDA Foods are considered "entitlements" and a specific dollar amount each year. The amount is according to the number of lunches the school district served the prior year.

If USDA Foods can take the place of a purchased item, it adds real value to the food and nutrition service program. Some USDA Foods are not easy to use, and some should be refused.

> Refusing some USDA Foods may save money in the end, if that product:
> - Requires excessive time and skill to prepare
> - Has poor acceptance
> - Results in lower participation

Processing USDA Foods may not be a wise use of the entitlement money. It requires careful analyses—it may not be a good buy. Is the school districts' labor cost higher than the manufacturers' labor cost? How much does the processed, delivered product really cost? The processed product may be costing far more than the commercial product. The fair market value (or the dollar amount of entitlement used) is part of the real cost. The goal is to use the USDA Foods entitlement wisely.

Bonus foods are extras that are available due to excess amounts on the market. Utilizing those foods can be like "freebies." The American Commodity Distribution Association provides useful information on processing and utilizing the foods available wisely.

Many states' USDA Foods distribution agencies (e.g., Colorado, Georgia, Texas, and Maryland) do excellent jobs of processing USDA Foods into more usable products. In California, groups of food and nutrition service directors have organized cooperatives that handle the USDA Foods processing and distribution. Local school district food and nutrition service directors can get involved in state processing contracts and often better utilize USDA Foods.

REDUCING THEFT

High food costs can be caused by theft—either of food/supplies or revenue (either will cause food cost percentages to increase). The most important safeguard against theft is a good system of accountability and using data reports to monitor usage. Such a system accounts for every item received and used, and will bring shortages or losses to the attention of the manager. Perpetual inventory is an excellent accountability tool, particularly when computerized and tied to the food "rung up" at the point-of-sale. The perpetual inventory should to be verified with a physical inventory at intervals.

Customer Theft

Customer theft is a major problem for some schools, particularly high schools. Unfortunately, displaying easy-to-pocket items is asking for problems. It has become necessary for staff to hand students a la carte items from behind the serving counter rather than allowing students to serve themselves.

Some of the most common theft is from students passing off counterfeit bills, pocketing a drink, and combining two servings of food into one container. Security cameras will reduce student theft. Fairfax County (VA) Public Schools installed security cameras and reduced student theft considerably.

It is important to have good a la carte accountability. This level of accountability means having a daily inventory of what is available to sell and an inventory of what is left. Then it is possible to determine whether the revenue is short. With this kind of accountability, the manager will have a realistic picture of theft.

Counting the day's receipts should be in a secure location, not in the dining room. A large high school may have between $1,500 and $3,000 per day, which is an attractive sum to steal.

Employee Theft

Embezzlement by cashiers is a widespread problem in the foodservice business, as well as in stores. It is probably a bigger problem for school food and nutrition service than is realized. Strict internal controls prevent theft of money and food. Comparing the data at the end of the day from computerized point-of-sale devices offers a lot of information. Moving employees' lockers away from the back door will make it harder for employees to store money or items in their locker during the day and take them home at the end of the work day.

Many schools have switched to using clear garbage bags. Boxes need to be broken down before taken out to the trash or allowing employees take the box home. Taking cans or packages of food and supplies out in the garbage are common ways of stealing.

Distributor Theft

A manager (or a manager's designee) should check in deliveries carefully against the actual order. When a manager does not carefully check in deliveries, the foodservice may be shortchanged, receive an inferior product, or not receive what was ordered. The Story at the opening of Chapter 6, "Procurement and Inventory Control," tells of this happening.

The price charged at the point of delivery and the price bid should be the same. The challenge may be to keep people honest with checks and balances. Preprinted delivery tickets that have the bid prices can help reduce price differences.

INCREASING REVENUE

Before offering new services or trying to expand services to offer, determine what the break-even point is for the service. Chapter 2, "Financial Management," has more information on break-even points.

How many meals/meal equivalents do you have to serve to break even? In order to offer any extra services, the school food and nutrition service employees have to be efficient and have high productivity. For some districts with high pay scales and benefits, providing extra services would be losing situations if labor hours have to be increased. In addition, the food cost may be too high. It is important to know the cost, as well as the revenue. Exhibit 11-4 illustrates how to determine revenue.

Finding Other Sources of Revenue

Numerous sources of revenue in addition to the lunch, breakfast, and snack programs are available. The revenue from other sources can help cover administrative and overhead costs. However,

Exhibit 11-4 Example of How to Determine Revenue for Lunch

Source	Elementary Paying Lunch	Secondary Paying Lunch	Free Lunch	Reduced-Price Lunch	Adult Lunch
Cash Sales	$2.7500	$3.0000	-0-	$.4000	$4.00
Federal Reimbursement[1] Supplement[2]	 .2800 .0600	 .2800 .0600	 $2.9300 .0600	 2.5300 .0600	 -0-
Entitlement Commodity Value[3] Bonus[4]	 .2325	 .2325	 .2325	 .2325	 -0-
State Funds[5]	-0-	-0-	-0-	-0-	-0-
Totals	**$3.3225**	**$3.5725**	**$3.2225**	**$3.2225**	**$4.00**

[1]Based on SY2014 reimbursement rates.
[2]Available for meeting federal meal requirements.
[3]Based on SY2014 USDA Foods entitlement rates.
[4]Varies from year to year, depending on surpluses.
[5]Some states provide cash supplements.

management needs to know the break-even point of each service provided. Additional revenue can help subsidize the lunch and breakfast programs. Below are some sources of revenue:

- Capitalize on grant opportunities (e.g., equipment, fresh fruit and vegetables, nutrition education)
- Provide food and/or services to other groups, such as
  - Charter schools, private schools, day cares
  - Head Start programs
  - Senior citizen programs, meals on wheels, adult day care centers
  - Detention centers
  - Administrative buildings in school district or city/county buildings
  - Sack lunches for field trips
  - After-school care programs

 - Concession stands at the local stadiums
 - Parks and other recreational areas
- Offer classroom catering
- Provide Summer Food Service Program—as a sponsor or vendor, or both
- Offer vending in schools, office buildings, and county administrative buildings
- Include interest and dividends earned on fund balance
- Participate in Community Eligibility Provision, if cost effective
- Include rebates from company on processed foods

Management needs to analyze cost before adding any additional services. If the cost of a labor hour is high, each additional service offered may result in increasing a deficit.

The Community Eligibility Provision is a form of a universal free meal program. Many benefits could be realized for all students entitled to free breakfasts and lunches. School districts in a few states are participating in a pilot program. Many of them have experienced increased participation in the School Breakfast Program (SBP) and National School Lunch Program (NSLP).

Effective for SY2015, the Community Eligibility Provision is available to schools/school districts in all states. A school district should carefully analyze the pros and cons of the program. It is important to know (1) what the financial impact will be, (2) how the district will meet the Title I data requirement and other programs that depend on free/reduced-price meal application data, as well as (3) the community attitude toward an all-free food program. The individual state agencies that administer the SBP and NSLP are the best sources of information.

Exhibit 11-5 provides the qualification criteria and some important information regarding Community Eligibility Provision.

If 62.5 percent or more of the student enrollment directly certify as qualifying for free meals, Community Eligibility Provision may be a winning situation.

Exhibit 11-5 Information and Cautions Regarding Community Eligibility Provision

Community Eligibility Provision applies by school, group of schools, or district. Applications must be in to state agencies by June 30 of one year for the following school year.

To Qualify for Community Eligibility Provision:

1. 40% or more of student enrollment must be identified as eligible through direct certification based on data as of April 1 to qualify the following school year.
   Example: Enrollment is 10,000 students; 4,000 students directly certified (data from the SNAP[1], TANF[2], and other programs such as Headstart, Migrant, Homeless)
   4,000 ÷ 10,000 = 40%
2. School or district must agree to serve all students a breakfast and lunch free.
3. Pay for any meals not free from sources other than federal funds the cost in excess of federal assistance.

Important Information:

Percentage of students who are directly certified is to be multiplied by USDA factor (1.6 in SY2014; factor holds for 4-year period; factor could be changed by USDA).

Example: 40% x 1.6 = 64% of meals served will qualify at the federal free meal reimbursement rate

6,000 of the students eat lunch x 64% = 3,840 of lunches qualify for free meal reimbursement rate

(3,840 x $3.01[3] = $11,558.40 for lunch)

2,160 students qualify for paid meal reimbursement rate

(2,160 x $.34[4] = $734.40 for lunch)

The threshold where 100% of the meals served are reimbursed at free meal reimbursement rates is 62.5%.

Example: 62.5% x 1.6 = 100% of meals served will qualify at federal free meal reimbursement rate

(6,000 x $3.01 = $18,060 from USDA based on free rates)

Entitlement USDA Foods value is based on number served lunch the prior year, multiplied by the current year's entitlement rate (in SY2014 the rate is $.2325).

Challenge:

Even if 62.5% or more of the students qualified as eligible, some challenges still remain. What is the break-even point? Will serving more students cost the district more? Can the foodservice program operate within the revenue available? To break even the cost of producing and serving the meal must be within the revenue available from federal and state reimbursement rates.

[1]Supplemental Nutrition Assistance Program.
[2]Temporary Assistance for Needy Families.
[3]Severe need school district rates SY2014 plus meeting meal requirement supplement.
[4]SY2014 paid lunch reimbursement plus meeting meal requirement supplement.

Summer Food Service can be an excellent source of revenue. The state agency will have current information on options available and the funding. Summer Food Service is not only a source of revenue for the school food and nutrition services program, but it benefits the children, community, and employees who want a job during the summer. A search on the USDA website provides many examples of successful, creative summer programs.

Before taking on additional services, administration needs to know the break-even point and whether the funding/revenue is adequate to cover the cost. The additional services offered may require more labor. If the district is overstaffed, it can provide work for staff and revenue to help justify labor hours. Even when staff is available, the revenue should be adequate to cover the cost the district will incur.

Raising Prices

After taking the preceding steps, if the revenue does not cover costs, it is time to consider raising prices charged for breakfast and lunch. The school district may not serve enough paying students for it to make a difference. After July 2011, many school districts increased lunch prices to comply with the federal mandate of "equity" in pricing. State agencies are the source of information on price requirements. Chapter 1, "Introduction," discusses the Paid Price Equity regulation.

If the price increase is beyond the "equity" requirement, a price increase should be used as a last resort or in combination with reducing costs. The factors to consider include the following:

- Costs of producing and serving the food
- Equity pricing requirements
- Economic situation in the community at the time
- What other school districts in area are charging

- When the price was last increased
- Whether the price increase can be justified publicly (e.g., in the media)
- What the customer considers a fair value
- Facts provided to superintendent and school board preceding the request for price increases (e.g., how using more nutritious foods increase cost)
- Community awareness of how the foodservice program is like a business (e.g., have a well-planned, factual article in local newspaper on how the program has increased productivity)
- Making the hard decisions (e.g., discontinue services that are losing money and let the public know why)

School districts that are managing financially sound programs have kept revenue at an adequate level to cover costs. In such cases, the school district should raise prices when necessary to maintain break-even programs.

Increasing Participation

When faced with financial problems, increasing participation and revenue can be part of the solution to those problems. A good marketing program will help increase participation. (Chapter 10, "Marketing," offers suggestions.)

Some ways to increase participation in the lunch and breakfast programs are to:

- Plan menus students like, improve food quality and service, and offer choices.
- Market, promote, and advertise programs to students, parents, teachers, and administrators.

- Change presentation (e.g., offer bag lunches, breakfast on the bus).
- Provide meals for field trips.
- Provide special menus for classroom parties.
- Coordinate menus with countries classes are studying.
- Consider the Community Eligibility Provision.
- Survey students, teachers, and parents to find out why the participation is not higher, and take corrective action.

SUMMARY

Resolving financial problems can be a difficult job for management, but the results can be rewarding. Involving employees in the process is a motivator and makes the results a team effort.

School food and nutrition service programs that depend on federal funds are challenging to manage. The federal reimbursement for the meals may not be adequate to cover the current cost. Extra food sales that were a source of additional revenue are limited. Hard decisions may be necessary to keep the programs financially successful.

Many food and nutrition professionals have dreamed of serving all students free for 50 or more years. Today, this scenario is a reality in the needy communities. At the same time, the media and education are helping the industry promote good nutrition. The future of serving good nutritious food at school is bright.

QUESTIONS AND ANSWERS

1. Cash-based accounting systems show all the revenue earned for the accounting period.
   a. True
   b. False
2. Inventory must be considered to determine food used.
   a. True
   b. False
3. Increasing productivity means working faster and harder.
   a. True
   b. False
4. Successful school food and nutrition service programs may need to increase revenue and reduce cost at the same time.
   a. True
   b. False
5. Student payment and federal reimbursements are the main sources of revenue for a lunch.
   a. True
   b. False
6. To determine percentage spent on food, divide the total food cost by total revenue.
   a. True
   b. False
7. Increasing prices charged for lunch should be the first thing to do when a financial problem arises.
   a. True
   b. False
8. Low productivity will increase the cost of labor per lunch served.
   a. True
   b. False
9. The two main expenditures are:
   a. Paper supplies and employee benefits
   b. Food and labor costs
   c. Food processing and technology
   d. None of those above
10. Labor costs should be kept below 45% of:
    a. Total revenue
    b. Total expenditures
    c. Both of the above
    d. Neither of the above

ANSWERS: 1.b., 2.a., 3.b., 4.a., 5.a., 6.a., 7.b., 8.a., 9.b., 10.a.

REFERENCES

Allison, G., Honegger, S., & Johnson, F. 2009. *Financial accounting for local and state school systems: 2009 Edition (NCES 2009-325).* National Center for Educational Statistics, Institute of Education Sciences. Washington, DC: U.S. Department of Education.

American Dietetic Association. 2005. Practice paper of the American Dietetic Association: A systems approach to measuring productivity in health care foodservice operations. *Journal of the American Dietetic Association,* 105, 122–130.

Barnes, R. 1968. *Motion and time study: Design and measurement of work,* 6th ed. New York: John Wiley & Sons.

Carr, D. & Cross, E. 2008. Vending reimbursable lunches to high school students: A study of two successes. *Journal of Child Nutrition & Management,* 1. Retrieved from *http://docs.schoolnutrition.org/newsroom/jcnm/08spring/carr/index.asp.*

Cater, J., Cross, E., & Conklin, M. 2005. *NFSMI financial management information system.* University, MS: NFSMI.

Dittmer, P. & Keefe, J. 2009. *Principles of food, beverage, and labor cost controls,* 9th ed. Hoboken, NJ: John Wiley & Sons.

Dopson, L. 2011. *Food and beverage cost control,* 5th ed. Hoboken, NJ: John Wiley & Sons, Inc.

Malustik, P. & DeBurgh, R. n.d. Commodity Processing. Retrieved from *http://www.djcoops.com/index.asp.*

McLaren, P. 2008. Winning ways for summer days. *School Nutrition,* 62 (10), 14–20.

NFSMI. n.d. *Revenue generation and cost control measures currently used in financially successful child nutrition programs.* University, MS: Author.

NFSMI. 2005. *Financial management: A course for school food service directors.* University, MS: Author.

Pannell-Martin, D. 2004. *Cost control manual for school foodservice. 3rd ed.* Santa Monica, CA: inTEAM Associates, Inc.

School Census Report. 2012. *Foodservice Director.* Retrieved from *http://www.foodservicedirector.com/trends/research/articles/2012-school-census-report.*

School Nutrition Association. 2005. *Operations survey: Final report.* Alexandria, VA: Author.

School Nutrition Association. 2013. *The little big fact book: The essential guide to school nutrition.* Harbor City, MD: Author.

USDA Food and Nutrition Service. 2008. *School lunch and breakfast cost study-II: Summary of findings: Executive summary.* Alexandria, VA: Author.

ONLINE RESOURCES

Foodservice Director 2012 School Census Report
http://www.foodservicedirector.com/trends/research/articles/2012-school-census-report

Governmental Accounting Standards Board
http://gasb.org

National Center for Education Statistics
http://nces.ed.gov/pubsearch

National Food Service Management Institute
http://nfsmi.org

NFSMI Financial Management: A Course for School Food Service Directors
http://www.nfsmi.org/ResourceOverview.aspx?ID=63

USDA Reimbursement Rates
http://www.fns.usda.gov/cnd/governance/notices/naps/naps.htm

U.S. Department of Education Financial Accounting for Local and State School Systems
http://nces.ed.gov/pubs2009/2009325.pdf

Glossary

A la carte – Food items that are priced and sold separately from a reimbursable meal.

Accounting system – System of measuring, communicating, and interpreting financial activity.

Accounts payable – The amount owed creditors for goods and services (e.g., food and supplies and unpaid payroll). "Prepaid" student tickets may be considered accounts payable.

Accounts receivable – The amounts that is owed the foodservice program for food and services rendered (e.g., federal reimbursement and contract meals).

Accrual-based accounting – A system of accounting in which revenues are recorded in the period earned and expenses are recorded in the period they occur.

Administrative review – A unified accountability system to ensure consistency and improve efficiency of the auditing process.

After School Snacks Program (ASSP) – Offered under the National School Lunch Program to students after the school day.

Aggregate bid – Bid that is awarded as a category or group of categories (e.g., milk and other dairy products to one vendor; bakery bread items to one bakery, canned and frozen foods to one vendor, etc.).

Allergen – Substance that causes an allergic reaction.

Allowable fund balance – A phrase referring to a federal regulation that limits a school district's net cash resources or fund balance. The limitation is to an amount that does not exceed three months of operation.

Anaphylaxis – Severe, life-threatening allergic reaction.

Annual household meal application – Refers to the application for school meal benefits.

Asset – Value of items owned by the foodservice operation or company.

"At risk" – Descriptor of students from needy family households.

Audit – The system used to evaluate a child nutrition program's compliance with laws and regulations.

Audit trail – A procedure that traces through all stages of an accounting system, starting from the source document (e.g., point of sale) and ending with the final report (e.g., monthly state claim for federal meals served reimbursements).

Balance sheet – A financial statement that shows the financial condition of a fund at a given point, a "snapshot."

Base or production kitchen – A kitchen where meals are prepared for serving on-site and for one or more other locations.

Baseline budget – A budget based on the assumption that all the previous year's expenditures were necessary and will reoccur.

Batch cooking – Cooking in small quantities for immediate service.

Bid – Formalized financial (and/or operating) proposal for a given service(s) or product(s).

Bioterrorism Act of 2002 – Abbreviation for the Public Health Security and Bioterrorism Preparedness and Response Act of 2002 that seeks to enhance national security by incorporating measures to prevent, prepare for, and respond to acts of bioterrorism or other public health emergencies.

Blog – A website for posting information, which allows a school district to provide longer descriptions or more detail about the programs and services.

Bonus USDA Foods – The food products that USDA purchases in addition to the entitlement food value.

Bottom line – Refers to financial statement, the difference in revenue and expenditures, either the gain or loss in fund balance.

Bottom-up budget – A decentralized approach to budget planning, whereby each cost center (school) plans a budget and the school district's budget is made by combining all the budgets together. This is also called "Bottom-up approach."

Branding – Relying on name recognition or creating name recognition used in developing menus, promoting, and advertising the food.

Break-even point (BEP) – The point at which the amount of revenue covers the costs.

Budget – An organized financial plan for a specified period of time (usually a year) that projects the income, or revenue, and expenditures.

Budgetary fund – Revenue generally received from taxes (e.g., a school district's education budget or the "general fund"). The fund does not generate revenue as with a business and is generally preset budget amounts.

Bulk cold – Food is cooked, then chilled or frozen and transported for finishing off in the receiving (serving) school.

Bulk hot – Food is cooked and maintained hot through transporting and serving at the receiving (serving) school.

Cash-based accounting – A system of accounting recording revenues when received and expenses in the period they are paid.

Cash in lieu of commodities (CASH) – Alternative to the USDA Foods program in which the lunch program receives CASH entitlement instead of food. A limited number of schools and all the schools in Kansas receive CASH. CACFP has the option.

Celiac disease – An autoimmune disease in which the small intestines are hypersensitive to gluten resulting in difficulty in absorbing nutrients.

Central production kitchen or commissary – A kitchen where food is prepared to be served in a number of other locations.

Centralized purchasing – The school foodservice central office makes purchasing decisions for all schools in district.

Chef Move to Schools – A Team Nutrition program to facilitate the involvement of certified chefs in school foodservices.

Child and Adult Care Food Program (CACFP) – Program administered by USDA to provide meals and snacks served after school, on weekends, and during school vacation periods.

Child Nutrition Act of 1966 – Law that provides substantial funding for needy children's meals, guidelines to identify the needy, and a breakfast program.

Child Nutrition Label (CN Label) – Instituted in 1984 to provide buyers assurance of a product's contribution toward meal components.

Child Nutrition Program (CNP) – Includes the following programs: National School Lunch, School Breakfast Program, Fresh Fruits and Vegetables, Special Milk, Summer Food Service, and Child and Adult Care Food.

Child Nutrition Women Infant and Children (WIC) – This special supplemental program provides federal grants to states for supplemental food, health care referrals, and nutrition education for low-income pregnant, breastfeeding, and nonbreastfeeding postpartum women and infant and children up to age five, who are considered specially needy.

Collective or cooperative purchasing – When a group of school districts form a legal entity for the purpose of purchasing food, supplies, equipment, and services.

Commodities (USDA Foods) – Agricultural food items made available by the U.S. Department of Agriculture to schools under the National School Lunch Program.

Commodity Letter of Credit (CLOC) – Alternative to the USDA Foods; the school district receives vouchers worth established amounts for a category of food. Once the school districts purchase the category of food (e.g., beef), the voucher cashes out. Only a few school districts qualify.

Community Eligibility Provision – A method of approving students for free meal benefits based on at least 40 percent of students in a school or school district qualifying for free meals through direct certification. All students receive meals free but nonfederal funds pay the difference in federal assistance received.

Competitive foods – Any food sold at school that is in competition with the National School Lunch Program or School Breakfast Program.

Conflict of interest – When the buyer has a personal interest in the company selected for bid award.

Contribution margin (CM) – The percent of the revenue used to pay the fixed costs.

Convenience foodservice system – Using a maximum amount of processed foods from partially prepared to fully prepared at another site and requires minimal preparation on site where served.

Conventional food production system – Preparation of food at school where served using a combination of fresh ingredients and convenience foods

Cook-chill/freeze system – Food is prepared, chilled or frozen, and reheated and served at a later time.

Coordinated review effort (CRE) – The accountability system used by government agencies to conduct administrative reviews of local program sponsors to ensure that the NSLP regulations are carried out properly.

Cost-plus-fixed-fee – A written contract where the fee for service is added to the price the vendor paid for the product plus freight.

Critical Control Point (CCP) – The point in the flow of food when an action may be taken that may prevent or eliminate a food safety hazard.

Cycle menu – Set of menus that repeat (e.g., every two or three weeks).

Data-driven decision making – Decisions made using data to support.

Decentralized – Foodservice administration is done by each school. This may includehe menu planning and purchasing.

Dietary Guidelines for Americans – Guidelines published by the U.S. Department of Agriculture and Health and Human Services every five years that provide evidence-based recommendations to help individuals select foods that provide optimal nutrition and build healthy eating patterns.

Dietary Reference Intakes (DRI) – Guidelines for nutrient intake(s) needed for planning and assessing diets of healthy people.

Direct certification – The process of establishing children's categorical eligibility for benefits by obtaining documentation directly from the state or local agencies confirming that the children are from households currently receiving SNAP, TANF, or FDPIR benefits.

Direct costs – Items of cost that can be specifically identified (e.g., food and paper supplies and equipment maintenance).

Disposables – Single-service items made from paper, plastic, and other products.

District profile – Information provided as a part of a formalized bid process that describes the size and requirements of the school district.

Enterprise fund – Revenue generated by producing goods and services sold (e.g., school foodservice and book store; sometimes referred to as a proprietary fund).

Entitlement USDA Foods – *See USDA Foods.*

Expenditures (liabilities) – The costs incurred for food, supplies, services, etc.

Facebook – A popular free social networking website that allows registered users to create profiles.

Federal reimbursement (rate) – Subsidy established annually for school meals/ snacks meeting federal requirements.

Finishing Kitchen – A kitchen that receives partially prepared foods that need heating, finishing off, or reconstituting before serving.

Fiscal year (FY) – The 12-month period used for accounting purposes (e.g., Jan–Dec, Jul–Jun, etc.).

Fixed costs (FC) – Costs that remain relatively constant or the same during for a given period of time regardless of the number served.

Fixed price – In bid purchasing, the price quoted for a period of time as part of a contractual agreement.

Fixed price with escalator or market-based clauses – Used mostly with perishable products allowing for long-term contracts on items that otherwise require frequent bidding.

FNS certificate program – A component of the professional standards requirements under the Healthy Hunger-Free Kids Act of 2010.

Food allergy – The immune system's response to an allergen resulting in the release of histamine and other chemicals in the body.

Food defense – Protecting food from intentional contamination with intent of harm or death.

Food and Nutrition Service (FNS) – A branch under USDA that provides regulations and guidance materials for the nutrition programs.

Food safety – Protection of food from unintentional contaminants and controlling biological contaminant growth with time/temperature control.

Foodborne illness – A disease transmitted to people through food.

Foodservice management company – A commercial enterprise or nonprofit organization that manages the food and nutrition service programs under contract for a fee.

Free meals – Meals served children at no cost because they have an approved meal application, are certified based on another government program, or qualified under the community eligibility provision.

Fresh Fruit & Vegetable Program (FFVP) – Federal grant program intended to encourage consumption of fresh fruits and vegetables.

Fund balance – The amount of revenue available after liabilities have been paid; the fund is restricted by USDA and must be kept separate from general funds.

Global Trade Item Number (GTIN) – A unique 14-digit number used to identify products such as a specific brand, unit of measure, and product code.

Gluten – A protein found in wheat, barley, and rye.

Gluten-free – A diet avoiding wheat, barley, and rye.

Group purchasing organization (GPO) – An organization of food and nutrition service directors whose purpose is to increase the buying power of the members.

GS1 – Not-for-profit organization that creates standards for identifying products and assists businesses in implementing the standards.

Hashtags – Key words or phrases with the prefix "#" in front of the text used with Twitter.

Hazard Analysis & Critical Control Points (HACCP) – A food safety system comprised of seven principles designed to identify, evaluate, and control food safety hazards.

Healthy Hunger-Free Kids Act of 2010 – This legislation reauthorized funding and sets policy for the core Child Nutrition programs. The legislation restricts food served throughout the school day on school campus, tightens food safety requirements, and establishes professional standards for school nutrition personnel.

Indirect costs – Costs that cannot be directly identified because the amount is prorated across several programs (e.g., cost of a school's utilities).

Inventory – A list of each item in storage at a given time along with the quantities.

Inventory turnover – Number of times the inventory turns over during a month. Number of turnovers is determined by (1) arriving at food cost for month, (2) dividing the total food by number of serving days, and (3) dividing the ending inventory by the average daily food cost.

Invitation for bid (IFB) – A solicitation to prospective vendors containing contract requirements and product or service specifications. Contracts are awarded to the lowest responsive, responsible bidder.

Line of authority – Chain of command within the Child Nutrition Programs.

LinkedIn – Social media that allows users to network with other people or businesses.

Local Educational Agency (LEA) – A term established by the USDA that refers to school district level management, sometimes called School Food Authority.

Loss (deficit) – The expenditures exceed the revenue and result in a loss or decrease in the fund balance.

Marketing – The process of promoting, advertising, merchandising, and selling.

Meal equivalent (MEQ) – A means of converting the amount of work involved in producing and serving meals, snacks, and revenue to a common denominator.

Meal reimbursement – A federal cash payment for breakfast and lunch meals. *See Federal reimbursement.*

Meals per labor hour (MPLH) – Formula commonly used to measure productivity rate of employees.

Menu cycle – A set of menus that repeat (e.g., every two or three weeks). The length of the cycle is usually tied to the number of daily entrée choices.

Modified diet – A menu requiring a change in the consistency or content of food due to medical conditions.

National School Lunch Act – The law signed by President Harry S Truman in 1946 creating school lunch programs.

National School Lunch Program (NSLP) – The largest student nutrition program in the United States and the first such mandated by Congress.

Nutrient – Substance that provides nourishment essential for growth and sustaining life.

Nutrient Standard Menu Planning (NSMP) – An approach to menu planning based on meeting defined nutrient targets.

Offer versus serve – Regulation under the National School Lunch and Child Nutrition Programs that allows students to refuse some of the offerings.

Open source – Hardware designed with software that is available to any developer in order for the product to work with a wide range of software products.

Overhead – Considered fixed costs and refers to expenditures such as administrative costs, management salaries, and miscellaneous operating costs of the programs.

Paid Lunch Equity Provision (PLE) – A federal regulation that requires paid lunch prices be similar to free federal reimbursement rates minus the paid reimbursement rate.

Performance Standard 1 and 2 – Part of the Administrative Review to ensure compliance.

Perpetual inventory – An up-to-date, running record of each item on hand that provides ready information to a manager for placing orders; easily maintained with the use of computers, scanners, and bar codes.

Physical inventory – An actual count of goods in stock; used to assist in more accurate ordering; should be taken monthly.

Point-of-sale (POS) – When a determination is made that a reimbursable free, reduced-price, or paid meal served to an eligible student and payment takes place based on that determination.

Postcost – The actual cost of producing and serving of food based on actual amount of food used.

Precost – The cost of food based on the planned ingredients.

Pre-plated cold (bag) – Food prepared and bagged or pre-plated ready for distribution at the receiving (serving) school.

Pre-plated frozen – Food prepared, portioned, and frozen, and then transported ready for heating for service.

Pre-plated hot – Food prepared, portioned, and transported on the day of service, hot food hot (and cold food cold) ready-to-eat.

Pre-plated meals – Meals ready to serve or ready to reheat and serve.

Procurement – Planning that goes into the buying of the right amount of products, at the right time, and at the price afforded.

Professional standard – Education and training criteria for school nutrition personnel at state and local levels as required under the Healthy Hunger-Free Kids Act of 2010. It also requires continuing education.

Production record – Report of forecasted number for each menu item, actual food produced, quantity, portion size, and actual number served.

Productivity rate – Measure of employee output usually stated/measured (i.e., meals per labor hour).

Profit (gain) – The revenue in excess of the expenditures, resulting in an increase in the fund balance.

Profit and loss statement (P&L) – Also called statement of revenues and expenditures; a financial report of revenues and expenditures for a given period of time showing either a profit or loss.

Proprietary hardware standards – Technology equipment designed to work exclusively with a specific software product.

Provisions 1, 2, and 3 – An alternative method of determining student eligibility for meal benefits and counting of meals for reimbursement claims.

Ready-to-serve – An item that will receive no further cooking.

Recalls – A voluntary action taken by manufacturers to stop usage of products deemed as unsafe.

Receiving kitchen – The school kitchen that receives food ready to serve; food may be delivered in bulk or in individual servings.

Recommended Dietary Allowance (RDA) – The nutritional basis for the original National School Lunch Program requirements.

Reduced-price meals – The meals served to students who do not qualify (because of family income) for free meals but do not have sufficient family income to pay full price.

Request for proposal (RFP) – A document to solicit proposals for goods and/or services that describes in a general way the needed items and requests that vendors submit a proposal for serving the needs of the district. Contracts are awarded based on criteria defined in the solicitation document.

Revenue (income) – Money received for food and services and accounts receivable.

Safety data sheets (formerly MSDA) – A document required by the Occupational Safety and Health Administration (OSHA) to communicate the hazards of chemicals.

Satellite food production system (satelliting) – Food prepared at one location for serving at another.

School Breakfast Program (SBP) – Federal program that provides funding based on the income of the students.

School Food Authority (SFA) – The school district's governing body, as denoted by USDA and state agencies, to be held responsible for carrying out the federal regulations of federally subsidized meal programs.

School Nutrition Specialist (SNS) – A credential established by the School Nutrition Association and obtained by individuals who meet educational requirements and pass a written exam.

Sealed bid – A vendor's sales proposal in response to a publicly advertised request for proposal (RFP) or invitation to bid (IFB). The proposal is delivered in a sealed package by the specified date and time.

Severe need breakfast school – Designates that the school has served the second preceding year 40 percent or more of the lunches free or at reduced price. The school qualifies for a higher rate of reimbursement for the breakfast served free and at reduced price.

Severe need lunch school district – Designates that the school district served the second preceding year 60 percent or more of the lunches free and at reduced price. The federal reimbursement as of SY2013–2014 is 2¢ for each lunch served.

Social media – Refers to the web-based software used to communicate and share information with other users.

Special need students – Refers to students with a disability or otherwise unable to eat school meals planned for the regular school population. This may also include students who have a physical disability (e.g., wheel chair) that may need to be accommodated in the serving line or in the dining room.

Specification – A written description of products and/or services desired by the buyer and included in a bid solicitation document.

Standard of identify – Outlines what ingredients a product must contain, which ingredients it may contain, and any requirements of manufacturing.

Standard Operating Procedure (SOP) – Set of detailed written instructions to provide consistency in the performance of a task.

Standardized recipe – Recipe that has been tested for consistency and yield.

Statement of revenues and expenditures – a financial report of revenues and expenditures for a given period of time showing an increase or decrease in funds.

Summer Food Service Program (SFSP) – Provides meals to low-income students during the summer in schools, parks, community centers or wherever children (up to 18 years of age) congregate.

Supplemental Nutrition Assistance Program (SNAP) – Formerly known as the Food Stamp Program, provides assistance for food to low-income households.

Supply chain – A set of three or more organizations directly involved in the upstream or downstream flow of products, services, finances, and/or information from the products' original source to the end consumer.

Team Nutrition (TN) – A program developed by the USDA to promote lifelong healthy eating and physical activity habits in school children.

Temporary Assistance for Needy Families (TANF) – A state-funded program under Part A of Title IV of the Social Security Act that provides benefits to low-income families with children to help them become self-supporting.

Track – The ability to identify the origin, attributes, or history of a product by reviewing records from each organization the product flowed through. Also referred to as trace.

Turnkey – A description used when implementing a project where one company is responsible for supplying all purchased products and/or services of the project.

Twitter – A popular instant-messaging system that lets a person send brief text messages of up to 140 characters through social networking.

Type A lunch – Under the National School Lunch Program, the lunch requirements from 1946–1977.

Universal Product Code (UPC) – A unique bar code number assigned to a product that identifies the item.

USDA Foods – Formerly known as "commodities" or "donated food," food products purchased by USDA and distributed to child nutrition programs to help defray food costs as well as remove surplus domestic food from the marketplace.

Variable costs (VC) – Costs that vary in direct proportion with volume of sales or number of customers served (e.g., food and disposable products).

Verification – A method of confirming eligibility for free and reduced-price meal benefits under the School Breakfast and National School Lunch Programs.

Wellness policies – A school board policy outlining nutrition and physical activity expectations for the school district students and staff. Beginning with the 2004 National School Lunch Program reauthorization, school districts are required to established wellness policies.

Whole grain-rich – A product containing 50 percent or more whole grain, or whole grain is the first grain listed in the ingredient list, or the product contains at least 8 grams of whole grain.

Work schedules – A detailed plan that indicates all employee tasks, when they are to be performed, and how long it takes to complete the task.

Youth Advisory Council (YAC) – A student organization that provides feedback to the Food and Nutrition Department regarding products, menu concepts, and services offered

YouTube – Large video-sharing site on the Internet.

Zero-based budget – A budget planned as if for the first time by determining revenue for number served and sources of revenue and determining expenditures by costing out all line items.

INDEX

Note: Page numbers with *e* indicates exhibits.

N

O

P